Introductory
Statistics for the
Behavioral Sciences

Joe D. Cornett
Texas Tech University

Weldon Beckner
Texas Tech University

Charles E. Merrill Publishing Company
A Bell & Howell Company
Columbus, Ohio

Published by
Charles E. Merrill Publishing Company
A Bell & Howell Company
Columbus, Ohio 43216

Library of Congress Catalog Card Number: 74–14424

ISBN: 0–675–08757–0

1 2 3 4 5 6 7 8 / 79 78 77 76 75

Printed in the United States of America

To our wives
Elayne and Betty

Contents

Preface

This book is designed as a basic text for students taking a first course in statistics for education, psychology or other behavioral sciences. We have written the book to help students accomplish three goals:

1. To read and interpret the research literature in the behavioral sciences;
2. To apply statistical techniques to the study of behavioral science problems;
3. To serve as a foundation for a more intensive study of the subject.

Throughout the book, we have assumed that students taking a course in introductory statistics have had only a minimum exposure to this area of study. With this in mind, we begin with a rather elementary treatment of the basics of statistics and then proceed to more difficult material. Application and interpretation are stressed throughout, however, and frequent illustrations and examples are employed. Our major theme, if we can be said to have one, is that statistics is a tool which any student can master well enough to apply successfully. In brief, the book makes the point that a person does not have to be a statistician to be an effective user of statistics.

We are indebted to many people for their help and encouragement during the preparation of this book, especially Dale Erickson, John

Cadena, and Gene Medely. We also want to thank Professor John Foll-
man for his careful criticism of the manuscript at various stages, and
Don Fisher for his assistance in checking our computations and offering
helpful advice. We are also indebted to the literary executor of the late
Sir Ronald A. Fisher, F.R.S., to Dr. Frank Yates, F.R.S., and to Long-
man Group Limited, London, for permission to reprint tables III, IV, and
VII from their book *Statistical Tables For Biological, Agricultural and
Medical Research*.

To the Student

A study[1] that appeared in a recent research journal was designed to determine the effect of pausal cueing on the free recall of educable mentally retarded and nonretarded children. It was assumed that the language of the retarded child is governed by the same rules as those for his nonretarded peers. Therefore, making phrase boundaries distinctive through pausal cueing should improve chunking and increase recall of sentences by EMR children.

Subjects for the study consisted of twenty-four randomly selected retarded children and twenty-four randomly selected nonretarded children. Each group consisted of thirteen males and eleven females. Retarded Ss were randomly selected from chronological ages ranging from 8.8 to 13.5 years with IQ ranging from 57 to 80. Nonretarded subjects ranged in age from 6.5 to 8.7 years with IQs ranging from 90 to 130. Table 1 summarizes the distribution of CA, IQ, and MA for the six subgroups.

Table 1, a portion of which is presented, provides the basic differences between the two groups being studied. Table 2 presents a portion of the analysis of these data on which the conclusions of this study were based.

---

1. M. C. Sitko and M. I. Semmel, "The Effect of Phrasal Cueing on Free Recall of EMR and Non-retarded Children," *American Educational Research Journal,* Spring 1972, pp. 217–29.

TABLE 1. Means and Standard Deviations of CA, MA, and IQ for
          Subgroups

Group	Variable	Statistic	Cueing Conditions		
			Distorted	Phrasal	Linear
Retarded Subjects	IQ	$\bar{X}$	72.12	70.00	71.25
($N = 24$)		SD	7.16	7.29	6.25
	CA	$\bar{X}$	.	.	.
		SD	.	.	.
	MA	$\bar{X}$	.	.	.
		SD	.	.	.
Non-retarded Subjects	IQ	$\bar{X}$	104.50	104.38	104.38
($N = 24$)		SD	11.84	10.97	10.88
	CA	$\bar{X}$	.	.	.
		SD	.	.	.
	MA	$\bar{X}$	.	.	.
		SD	.	.	.

From Table 2, the researchers concluded that the main effects of
groups (nonretarded vs. retarded Ss), and degree of syntactic structure
(standard vs. distorted syntactic structure) were significant ($p < .05$;
$p < .001$). The two-way interaction of cueing conditions with degree of
syntactic structure was also found to be significant at the .05 level, as was
the triple interaction of groups with cueing conditions and of syntactic
structure ($p < .01$).

Although only a very sketchy summary of this study was presented, if
after reading it you understand the terminology, symbols, concepts, and
techniques employed, as well as those that were left out, then YOU ARE

TABLE 2. Analysis of Variance of Recall for the Four Factors Studied*

Source	df	MS	F	p
Between Ss	47			
Groups (A)	1	2775.521	4.562	.05
Within Ss				
Degree of Syntactic Structure (A)	1	23,012.521	226.339	.001
$B \times D$	2	502.693	4.945	.05
$A \times B \times D$	2	657.818	6.471	.01

* Only the significant sources of variation presented

GOING TO BE BORED IN AN INTRODUCTORY STATISTICS COURSE. However, if most of what you read was not at all clear, then you should profit by a course in statistics.

It might be of interest to note that in the short description of the study, the following statistical topics are employed:

Research design	Statistical significance
Statistical hypotheses	Degree of freedom
Sampling	Interaction
Variability	Inference
Mean	Analysis of variance
Standard deviation	F distribution

and others

To read and accurately interpret the full text of this report, these topics must be understood, at least to some degree.

In the current vogue, "research is where it's at." Professionals without some understanding of statistics find the door closed to a wealth of information that can help in the understanding and solution of a multitude of problems.

Symbols and Terminology

This section is designed to introduce the student to the basic symbols and terminology employed in the study and application of statistics. As with the study of most subjects, a peculiar set of symbols and terms are used to represent meaning. Some of the symbols and terms are mathematical in nature and can be found in most mathematics textbooks, while others are somewhat unique to the field of statistics. It is hoped that you will become acquainted with the symbols and terms prior to proceeding to the main body of the text where they are used, and more fully defined, in the context of a particular discussion. The initial list in this section is not intended to be all-inclusive, but rather it contains those items that appear most frequently throughout the text. At appropriate times, these items will be re-introduced along with others that apply to the particular subject under study.

BASIC SYMBOLS

The following are some of the more basic symbols utilized in the text. We should mention at this point that complete uniformity in the use of statistical symbols does not exist. This is unfortunate in that confusion is produced when consulting a variety of textbooks and when reading research reports in the behavioral sciences as well as texts and reports from other fields. The symbols used in this text, however, are those that the authors feel are most commonly used in analyzing and reporting behavioral science data.

Common Statistical Symbols

Symbol	Meaning	Explanation
$<$	less than	8 is less than 9 $8 < 9$
$>$	greater than	9 is greater than 8 $9 > 8$
$\sqrt{}$	square root	$\sqrt{36} = 6$
N	number of observations in population	data gathered from the total group under consideration
n	number of observations in the sample	data gathered from a subgroup of the total population
X	raw score	score made on a psychological examination
x	deviation score	the difference between a raw score and the mean $(x = X - \bar{X})$
$\bar{X}$	mean	the arithmetic average of a set of scores
Σ	the sum of	when preceding another symbol, it denotes addition
σ	population standard deviation	see explanation of standard deviation and variance in terminology section
s	sample standard deviation	
σ^2	population variance	
s^2	sample variance	
z	standard score	a converted score utilizing the difference between the mean and a raw score divided by the standard deviation
f	frequency	number of items in a category
d.f.	degree of freedom	number of observations allowed to vary around a particular value; see terminology section

BASIC TERMS

The following are some of the more basic statistical terms used in the text. The definitions are brief and to the point and are defined simply to acquaint the reader with the term. More detailed definitions and explanations, along with the introduction of additional terms, are provided in appropriate places throughout the text.

population: a statistical term that refers to the entire group of observations under study. Sometimes referred to as the universe.

sample: a subset of the population. Sample data are studied and the results are generalized to the population.

significant difference: differences that are unlikely to be due to chance.

statistical inference: data are studied on the basis of a representative sample of the population and the results are inferred to approximate those actually existing in the defined population.

variability: the amount of spread or dispersion of a set of data from a central point. This central point is usually the mean. The standard deviation and variance, for example, are means used to measure variability.

probability: the chances of a given event occurring from a total number of possible outcomes.

parametric tests: a set of statistical tests that are based on the assumption of independence and normality of population data. Techniques that fall into this category are normally those that deal with continuous data, i.e., age, weight, test scores, etc.

nonparametric tests: a set of statistical techniques that can be used when the population distribution is not known or when the data are expressed in terms of frequency counts.

power: the probability of rejecting the null hypothesis when in fact it is false.

parameter: a characteristic or measure of the population.

statistic: a characteristic or measure of a sample.

hypothesis: tentative propositions or statements that are subjected to statistical analyses for verification.

1

Descriptive Statistics

Study of the behavioral sciences requires at least a minimum knowledge and understanding of descriptive, inferential, and predictive statistics. Descriptive statistics use techniques and procedures to describe collections of quantitative information with precision and brevity. Inferential techniques facilitate testing hypotheses by drawing inferences and generalizations from small groups (samples) to larger groups (populations). Predictive statistics techniques are used to show how one measure is related to another, thus allowing prediction of one measure from another. For example, IQ and academic success are usually correlated, and through statistics a person can predict the probable academic success of a student whose IQ is known.

In this chapter we are concerned with descriptive statistics and the ways in which behavioral scientists may take disorganized masses of raw data and summarize or group them for orderly communication and interpretation. Three types of measures are most helpful in this respect: measures of position, central tendency, and variability. Various types of charts and graphs are also useful. Following a brief introduction to constants, variables, and measurement scales, we will discuss each of these three types of measures and the more commonly used types of graphs and charts which are convenient in their interpretation.

VARIABLES AND CONSTANTS

Behavioral science is based upon the observation of human behavior, and this observation must indicate how the objects of study change from time to time or person to person. Traits which are capable of variation, such as intelligence, weights, or action, are called *variables*. The behavioral sciences base their study on the relationships between these variables. However, any study of a group of individuals (a population) will describe that population in terms of characteristics that they have in common as well as those that vary. Those characteristics which do not vary from individual to individual within the particular group being studied are termed *constants*.

Variables are of two types: those that vary in *quality* and those that vary in *quantity*. Sex, for instance, is a qualitative variable, while intelligence is a quantitative variable.

In addition to differing as to being qualitative or quantitative, variables are either discrete or continuous. A *discrete* variable is one which can take on only a finite set of values, meaning that fractional values are usually not allowed. The population of a city, number of females in a group, or the score of a basketball game are examples of discrete variables. A *continuous* variable can take on any value, including fractional values, over a range of values. Intelligence, height, and weight are examples of continuous variables. These may for convenience be recorded as whole numbers (such as a weight of 115 pounds) but this does not mean that a person could not weigh 115.4 pounds. Some statistical procedures are appropriate for use with continuous variables, while others are appropriate only for use with discrete variables.

MEASUREMENT SCALES

We use numbers every day and tend to take for granted that their use in statistical techniques will be similar to that to which we are accustomed. Most measures generally lend themselves to normal arithmetic operations, but not always. As we learned early in our study of arithmetic, you can't add apples and oranges, and this is what we may attempt unless we are aware of the different properties that it is possible for numbers to have. Numbers represent something, and we must know what they represent before proper manipulation can occur.

Measurement is the assignment of numbers to objects or events according to certain prescribed rules. If we understand these rules we will understand the properties of the numbers and treat the numbers accordingly. To understand the properties of the numbers used in different kinds of measurement, it is common practice to use four kinds of scales that describe the varying levels of measurement. These are called measurement scales, and each scale represents a way of assigning numbers to objects or events. Different rules are applied to the use of each type of scale.

Nominal Scales

The nominal scale is the simplest form of measurement. It is a means to classify an object into some category. The object either is or is not a member of the category under consideration. Cars can be classified as to make, people may be classified as either male or female, dogs may be classified as to breed. These classifications may be given numbers, but the numbers are meaningless so far as arithmetical computations are concerned. This is a crude type of measurement, but it does enable us to discriminate one object or event from another. With refinement, nominal measurement is valuable, particularly in regression analysis.

Ordinal Scales

As implied in the term, ordinal scales include the establishment of orders among categories. Nominal scales show that things are different; ordinal scales show the direction of the difference. With their use, we can show relative position of one thing to another, but we cannot specify the magnitude of the interval between two measures. For example, we can rank objects or events according to height, weight, quality of performance, or order of finishing, but we cannot speak precisely as to the amount of difference between the rankings. Three people may be ranked according to their height, but we cannot tell from this operation how much taller one is than another. They may be ranked one, two, and three, according to height, but this certainly does not mean that the tallest person is twice as tall as the second tallest and three times the height of the shortest.

Nominal and ordinal scales have important uses in the behavioral sciences, but their meanings must be understood and their limitations taken into account. Statistical techniques which have been developed especially for use with nominal and ordinal scales are usually termed *nonparametric* statistics.

Interval Scales

Interval scales are different from nominal and ordinal types in that they have equal intervals between the units of measure. A score of 20 on an interval scale is half way between scores of 10 and 30. With interval measurements, the common arithmetic operations of addition, subtraction, multiplication, and division may be used. However, it cannot be said, for example, that a score of 70 on an interval scale is twice as good as a score of 35, because this type scale lacks a true zero. This is the case with intelligence tests, because we cannot meaningfully establish that any person has zero intelligence.

Ratio Scales

Ratio scales have the same qualities as interval scales, with the additional property of an absolute zero. Measures of weight, height, and age are ratio scales, so we can say that a person who weighs 100 pounds is twice as heavy as one weighing 50 pounds. On the other hand, we cannot say that a person with an IQ score of 100 is twice as intelligent as one with a score of 50, because zero intelligence cannot be defined.

Statistical procedures used with ratio scales will usually be the same as those used with interval scales. The techniques specified for use only with interval and ratio data are referred to as *parametric* statistics.

MEASURES OF POSITION

For rather simple organization and analysis of raw data, we may use techniques of frequency distribution and ranking. At this point it seems appropriate to consider only simple frequency distributions, simple ranking, and percentile ranking.

Frequency Distribution

A mass of raw data, such as student test scores or questionnaire responses, is of very little use until it is organized for analysis and interpretation. A frequency distribution arranges a collection of measures in graphic form to indicate the frequency of occurrence of each value. To construct a frequency distribution table, proceed in the following manner:

1. Construct a score column (X) in which raw scores are listed from high to low.
2. Tally the number of times each score appears in the distribution.
3. Check the number of tallies against the number of raw scores.
4. Make a frequency (f) column showing the number of tallies for each score.

Table 1–1 illustrates the above procedure.

TABLE 1–1.   Simple Frequency Distribution.

Raw Scores		X	Tally	f
61	69	69	///	3
63	61	68	/	1
69	60	67	//	2
64	63	66	/	1
65	68	65	////	4
65	67	64	/	1
66	65	63	//	2
69	61	62		0
65	67	61	////	4
60	61	60	//	2
$N = 20$				$N = 20$

Simple Ranking

Using the frequency distribution in table 1–1, additional analysis may be accomplished through ranking the data. Each score is given a position from high to low, with 1 indicating the highest rank. If there are two or more scores in one position, they are averaged to determine their rank. For example, in the above illustration of a frequency distribution, the score 67 occurs twice, occupying ranks 5 and 6. Taking the sum of these two ranks (11) and dividing by 2 yields an average rank of 5.5. The rank of the last score should equal the value of N (total number of scores) unless the last position contains duplicate scores, in which case the last position will be the result of averaging. Table 1–2 shows the results of ranking the frequency distribution shown in table 1–1.

TABLE 1–2.   Ranked Data.

X	f	Rank
69	3	2
68	1	4
67	2	5.5
66	1	7
65	4	9.5
64	1	12
63	2	13.5
61	4	16.5
60	2	19.5

Percentile Ranking

A score on a test or some other measuring instrument has little meaning unless it is related to other scores. Knowing that a student made a score of 63 on a test does not tell much unless one knows what score other students made on the test so that comparison can be made. A useful way to do this is through the use of a percentile rank, which is a relative rank, a rank order score based on a scale of 100.

The *percentile rank* of a raw score is the percentage of scores below the particular score. For example, if 65 percent of a group of students score below a student, that student's percentile rank is 65. Thus, the percentile rank is a point on a scale ranging from 1 to 100.

The *centile* (sometimes inappropriately termed the percentile) is the point on a raw score scale which corresponds to a given percentile rank. For example, an IQ score of 100 normally is the fiftieth centile. Correspondingly, the fiftieth centile is 100. The percentile rank of an IQ score of 100 is normally 50.

To calculate a percentile rank, the following formula is useful:

$$PR = \frac{100}{N}\left(cf - \frac{f}{2}\right)$$

where N is the number of scores in the entire distribution, cf is the cumulative frequency, and f is the frequency of the score.

The cumulative frequency we have not discussed before. If we have a particular interval (or score), the cumulative frequency of that interval is the frequency of the interval plus the total of the frequencies of all intervals below the given interval. In the sample frequency distribution in table 1–1, a score of 64 has a cumulative frequency of 9.

Applying the formula for computing a percentile rank to the frequency distribution above, we may calculate the percentile rank of a score of 65 as follows:

$$PR = \frac{100}{N}\left(cf - \frac{f}{2}\right) = \frac{100}{20}\left(13 - \frac{4}{2}\right) = 5 \times 11 = 55.$$

Theoretically, the distribution of percentile ranks is uniform throughout the percentile score scale. If the distribution of scores is normal, there will be an equal number of scores below the tenth centile, between the tenth and twentieth centiles, or between the ninetieth and hundredth centiles. This may not be the case, however, if the number of scores is relatively small or unevenly distributed.

MEASURES OF CENTRAL TENDENCY

When we wish to refine our analysis of group data we employ measures that describe group performance as a whole. The three measures most often used to describe group performance are the mean, median, and mode.

Mean

The most common measure of central tendency is the mean, simply defined as the arithmetic average. In essence, it is the sum of all the observations divided by the number of observations. The formula for computing the mean is presented below.

$$\bar{X} = \frac{\Sigma X}{n}$$

Utilizing data that has a sum of 1295 and an n of 18, the mean of a distribution would be:

$$\bar{X} = \frac{1295}{18}$$
$$= 71.94$$

Although the mean is the most common measure of central tendency, it is subject to the influence of extreme observations. For a more meaningful account of group performance, further analysis of the data should be made.

Median

The median is that point in a distribution where half of the observations fall above it and half of the observations fall below it. For a distribution containing an odd number of observations, the median is simply the middle point. For example, the median of 1,9,12,14, 16 is 12. For a distribution containing an even number of observations, the median point is determined by inserting the mid-point between the two middle observations. For rather large distributions that have been organized in a frequency distribution, the following procedure could be used.

Utilizing the data in the following frequency distribution, and using the formula

$$Mdn = \frac{n+1}{2}$$

the median would be:

X	f
90	1
83	2
78	4
75	3
73	2
72	1
64	1
54	1

$$Mdn = \frac{15+1}{2}$$
$$= 8$$

The median for this distribution is 75, determined by counting eight frequencies starting from the bottom. When many persons have equal scores, the median score is not so easily determined. An estimate is usually sufficient for the purpose at hand, but if a more accurate calculation is desired, additional sources on this subject should be consulted.

The median is most useful for describing certain kinds of data in that it is not affected by extreme scores. Salary distributions, for example, can often be described more effectively by using the median rather than the mean.

Mode

The mode is defined as the observation occurring most often in a distribution and is determined by simple observation. It is possible that a distribution may have more than one mode. If two exist, for example, the distribution is considered bimodal. Use of the mode is usually limited to descriptive statistics, but it may be very useful in getting a quick, rough estimate of central value. It quickly shows what is the most typical case.

MEASURES OF VARIABILITY

It is evident from our discussion of the measures of central tendency that these measures have some limitations with regard to describing group performance. To get a more accurate picture, we need to know how the data are distributed; that is, how compact or how scattered are the data from a certain point, say the mean. In analyzing quantitative data, the concept of individual differences becomes an essential consideration. This is the function of the measures of variability.

Measures of variability provide a numerical index that measures the amount of spread or dispersion of a set of data and make it possible to judge the amount of homogeneity or heterogeneity of the observations. When the need arises to compare one set of data with another, we need to know the amount and nature of variability contained in each set of data.

The measures of variability covered in this section include the range, deviation scores, standard deviation, and sigma scores. Each of these measures performs basically the same function, measuring variability, but differs in the degree of precision.

Range

The most elementary measure of variability is the range, which is defined as the difference between the lowest and highest observation in the distribution. The primary purpose of the range is to provide a numerical value that will indicate the overall spread of a set of observations. For example, in a distribution that has a high score of 99 and a low score of 60 the range would be 39.

Deviation Score

A simple but useful measure of variability is the deviation score. This index provides a means for determining the distance of an individual observation from the mean. The procedure for determining the deviation score is presented below.

$$x = X - \bar{X}$$

where

x = deviation score
X = raw score
$\bar{X}$ = mean

In a distribution with a mean of 80, the deviation score for a raw score of 94 would be:

$$x = 94 - 80$$
$$= 14$$

Standard Deviation

The most precise measure of variability presented in this chapter is standard deviation. It is more precise because it takes into account the variability of *all* the observations in a distribution. To illustrate the usefulness of this index, consider the situation in table 1–3 where the means of the two sets of data are the same.

TABLE 1–3.

Group 1	Group 2
100	62
70	61
60	60
50	59
20	58
$\bar{X} = 60$	$\bar{X} = 60$

Both sets of data have the same mean. It is evident, however, that the performance of subjects in each group is not the same. In a pure descriptive sense, we would use standard deviation as a means for making a more accurate interpretation of these means. The concept of variability and its application to more sophisticated statistical techniques is discussed in more detail in chapter 2.

The procedure for determining standard deviation is described below.

$$s = \sqrt{\frac{\Sigma X^2 - \frac{(\Sigma X)^2}{n}}{n-1}}$$

where

$$n = \text{number of observations}$$
$$\Sigma X^2 = \text{sum of the raw scores squared}$$
$$(\Sigma X)^2 = \text{sum of the raw scores, quantity squared}$$
$$s = \text{standard deviation}$$

The standard deviations for the data provided in this section would be:

Group 1

$$s = \sqrt{\frac{21{,}400 - 18{,}000}{4}}$$
$$= \sqrt{850}$$
$$= 29.15$$

Group 2

$$s = \sqrt{\frac{18{,}010 - 18{,}000}{4}}$$
$$= \sqrt{2.50}$$
$$= 1.58$$

With this additional information at hand, we can more accurately interpret the means of the two sets of data. Basically, they are different because the variability of the sets of data is different. Again, the concept of variability is discussed in more detail in chapter 2.

Sigma Score

The sigma score (z) is a method of reducing scores to a common comparable unit of measure. For example, if an individual makes a score of 65 on a history test and 75 on an English test, the interpretation of these scores might produce an incorrect conclusion that the individual is more capable in English. The sigma score is designed to provide a weighted index conducive to meaningful comparison, taking into consideration the amount of variability contained in the two sets of data.

The following formula is used to transform raw scores into sigma scores.

$$z = \frac{X - \bar{X}}{s}$$

Given a mean of 80 and a standard deviation of 10.20, the sigma score for a raw score of 94 would be:

$$z = \frac{94 - 80}{10.20}$$
$$= \frac{14}{10.20}$$
$$= 1.37$$

The score of 94 is thus seen to be 1.37 standard deviations above the mean.

We will deal with the sigma score again in more detail in chapter 2. In the context of this section, we use the sigma score to equate data that otherwise might not be comparable in original form by showing how they compare in terms of standard deviations above or below the means.

GRAPHIC REPRESENTATIONS

Numbers and statistics are used to represent real information. They summarize masses of information so that we may better understand and use it. This process results in an abstractness that is often difficult to understand, especially for the novice. A useful technique for organizing and summarizing data in more understandable fashion is the graphic representation.

Information is communicated pictorially and becomes easier understood. In addition, graphic representations of information may facilitate the solution of many problems in research by portraying the form of a frequency distribution.

The graphs we will consider are constructed with reference to two perpendicular lines, one horizontal and one vertical, called the coordinate axes. The horizontal axis (the abscissa) normally represents scores or measures, and the vertical axis (the ordinate) represents frequencies or cumulative frequencies (such as percentage of cases). For a pleasing and functional effect, the size of units for a graph is chosen so that the length of the vertical axis is 60 to 75 percent of the length of the baseline (an exception to this is the ogive which is usually constructed with the baseline equal to or slightly longer than the vertical, or cumulative frequency, axis).

Histogram

The histogram is basically a bar graph in which frequencies are represented by areas in the form of vertical bars. The horizontal axis is laid out to provide for all needed scores and the vertical axis includes frequencies from zero to the highest frequency in the particular distribution. If there is a fairly wide range of scores, they will probably need to be grouped in some fashion. In table 1–4 we have taken a group of performance scores on a physical fitness test and grouped them for graphic representation through the use of a histogram (figure 1–1).

TABLE 1–4.   Number of Sit-Ups in Two Minutes by 100 7th-Grade Girls.

Number of Sit-Ups	Frequency
0–10	2
11–20	5
21–30	9
31–40	7
41–50	13
51–60	27
61–70	11
71–80	11
81–90	4
91–100	7
101–110	3
111–120	1

Frequency Polygon

Frequency distributions may also be shown by using a frequency polygon, which is a graph with straight lines connecting points located above the

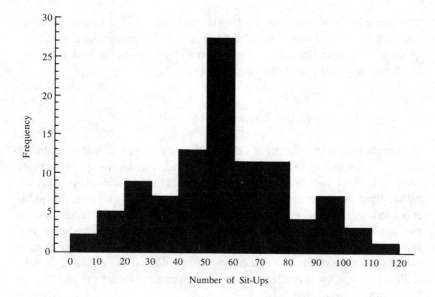

FIGURE 1–1.   Histogram.

midpoints of the intervals at heights corresponding to the frequencies. An empty interval is left at each end of the distribution with the line brought to the horizontal axis at the midpoint of these two intervals. The total area enclosed is the same as the histogram for the same data, but the area of each interval is not precisely indicated as in the histogram. The frequency polygon has the advantage of indicating that the trait portrayed is

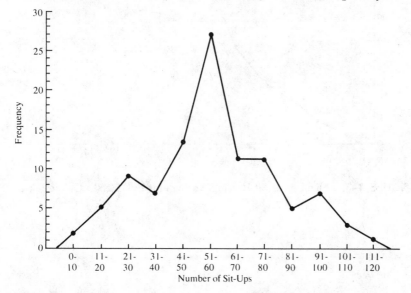

FIGURE 1–2.   Number of Sit-Ups in Two Minutes by 100 7th-Grade Girls.

continuously distributed, which is often the case, and it is also useful in showing two distributions on the same graph for comparison purposes.

Using the same data as the histogram in figure 1–1, we may construct the frequency polygon shown in figure 1–2.

Cumulative Frequency Curve (Ogive)

A cumulative frequency curve (often called an ogive) is useful when the intent is to represent the number of measures falling below specified score values. It conveniently shows the position of an individual in a group, rather than the general form of group performance. The vertical scale is recorded in cumulative frequencies, relative cumulative frequencies, or percentile ranks, and the plotting points are located above the upper real limits of the intervals rather than above the midpoints. Such a graph may also be used to estimate centiles and percentile ranks. Again using the data on sit-ups by seventh-grade girls, we may construct the cumulative frequency curve of figure 1–3.

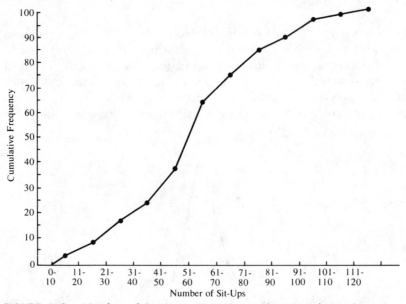

FIGURE 1–3. Number of Sit-Ups in Two Minutes by 100 7th-Grade Girls.

FOR REVIEW AND FURTHER STUDY

1. Give additional examples of the following:
   a. constants;
   b. variables: quantitative, qualitative, discrete, continuous.

2. Explain how each type of scale differs from the others and give examples of each.

3. Construct a simple frequency distribution, using the following data on the heartbeat of 30 subjects after running 880 yards.

142	140	148	142	143	157
156	161	158	150	156	155
161	141	162	170	162	157
143	152	164	143	167	169
157	158	168	143	156	169

4. Rank the data from the frequency distribution obtained in exercise 3.

5. Calculate the percentile rank of 164 in the frequency distribution of exercise 3. Calculate other percentile ranks in the distribution.

6. Calculate the mean, median, and mode for the data in exercise 3. Which is the most appropriate measure of central tendency in this case?

7. What are the strengths and weaknesses of each of these three measures of central tendency?

8. What is the range of the distribution in exercise 3?

9. Calculate from the data in exercise 3 the deviation score of 167 and of 150.

10. Calculate the standard deviation of the data in exercise 3.

11. Using the data in exercise 3, calculate the sigma score of 161, 148, 168.

12. A student's score, the mean, and the standard deviation on the test are given for an English test and a mathematics test. From this data, what conclusion might be reasonably drawn concerning the student's relative achievement in English and mathematics?

    Math: student score $= 85$; mean $= 75$; $s = 10$
    English: student score $= 95$; mean $= 85$; $s = 30$

13. Draw a histogram, a frequency polygon, and a cumulative frequency curve (ogive) of the following scores on a Stanford-Binet intelligence test for 75 adults.

94	141	121	97	112	134	121	123
102	132	92	106	113	103	107	107
95	110	100	83	92	148	102	107
97	107	105	127	108	96	106	129
115	95	110	108	129	139	89	123
130	109	110	104	113	111	98	
101	92	104	87	114	118	138	
146	102	124	124	106	133	101	
108	114	118	135	105	101	116	
105	127	131	105	86	91	105	

2

Variability and Probability

In this chapter, we will include a discussion of the concept of variation, variation and its role in statistical analyses, standard scores and the normal curve, and a brief introduction to the notion of probability. These concepts are employed throughout the text, since they represent the central basis for the use and interpretation of statistical analyses of behavioral science data.

VARIABILITY DEFINED

Variability refers to the spread or dispersion that exists in a set of data drawn from the measurement of any characteristic. If a personality test is given to a group of adults, all the scores will not be the same. If the attitudes toward a given political issue are measured, the attitudes will not all be the same. If a performance test is given, the scores on the test will not all be the same. A certain amount of variation will exist from the measurement of any characteristic if the instrument being used in any way measures what it is designed to measure. Characteristics that are not measured by tests, such as height, weight, speed, etc., also produce variation unless subjects are picked on the basis of a commonality, such as persons of the same height.

Recently, a test was given to a group of pre-school children in an attempt to measure their vocabulary. The subjects who took the test consisted of twenty-eight children ranging in age from three to five. The subjects were considered rather homogeneous in other factors, such as home background, ethnic makeup, and physical well-being. Their scores are shown in table 2–1.

TABLE 2–1.   Peabody Picture Vocabulary Scores of Twenty-Eight Pre-School Children.

93	37	10	2
73	24	10	2
62	18	7	2
60	18	6	1
60	15	6	0
51	12	3	0
44	12	2	0

Simple observation tells us that a considerable amount of variation exists within this set of scores. We can say, then, that regardless of testing error or other matters, some of the subjects had a greater vocabulary than others. This same type of outcome would occur regardless of the characteristic being measured. Variability can be increased or decreased by the way subjects are selected and by the number of subjects used, but variability cannot be eliminated unless, again, the subjects are preselected on some exact basis. We could, for example, reduce the amount of variability in the language development scores by reducing the age range. On the other hand, we could increase the variability by adding a group of six-year-olds to the total group.

VARIABILITY AND STATISTICAL ANALYSES

Variability is of concern in statistical analyses in two ways. First, we use variability to help describe a set of data. Variability was treated in chapter 1 in this way. Another example may help indicate the usefulness of variability concepts in describing data. Keep in mind that we are only interested at this point in helping a person to get a picture of the basic characteristics of a mass of data. The study of inferences and relationships will be considered later.

If the members of two golf clubs wished to compare the scores of the members of one club with those of the other, they might over a period of time record the scores of each member. Let us consider first what might happen in observing the scores of any one member. Table 2–2 shows

TABLE 2–2.

Scores of Golfer A:		
84	97	
93	79	
80	84	$\bar{X} = 87$
82	85	$Range = 18$
90	88	x of 97 (highest score) $= 10$
87	87	x of 79 (lowest score) $= 8$
86	89	$s^2 = 26.83$
92	81	$s = 5.18$
80	91	
95	90	

what his scores for twenty rounds of eighteen holes might be. Just from observing the list one may conclude that this particular golfer has a rather wide range of scores—he is not very consistent. However, a better picture of the situation may result by calculating the mean, the range, the deviation of high and low scores from the mean, the variance, and the standard deviation of the group of scores. Calculating these as indicated in chapter 1 reveals the information indicated beside the scores.

TABLE 2–3.

Scores of Golfer B:		
89	88	
85	85	
90	84	$\bar{X} = 87$
87	85	$Range = 7$
88	87	x of 90 (highest score) $= 3$
89	88	x of 83 (lowest score) $= 4$
86	89	$s^2 = 4.41$
90	86	$s = 2.10$
85	87	
83	89	
87	90	

Table 2–3 shows the scores of another golfer who played twenty times. A cursory examination of this group of scores indicates a golfer who is more consistent than the first one we discussed. Calculating the mean, the range, the deviation of high and low scores from the mean, and the standard deviation of the group of scores will give a better description of the golfer's performance.

If each golf club had a total membership of three hundred, a random selection of fifteen golfers from each club might result in scores on a given day as shown in table 2–4. We will calculate the mean, range, deviations

TABLE 2.4.

Scores of Club A Members:		Scores of Club B Members:	
72	$\bar{X} = 87$	84	$\bar{X} = 87$
80	$Range = 42$	93	$Range = 18$
94	x of $110 = 23$	79	x of $96 = 9$
68	x of $68 = 19$	87	x of $78 = 9$
85	$s^2 = 128.71$	89	$s^2 = 30.71$
94	$s = 11.35$	81	$s = 5.54$
110		95	
87		78	
93		96	
77		88	
92		82	
101		91	
88		85	
74		87	
90		90	

of high and low scores, and standard deviation for the scores representative of each club.

It is not difficult to recognize the fact that although the mean score for each group of golfers was the same, there is quite a difference in the membership of the two golf clubs.

Describing the scores of two golfers and scores by members of two golf clubs by means of statistical variability gives us a better picture of the situation in each case. In addition to description, variability may also be used for further analysis of data for purposes of inference, such as comparing means, determining relationships, or making predictions. Let us now consider some of these possibilities.

By looking at the twenty different scores of the two individual golfers, some rather simple inferences may be drawn. One is much less consistent than the other and less predictable from day to day. He probably plays less often and makes more poor shots. Prediction of his score on a given day would be more difficult and subject to error. Comparison of means does not tell us this type of thing; it must be inferred from the range, deviations, and standard deviation. Most people would consider golfer B the better golfer of the two.

Inferences to be drawn from analysis of the variability statistics of the members' scores from two golf clubs indicate that, although the mean score of the golfers from each club is the same, there is considerable difference in the type of golfers who are members. One might even make an inference as to which group belonged to a country club and which group played at a public course. Prediction of a score of a member of Club A would be more subject to error. If the members of each group were given some lessons, which group of scores would probably improve the most?

Some inferences about age range of the golfers might also be drawn. It is not difficult to see that much more use can be made of data such as this if variability analysis is utilized.

MEASURING VARIABILITY

Several types of mathematical calculations may be used with deviation scores—the scores calculated as the difference between a raw score and the mean ($x = X - \bar{X}$). The simplest of these is the mean deviation, in which the deviations from the mean (either positive or negative) are added together, disregarding negative or positive aspects of the deviation, and divided by the number of scores. The mean deviation is used very little because of mathematical restrictions upon the use of absolute values (disregarding negative and positive aspects of values). It may be useful if the investigator wants to know how far, on the average, the scores of a distribution depart from the mean of the distribution. The primary use of the mean deviation is to introduce additional measures of dispersion.

The Sum of Squares (SS) measure of dispersion avoids the problems of using absolute values by squaring the deviations before summing. This measure of dispersion enters into many statistical calculations, including the variance and standard deviation which are discussed next, but it is not usually reported as a descriptive index. The variance and standard deviation are the most important measures of dispersion in both descriptive and inferential statistics.

Variance

The standard deviation is the most widely used measure of dispersion, but to more fully understand it we shall first briefly consider what is called the variance. The variance may be defined as the mean of the sum of all squared deviations from the mean of any distribution of scores, or more briefly, the mean of the squared deviations from the mean. This definition is usually abbreviated to mean square. In formula form this becomes

$$S^2 = \frac{\Sigma(X_i - \bar{X})^2}{n} .$$

For a total population, the variance is computed by dividing the sum of squared deviations by the number of subjects (SS/N). Using this same procedure to make inferences from a sample would result in inaccuracies due to biased sampling, particularly with smaller samples. To correct for this and allow a sample variance to be used as an estimate of the population variance, the formula is adjusted by substituting $n - 1$ for N. The formula for calculating a sample variance thus becomes

$$s^2 = \frac{SS}{n-1}$$

where

$$SS = \frac{\Sigma(X_i - \bar{X})^2}{n}.$$

The variance may be calculated as indicated above, or with a calculator, using the raw score formula:

$$s^2 = \frac{\Sigma X^2 - \dfrac{(\Sigma X)^2}{n}}{n-1}$$

As an example of how variance is calculated, consider the data in table 2–5.

In doing research, examination and comparison of the variance of the data being considered often has significant advantages over examination of means or other similar measures. As we have seen in earlier comparisons of the scores of individual golfers and the members of two different golf clubs, when two samples have equal means it does not necessarily mean that they are similar in other respects. Comparison of mean scores in these instances indicates considerable similarity, but further examination of the variances of the scores indicates a great deal of difference (see p. 24). On the other hand, two arrays of data with different means might actually be more similar than our golfers' scores if consideration is given to variance as well as measures of central tendency. Much of the discussion and many of the statistical techniques included in the chapters which follow are based on comparisons of variance and relating these comparisons to establishing similarities and differences in samples and groups or to making predictions and inferences on the basis of sampling and probability.

Standard Deviation

As stated above, the standard deviation is the most widely used measure of dispersion for data that are interval or ratio in nature. This measure is simply the square root of the variance. In most cases, the standard devia-

TABLE 2–5.

X	x	x^2
31	18	324
43	6	36
62	13	169
46	3	9
58	11	121
30	19	361
28	21	441
74	25	625
54	5	25
57	8	64
43	6	36
61	12	144
35	14	196
50	1	1
52	3	9
57	8	64
47	2	4
38	11	121
51	2	4
63	14	196

$$\bar{X} = 49$$
$$s^2 = \frac{\Sigma(X_i - \bar{X})^2}{n-1} = \frac{2950}{19} = 155.26$$
$$s = \sqrt{155.26} = 12.46$$

or:

$$s^2 = \frac{\Sigma X^2 - \frac{(\Sigma X)^2}{n}}{n-1} = \frac{50930 - \frac{(980)^2}{20}}{19}$$

$$= \frac{50930 - 48020}{19} = \frac{2910}{19} = 153.16$$
$$s = \sqrt{153.16} = 12.38$$

tion is more useful than the variance because it is expressed in the same units as the original measures. For example, looking again at the scores of golfers A and B mentioned earlier, the variance of each (26.83 and 4.41) doesn't tell us very much, but the standard deviation (5.18 and 2.1) is more usable because it is expressed in the same terms as the original scores (number of strokes). We can see that golfer A varies in his scores more than twice as much as does golfer B.

The standard deviation tells us how much the scores in a distribution deviate from the mean. If the standard deviation is small, there is little variability, and most of the scores are tightly clustered about the mean. If the standard deviation is large, the scores are more widely scattered. By using the standard deviation to compare two groups, we can easily see how they differ in variability.

A quick check of calculations on the standard deviation can be made by comparing it to the range of a distribution. With larger groups, approximately six standard deviations will equal the range of scores. As N decreases, the number of standard deviations needed to include all of the cases decreases. This has been estimated by L.H.C. Tippett and is shown in table 2–6.

TABLE 2–6.

N	Number of Standard Deviations Included in the Range
5	2.3
10	3.1
25	3.9
30	4.1
50	4.5
100	5.0
500	6.1
1000	6.5

THE NORMAL CURVE AND PROBABILITY

The standard deviation becomes even more useful when it is studied in relation to what is known as Tchebycheff's theorem, which states that the proportion of the scores in any frequency distribution which are within h standard deviations of the mean is at least $1 - 1/h^2$. This means that at least 75 percent of the scores in any collection will lie within two standard deviations from the mean, and at least 85 percent of the scores will lie within three standard deviations from the mean. Referring again to golfer A, according to this theorem we can safely predict that at least 75 percent of the time his golf score will be between 77 and 97 (87 ± 10). In the case of golfer B, we can predict that at least 75 percent of the time his golf score will be between 83 and 91 (87 ± 4).

If we know more about the type of distribution, we can make more exact statements concerning the frequency of cases which lie within certain standard deviations from the mean. If the distribution is the Gaussian or normal-curve type, then 68.2 percent of the scores will lie within one standard deviation of the mean, 95.4 percent of the cases within two standard deviations of the mean, and 99.7 percent of the cases within three standard deviations of the mean. Using our golfers as examples again, if we can assume that their scores over a period of time will be normal in their distribution, we can predict that at least 68.2 percent of the time (usually roughly figured as two-thirds) golfer A will score between 82 and 92 (87 ± 5); and about 95 percent of the time his score will be between 77 and 97 (87 ± 10). Golfer B, who is more consistent and has a score standard deviation of approximately two, can be predicted to score between 85 and 89 two-thirds of the time, and 95 percent of the time he will score between 83 and 91. Similar predictions can be made about scores of golfers from the two golf clubs or scores of a student on a test similar to that from which the scores in table 2–5 were drawn.

These examples provide illustrations of the importance of variability and the standard deviation in making inference and predictions. We can predict a future score of golfer B with much more accuracy than we can one for golfer A because of the differences in variability of the two golfers' scores. What inferences can be made about the golf scores of members of the two golf clubs mentioned earlier? Assuming the array of scores in table 2–5 is that for a student's English test grades, what predictions can be made about his future test scores?

The normal curve concept is very important in understanding the use of statistics and so deserves some additional discussion. Direct measures used in the behavioral sciences (such as the height and weight of adult humans) and most psychological measures (such as IQ scores and reaction times) have been found to approximate closely a mathematical model called the *normal distribution*. The graph of this normal distribution is a continuous, symmetrical, bell-shaped curve. Frequencies tend to concentrate around the median and become fewer and fewer at either end, resulting in a frequency curve which is high in the middle and low at the ends.

Frequency distributions are not always of the normal curve type, of course, and the terms *skewness* and *kurtosis* are used in describing abnormal distributions. In a normal curve, the right and left halves of the curve are mirror images of each other. If this is not the case, the curve is said to be *skewed*, either *positively* (to the right) or *negatively* (to the left). Thus, if the scores tend to be concentrated toward the high end of the score scale, the curve is negatively skewed. If they are concentrated toward the low end of the score scale, they are positively skewed. Both types of skewness are illustrated in figure 2–2.

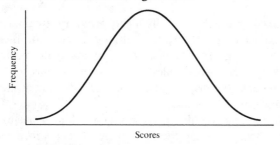

FIGURE 2–1. Theoretical Normal Curve of Distribution.

Kurtosis refers to the relative peakedness or flatness of a curve in the center of the distribution. If the curve is flatter than normal (fewer scores near the mean), it is said to be *platykurtic;* if it is more peaked than normal (more scores near the mean), it is said to be *leptokurtic* (figure 2–3).

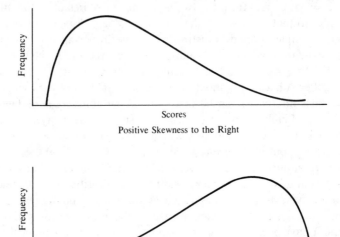

Positive Skewness to the Right

Negative Skewness to the Left

FIGURE 2–2.   Skewness.

There are measures of skewness and kurtosis, but they are seldom used by behavioral scientists. We will not discuss these measures, but it is important for the student to have a basic understanding of skewness and kurtosis as they apply to frequency distributions and related matters in statistical analysis.

Standard Scores

Scores obtained on tests are usually highly arbitrary. Real meaning of the scores can be achieved only by comparing one score to others or to the general tendencies of the test scores. Comparison of raw scores of two or more tests is not very useful unless there is some means of standardizing the scores, because the dispersion or central tendencies of the test scores are not necessarily very similar.

Percentile ranking was discussed in chapter 1 as a means of relating meaning to a score showing the percentage of scores in the distribution which are smaller. Another common procedure, the *z*-score, was briefly

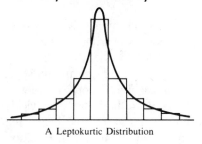 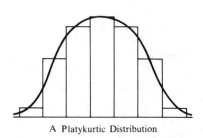

| A Leptokurtic Distribution | A Platykurtic Distribution |

FIGURE 2–3. Kurtosis.

described in chapter 1. It indicates the placement of the score with respect to the mean of the distribution by stating the score in terms of standard deviations above or below the mean. This and other score distributions which have been altered to produce means and standard deviations of standard value are called *standard scores*. They are very useful in the interpretation of test data, and we will discuss their basis and use in a little more detail at this point.

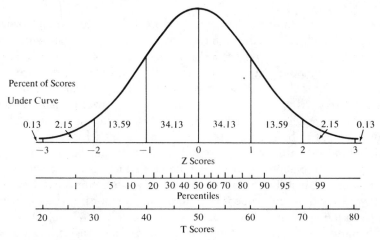

FIGURE 2–4. Normal Curve and Derived Scales.

The whole process of standard score derivation and use is related to the normal curve and areas under it. We mentioned earlier the fact that if a distribution is of the normal-curve type, then approximately two-thirds of the scores will lie within one standard deviation of the mean, about 95 percent within two standard deviations, and over 99 percent within three standard deviations of the mean. This may be illustrated, as in figure 2–4, by showing the percentage of cases lying under a normal curve within standard deviation or z-score units of the mean. Corresponding percentile equivalents are also indicated.

Comparing scores from two different distributions by means of z-scores is very useful, but it has the disadvantage of awkward negative score values for scores below the mean. This may be remedied by converting the z-scores to a new distribution having any convenient mean and standard deviation. For example, what has been called a T-score is achieved by multiplying the z-score by ten and adding 50 to the result. This yields a mean of 50 and standard deviation units of 10 above and below the mean, as shown in figure 2–4. Another commonly used score distribution has a mean of 500 and standard deviation of 100. Modern intelligence tests are commonly scaled in this way with a mean of 100 and standard deviation of 15. Any score of this nature (commonly referred to as Z-scores, using the capital letter) may be obtained with the formula: $Z_i = M' + z_i S'$, where M' is the mean and S' the standard deviation desired in the new distribution.

THE NOTION OF PROBABILITY

Most analysis of statistical data requires some knowledge and understanding of probability. To make an intelligent judgment about the significance of a person's score on an academic achievement test, for example, we must know something about the probability of his making that score. If 100 people took the test, how many would be likely to make the same or a similar score? If we have some estimate of the answer to that question, then we can reach a reasonable understanding of the significance of the score. Would it be accurate to predict that a high school senior boy would run 100 yards in 9.6 seconds? To answer that question we must know something about the average time needed for such a person to run 100 yards, the distribution of running times when a number of boys run 100 yards, and the consequent likelihood that a senior boy could run 100 yards in 9.6 seconds. We can achieve an estimate of this likelihood, or probability, by calculating standard deviations and considering the percentages under the normal curve.

In the above two examples we have illustrated two of the major ways probability theory is utilized in statistical analysis. To *judge the significance* of an event, we must have an estimate about the probability that the event would occur under normal circumstances. To *predict the likelihood* of an occurrence, we must have an idea about the probability of its occurrence under normal conditions. It is readily apparent that both kinds of situations are directly related to the normal curve, areas under the curve, and standard deviations.

We can see how probability is related to the normal curve if we remember that the normal curve is a theoretical distribution of frequency of occurrence. The curve's bell shape indicates that the greater the deviation of an event from the mean of all events, the less the frequency of occurrence decreases.

Probability may be expressed as the number of chances in 100 or as a proportion. In a normal distribution, events that deviate more than 2.58 standard deviations from the mean occur one percent of the time. The chances of such an event occurring are 1 in 100. The same probability can be expressed as a proportion (P) by saying that $P = .01$. In similar fashion, with a normal distribution five percent of the cases deviate 1.96 standard deviations from the mean. The chances of such events are 5 in 100 (1 in 20), or it can be stated that $P = .05$.

We may explore the meaning of probability in another way by considering the flipping of coins and the throwing of dice. When we pitch a coin in the air, we know that the chance of its coming down tails is one-half or fifty percent. We know this because a coin has only two sides. When we roll a die, we know that the chance of the number t appearing is one-sixth or one in six. We know this because a die has six sides, each with a different number.

We can say, then, that every time a coin is flipped it will come down either heads or tails. If we flipped a coin a large number of times we would expect the number of heads and tails that come up to be approximately equal. In similar fashion, if we roll one die a large number of times, we can expect the number 5 to appear about one-sixth of the time.

When we deal with probability, we are considering the ratio of the number of occurrences to the possible number of events (the number of heads turned up to the number of flips, for example). In tossing a coin, as the number of flips increases, the ratio comes closer to the true value of one-half. It is rare, however, for a perfect 50-50 split to be achieved. As we will see later, this is an important point when attempting to predict the probability of an event as a result of a statistical analysis.

We will avoid getting too technical, but let's look at a situation where we flip two coins at the same time and desire to determine the probability of getting both heads, both tails, or one head and one tail. When we flip the two coins, each one can come down in two ways with equal probability. There are four possibilities, each with a probability of one-fourth. We could expect either two heads, heads on the first and tails on the second, tails on the first and heads on the second, or both tails. The probability of getting two heads or two tails is one-fourth, while the probability of getting one head and one tail is one-half. This may be expressed as 1 in 4 ($P = .25$) and 1 in 2 ($P = .50$).

From the above illustrations we can arrive at a workable definition of probability, although an understanding of the concept is more important than memorizing a definition. Stating it as simply as possible, probability is the ratio of the number of ways a specified event can happen divided by the total number of ways all events under consideration can occur. The following more important applications of this concept are commonly found in statistical analysis and research procedures.

1. The probability of occurrence of any one of a set of equally likely events is one divided by the number of events. As an example, if we take a team of five basketball players, place their numbers on separate pieces of paper, place these in a hat and draw a number, the chances are 1 in 5 that a particular player's number will be drawn.

2. In a frequency distribution, if there is more than one object or event in a given class, the probability of drawing an object of a particular class is equal to the class frequency divided by the number of objects. In a game of cards, your hand contains 3 Spades, 4 Hearts, 2 Diamonds, and 5 Clubs. You have one too many cards and your opponent draws one card from your hand. The probability of his drawing one of your Clubs is 5 in 14.

3. The probability of an event occurring plus the probability of its not occurring is equal to one. In the card game situation above, the probability that your opponent will not draw a Club from your hand is 9 in 14.

4. The probability that any one of a set of mutually exclusive events will occur is the sum of the probabilities of the separate events. In the card game situation above, the probability that your opponent will draw either a Spade or a Heart is 7 in 14 or 1 in 2. This is known as the addition rule of probability, and, as stated above, for it to apply the events must be mutually exclusive—when one occurs the other cannot occur. When a card is drawn, for example, it will be either a Spade, a Heart, a Diamond, or a Club.

5. The probability that a combination of independent events will occur is the product of the separate probabilities of the events. Independent events means that the occurrence or nonoccurrence of one has no effect on the other. To illustrate this principle, consider the probability that a student will randomly guess at the answer on a true-false question. The probability that he will answer it correctly is 1 in 2. The probability that he will guess the correct answer on the second question is also 1 in 2. Applying this principle, the probability that he will guess both of the answers correctly is 1 in 4. The probability that he will guess the correct answers to the first three questions is 1 in 8, and to the first four questions 1 in 16. This is known as the multiplication rule of probability.

Additional application of these concepts about probability and related statistical significance will be discussed in chapter 4.

FOR REVIEW AND FURTHER STUDY

1. A research study[1] was carried out to determine the effectiveness of predicting student teacher success from student teacher responses to selected
   videotaped critical incidents in teaching. As a part of this study, the
   student teachers were scored by their university supervisor and their
   cooperating teacher, using an evaluation instrument. The evaluation scores
   were as follows:

University Supervisor	Cooperating Teacher	University Supervisor	Cooperating Teacher
177	186	148	140
158	165	177	174
160	126	189	189
160	179	146	114
195	194	178	159
183	165	161	146
174	178	156	161
181	180	198	168
190	178	176	181
197	177	156	154
143	139	168	161
181	168	185	173
171	170	183	176
166	167	167	143
175	178	182	170
183	173	182	155
191	194	135	158
180	166	192	183
133	126	151	156
150	156	195	179
181	178	150	158
181	170	173	162
180	190	107	116
170	185	195	196
198	186	187	170
130	145		

$$N = 51$$
Mean $= 171$	166
Range $= 68$	82
X of high score $= 27$	30
X of low score $= 41$	52
$S^2 = 3920$	374
$S = 62.6$	19.3

   a. Describe and make simple inferences about the students, the scores
      on the evaluation, and comparisons of the two sets of scores by
      calculating the mean, range, deviation of highest and lowest scores,
      variance, and standard deviation.

---

1. David Lesley Henderson, "Predicting Student Teacher Success with Videotaped Critical Incidents." 1970.

b. Assuming a normal distribution, between which scores by the co-operating teachers would you expect two-thirds of the evaluations to fall? Between which scores would you expect 95% of them to fall?

c. If the scores were skewed to the left (negative), how would this affect your predictions in exercise b? What would be the effect on predictions if it were skewed to the right (positive)?

d. What effect on your predictions in exercise b would result if the distribution of scores was platykurtic? leptokurtic?

e. Consider the evaluation scores by the cooperating teachers and the university supervisors, assuming they are normally distributed.

   (1) Calculate the score equivalents to a z-score of 1, 2, 3, -1, -2, -3.

   (2) Compare the similarity of a score of 180 given by university supervisors and cooperating teachers by calculating the z-score and T-score.

f. Which group of scores by the university supervisors in this study would be likely to occur no more than 5% of the time? 1%? 33%?

g. What is the probability that the score given by a cooperating teacher to a student would be 128? 116? 185?

2. If in a group of 100 people there are 10 children (ages birth to 12), 15 adolescents (ages 13–18), 25 young adults (ages 19–35), 30 middle-aged adults (ages 36–55), and 20 older adults (ages 56 and above):

a. What is the probability that a random selection of a person from the group will produce an adolescent? a child?

b. What is the probability that random selection of two persons will produce either a child or an adolescent?

c. What is the probability of randomly choosing a specific young adult and a specific older adult in two consecutive selections?

3. A study[2] was conducted of the leisure-time reading preferences of ninth-grade students. Each of sixty pupils was asked to list his favorite magazines. The responses were grouped according to twelve magazine categories. The number of respondents that included each category among their preferences was as follows:

Category of Magazine	Number of Respondents Indicating This Category as Their Preference
Teen-Age	60
Comic	55
Stage and Screen	45
True Romance	40
Mechanical	35
Weekly Pictorial	33

2. John Q. Adams, "A Study of Leisure-Time Reading Preferences of Ninth Grade Students," *The High School Journal* 46:67–72, November 1962. (In *World Book*, p. 17 ff.)

Category of Magazine	Number of Respondents Indicating This Category as Their Preference
Weekly	26
Outdoor Sports	25
Digest	24
Women's Fashion	21
Women's Home	14
Suggestive	9
Travel	7
Science-Fiction	6
Scandal	5
Current Events	5
Men's Adventures	4
Church	3

Assuming that the sample for this study is typical of the total population of ninth-grade students in the United States:

What is the probability that a ninth-grade student will include in his preferences the reading of sports magazines? teen-age magazines?

4. Assume that in a study similar to that above, 100 randomly selected nineth-grade students were asked to name their favorite type of magazine for leisure-time reading, with the following results:

Category of Magazine	Number of Respondents Indicating This Category as Their Preference
Teen-Age	26
Comic	21
Outdoor Sports	18
True Romance	14
Adventure	11
Mechanical	6
Other	4

a. What is the probability that a ninth-grade student will prefer to read teen-age magazines? adventure magazines?

b. What is the probability that a student will prefer to read something other than comic magazines?

c. What is the probability that a student will prefer to read either true romance or adventure magazines?

d. What is the probability that four students selected at random will all prefer to read magazines other than those listed?

e. What is the probability that if two students are selected at random one will prefer teen-age magazines and the other will prefer comic magazines?

3

Sampling

During a recent period, the following information was reported on items of concern to the American people.

Item 1

On the eve of the 1972 election for President of the United States, Richard Nixon holds a lead of landslide proportions over Senator George McGovern. The final Gallup Poll[1] taken just prior to the election predicts the following outcome.

Nixon—61 percent of the vote

McGovern—35 percent of the vote

Other Parties—1 percent of the vote

When the undecided vote is allocated, the final outcome of the election will be:

Nixon—62 percent of the vote

McGovern—38 percent of the vote

Post election results revealed that, with 97 percent of the vote counted, Nixon carried the election with 61 percent and McGovern won 38 percent.[2]

---

1. Reported by the Associated Press, November 6, 1972.
2. Reported by the Associated Press, November 8, 1972.

Item 2

A recent survey[3] reported information relating to attitudes currently held by the American public toward various aspects of the school system. A sample of the results is presented below.

41 percent of the adult public feel that public school students have too many rights and privileges.

73 percent of the adult public feel that students who are 18 years of age should not have more rights and privileges than other students.

56 percent of the adult public would not vote for raising taxes to provide more money for the schools.

61 percent of the adult public disapprove of tenure for teachers.

64 percent of the adult public oppose children starting school at age four.

67 percent of the adult public would like to see their children take up teaching as a career.

Item 3

With reference to what people are watching on television, a recent report,[4] referred to as the Nielsen Ratings, provided the following information.

Nielsen Ratings for the two-week period ending the first of November revealed that the Summer Olympics took the first seven positions on the ratings. In addition to the top seven, the Olympic games tied for the number nine spot and was also number sixteen. Holding down the twenty-fifth spot in the ratings was "Cade's County."

The three items of information presented above all give the impression of representing the views and preferences of the general public as a whole. The impression is given on purpose, in that the statements are designed to represent the public, or that part of the public that the information was designed to represent. The items also give the impression of providing information based on responses of *all* persons to whom the information was directed. However, this is not the case. For example, the Gallup Poll prediction, concerning the outcome of the election, was based on the preferences of approximately 3,500 persons questioned just prior to the election. The Gallup Poll of public attitudes toward education referred to in item two was based on responses from 1,614 adults. The information relative to what television viewers watched during a specified period of time was based on approximately 1,100 contacts.

---

3. George H. Gallup, "Fourth Annual Gallup Poll of Public Attitudes Toward Education," *Phi Delta Kappan* 54 (September 1972): 33–46.
4. Reported by the Associated Press, November 5, 1972.

THEORY AND PRACTICE OF SAMPLING

The technique of sampling used to obtain the information reported in the previous section is one of the most useful tools available for research in the behavioral sciences. Sampling allows the researcher to work with relatively small samples and then generalize the information obtained to a larger defined population. In the political poll, for example, information was gathered from approximately 3,500 persons designated to be representative of the millions of persons qualified to vote in this country. In other words, the preferences of the American people reported in the survey were derived from the measurement of preferences of a small proportion of the total population of voting age.

Two terms should be defined at this point. First, the term "population" is used to denote the defined limits placed on the group from which the sample is to be taken. The second term, "sample," refers to the subgroup drawn from the defined population and is assumed to approximate the larger group on whatever is to be studied. Once the sample has been drawn and used it ceases to be of interest, since whatever is found is assumed to approximate, within a measurable degree of error, that possessed by the larger group. For example, if some characteristic was measured using a sample of residents drawn from the total population residing within a city limits, then it would be assumed that whatever was discovered concerning this characteristic could be generalized to all residents of that city.

Some Basic Assumptions

There is, of course, considerably more to sampling than simply gathering a small group of subjects together for the purpose of facilitating research. Some of the key assumptions underlying the use of samples are described in the sections that follow.

Defining the Population. The first task of the sampling process is to define the population both in terms of numbers involved and the distribution of the characteristic that will be involved in the study. For finite populations, i.e., those that can be specifically identified in terms of the total number involved, limits can be placed on the population without much difficulty. For infinite populations, i.e., those for which no definite limits can be established, the validity of sampling becomes questionable. In essence, the task is simply one of setting the limits from which the sample will be drawn and the findings generalized. This idea is illustrated in figure 3–1.

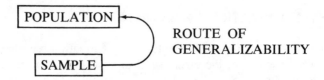

FIGURE 3–1.   Relationship of Samples to Populations.

To define the population in terms of the distribution of variables under study, or those related to it, the concept of distribution curves must be employed. (Distribution curves are discussed in chapter 1.) This is to say that, in the process of defining the population, an assumption must be made regarding the distribution of the variables one wishes to sample in the population, which, in turn, allows the assumption regarding the distribution of the variables in the sample. For example, if we were interested in determining the average IQ of a group of citizens in a city, we would begin by assuming that the intelligence level of the people would be normally distributed according to the scale illustrated in figure 3–2. The assumption that a variable is normally distributed in a population or not normally distributed is made on the basis of either logic or research evidence.

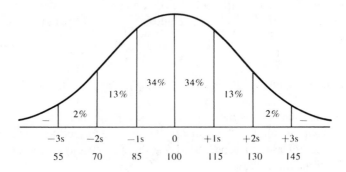

FIGURE 3–2.   A Normal Distribution of IQ Scores.

We would interpret this distribution to mean that one would expect, based on prior information concerning the IQ distribution in a normal population, approximately 13 percent of the population to possess IQs between 115 and 130 and a corresponding percentage to possess IQs between 70 and 85. The remainder of the scale is interpreted in the same manner.

If the population was known, or expected to have an abnormal distribution, say, a school for the mentally retarded, a group of high school seniors, or a group of graduate students, then the distribution would be assumed to take a different form from the one described in figure 3–2. The type of distribution one might expect in situations like these would be one that is skewed either in a negative direction, as in the case of graduate students, or skewed in a positive direction, as in the case of a school for the mentally retarded. These two types of distributions are illustrated in figures 3–3 and 3–4.

FIGURE 3–3. A Negatively Skewed Distribution, i.e., Graduate Students.

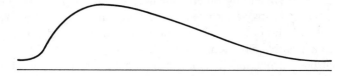

FIGURE 3–4. A Positively Skewed Distribution, i.e., Retarded Students.

If some other variable was used and the distribution of this variable in the general population was not known, we would have to draw on the theory of probability in order to make an assumption about normality. For example, if we were interested in determining the attitudes of citizens in a given city regarding a proposal to liberalize the liquor laws, a sampling procedure would be used to obtain this information. The population might be defined as all the citizens of voting age living within the city limits. In this case, it might be assumed that the attitudes toward this issue would be distributed in a manner as shown in figure 3–5.

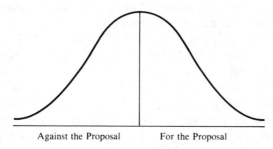

Against the Proposal   For the Proposal

FIGURE 3–5. Normal Distribution of Attitudes toward Liberalizing Liquor Laws.

This distribution would be interpreted to mean that approximately 34 percent of the population might be expected to slightly favor liberalizing the existing laws, while a corresponding 34 percent might be expected to be against the proposal in a moderate way. In other words, approximately

68 percent might be expected to hold a middle ground on the proposal and could possibly be swayed to one side or the other. Approximately 13 percent of the population might be expected to strongly favor the proposal to the extent that efforts to change their position would probably be to no avail. A corresponding 13 percent might be expected to be against the proposal to the same degree as their counterparts favoring it. The remaining percentage might be expected to occupy the extreme positions on both sides of the issue; that is, those that might stop at nothing to either see the proposal pass or see the proposal fail. Approximately 2 percent of the population might be expected to fall into these categories.

The distribution of attitudes toward the proposal might, however, be perceived to be something other than normal, i.e., a population center whose economy is strongly rooted in the liquor industry. If this was the case, the distribution of the variable in the population might be assumed skewed in a negative direction.

The purpose of making an assumption about the distribution of a variable in the population is to serve as a bench mark when assessing the observed distribution of the variable in the sample. A sample is useful only if the distribution of the variable in the sample approximates the distribution of that variable in the population.

Conditions of Sampling.   In order to obtain a sample that approximates the population, two conditions must be met when selecting the sample. These are *equal chance* and *independence*.

The concept of equal chance simply means that every subject in the defined population must be given an equal chance of becoming a part of the sample. In other words, the sample distribution must be a miniature of the population distribution in so far as it is representative of the larger population. If certain portions of the population are excluded, the sample becomes biased. The classic example of violating the concept of equal chance is the Literary Digest's prediction concerning the outcome of the 1936 election between Alfred Landon and Franklin D. Roosevelt. Although this example is rather out of date and overused, it still makes the point. The Digest, now defunct, predicted, incorrectly of course, that Alfred Landon would win. The error occurred when telephone directories were used to obtain the sample, and in doing so, automatically excluded from the sample persons who did not have a telephone and were not listed in the directory. Since the depression years prohibited many from having a telephone, the very people excluded from the sample were those that were most likely to vote for Roosevelt because of the New Deal provisions for the poor. The prediction was far off base simply because it was not based on a representative sample of the total population, which, in this case, would have significantly altered the prediction. Apparently the Gallup Poll, referred to in the first part of this chapter, did not make this kind of mistake in the selection of a sample in the 1972 election.

A second condition that must be met in order to obtain a representative sample is independence. Although this is not usually a problem when equal chance is adhered to, the selection of one subject for the sample must not be dependent on the selection of another subject. For example, if the mean income of citizens residing in a community is to be calculated from sample data, the selection of every corner house to use as a basis for calculating family income may violate the concept of independence. The violation would occur because corner lots usually cost more and therefore persons buying homes on corner lots may have higher incomes. If this was the case, the selection process and the variable, income, would not be independent.

Sample Size

Although we indicated in the previous section that two conditions must be met to insure representativeness in the sample, the size of the sample must also be considered. In general, any number less than the total population will produce some degree of error, therefore, precision and accuracy increase as the size of the sample approaches the size of the total population.

Since the object of sampling is to get a miniature population that is representative of the larger group, the sample must contain a distribution of the characteristic under study approximately the same as it actually exists in the total population. To accomplish this, the size of the sample must be large enough to insure the probability of including the extremes in the population. In the IQ illustration, for example, the chances of including a proportionate number of persons with IQs between 85 and 115 would be quite good since this range constitutes 68 percent of the population. In other words, 68 out of every 100 selected should fall within this range. But to get an adequate proportion of persons with IQs between 130 and 145 would be more difficult because this range represents only 2 percent of the population.

Determining sample size has been simplified somewhat by the development of a table based on a formula derived by the research division of the National Education Association.[5] The formula is presented and briefly described below.

$$s = \chi^2 NP\,(1 - P) \div d^2\,(N - 1) + X^2 P\,(1 - P)$$

where

s = required sample size

---

5. "Small Sample Techniques," *The NEA Research Bulletin* 28 (December 1960): 99.

χ^2 = the table value of chi-square for 1 degree of freedom at the desired confidence level (3.841)

N = the population size

P = the population proportion (assumed to be .50 since this would provide the maximum sample size)

d = the degree of accuracy expressed as a proportion (.05)

Table 3–1 presents the table derived from the above formula.[6] Sample size, within a 5 percent error range, is simply determined by entering the table with a known population size (N) and reading across under the heading (s). For example, if the known population size is 4000, the appropriate sample size needed to insure the probability of getting a representative sample is 351.

TABLE 3–1. Table for Determining Sample Size from a Given Population.

N	S	N	S	N	S
10	10	220	140	1200	291
15	14	230	144	1300	297
20	19	240	148	1400	302
25	24	250	152	1500	306
30	28	260	155	1600	310
35	32	270	159	1700	313
40	36	280	162	1800	317
45	40	290	165	1900	320
50	44	300	169	2000	322
55	48	320	175	2200	327
60	52	340	181	2400	331
65	56	360	186	2600	335
70	59	380	191	2800	338
75	63	400	196	3000	341
80	66	420	201	3500	346
85	70	440	205	4000	351
90	73	460	210	4500	354
95	76	480	214	5000	357
100	80	500	217	6000	361
110	86	550	226	7000	364
120	92	600	234	8000	367
130	97	650	242	9000	368
140	103	700	248	10000	370
150	108	750	254	15000	375
160	113	800	260	20000	377
170	118	850	265	30000	379
180	123	900	269	40000	380
190	127	950	274	50000	381
200	132	1000	278	75000	382
210	136	1100	285	1000000	384

Note: N is population size. S is sample size.

6. Robert V. Krejcie, and Daryle Morgan, "Determining Sample Size for Research Activities," *Educational and Psychological Measurement* 30 (August 1970): 607–10.

This procedure is further illustrated in figure 3–6 (p. 48). It can be noted that as the population increases the sample size increases at a diminishing rate and remains relatively constant at slightly more than 380 cases.

Methods of Sampling

There are several approaches available to insure the probability of obtaining a representative sample. The methods to be discussed here are random sampling, stratified random sampling, and cluster sampling.

Random Sampling. In situations where the characteristics under study are assumed to be normally distributed, or some other assumed distribution, the most common and efficient method of obtaining a sample is by random selection. The key condition of random sampling is that each member of the defined population must be given an equal chance of being selected for the sample. This may be accomplished in several ways. Probably the most efficient and less time consuming is to use a table of random numbers, a portion of which is presented below. A more complete table is provided in the appendix.

34	50	57	74	37
85	22	04	39	43
09	79	13	77	48
88	75	80	18	14
90	96	23	70	00

To use a table of random numbers, which consists of a randomly generated set of numbers which has no order or structure, first assign each member of the population a number. Then, after the appropriate sample size has been determined, select those members of the population whose numbers occur first as you read down a column or across a row of the table of random numbers. For example, if the population size was 500, the numbering would range from 001 to 500. The actual sample selection would involve beginning with any three digits and proceeding through the table in an orderly fashion. It is important that the same pattern be followed throughout the table. With a population size of 500 we could start with 345, the first three digits of the example table, and proceed downward until we reach 909. We could then return to the top and proceed downward again from 057. Once a pattern is set, it should be followed throughout the selection process. The numbers falling between 001 and 500 would be singled out to be included in the sample. The justification for using a table of this type is that the numbers do not follow any set pattern, therefore allowing each number an equal chance of being selected.

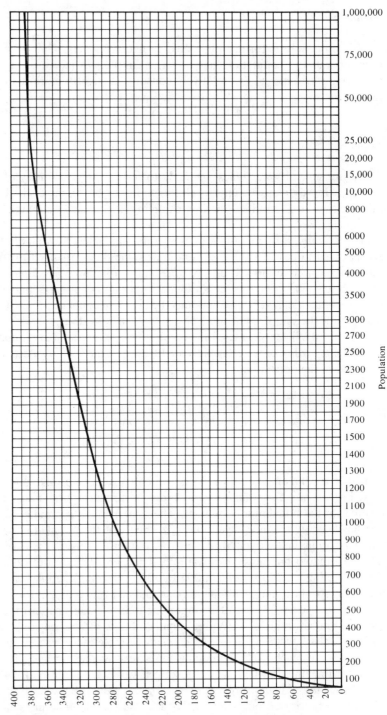

FIGURE 3–6. Relationship between Sample Size and Total Population.

48

Although the table of random numbers is probably the most efficient method of obtaining a random sample, other procedures may be used. Numbers can be written on cards or some other object, placed in a container, and then extracted from the container. We could also use a system of numerical intervals by listing all the observations in the population, then selecting every fifth, tenth, etc. interval that will produce the desired sample size. Even though the latter two methods will produce a representative sample, using a table of random numbers appears the most efficient way to accomplish this task.

Stratified Random Sampling.   In situations where variables under study may not be normally distributed in the population, the common procedure is to divide the population into natural groupings or strata prior to sampling. This is done to insure a more representative sample according to some preconceived notion that different versions of the variable would be present in the different strata. For example, in an attempt to determine the attitudes of a group of persons relative to an increase in retirement costs, the age of a person might have something to do with the way he feels about paying more for retirement. If this were the case, the population could be subdivided according to age prior to sampling. In any situation where it might be assumed that the composition of some category (age, sex, geographical location, etc.) in relation to the variable under study could have an effect on the outcome of the study, then stratification could be employed to insure a more representative sample.

Cluster Sampling.   Another extension of basic random sampling is called cluster sampling. This involves subdividing the population into clusters or large blocks of subjects prior to sampling. For example, a cluster might be defined as wards within a city, school districts within a given area, or any other large block of subjects.[7]

SAMPLING ERROR

A sample mean is an estimate of the true population mean. This is to say that, when a sample value is computed and the object is to generalize this value to the parent population, the chances are great that the sample value is not the same as the true population value. However, this does not prevent the use of sample values to estimate parameter values because the amount of error can be measured.

Suppose we have a very large population, such as all students enrolled in an introductory psychology course in four-year institutions in the

7. For a more detailed account of cluster sampling see: Russell Actoff, *The Design of Social Research* (Chicago: University of Chicago Press, 1953), p. 114.

United States. With a population of this magnitude, numerous samples could be drawn in an effort to study them. If this was the case, we might decide to draw a sample of thirty students from one of the institutions and administer some kind of test. After giving the test, a mean and standard deviation could be calculated. We could then draw another sample of the same size and compute another mean and standard deviation and continue this procedure until we had exhausted the population. For example, if we drew 4000 samples of size thirty, we would have 4000 means and 4000 standard deviations. A distribution of these sample values would provide us with a sampling distribution. The variability of this distribution would be measured by the standard error of the mean. Figure 3–7 illustrates this idea. It is an example of the *central limit theorem* which states:

> If a population distribution has a mean $\bar{X}$ and a standard deviation σ, then the distribution of random sample means drawn from this population approaches a normal distribution with a mean of $\bar{X}$ and a standard deviation of $\sigma/\sqrt{N}$ as the sample size N increases.

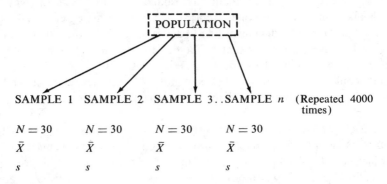

FIGURE 3–7.

It should be noted that when the sample size is less than thirty, the sampling distribution of means is not accurately represented by the normal curve table. If samples less than thirty are used, the distribution of the t probability must be employed. It is good practice, if at all possible, to keep sample sizes thirty or above.

Correcting for Sample Bias

Since the sample standard deviation is considered to be a biased estimate of the population standard deviation, steps must be taken to determine just how much error is present. The importance of this operation is that knowledge of the standard error of the mean must be determined if an accurate estimation of the parameter value is to be made.

If a relatively small sample is selected from a large population, the chances are good that the sample observations will represent the center of the distribution. This will produce a sample range that is less than the range for the parent population. The standard deviation will also be smaller for the sample than is actually present in the total population. As the size of the sample increases, the chances become better for obtaining scores from the extremes of the distribution and, therefore, the sample standard deviation comes closer in line.

To obtain the correction for this bias, the following steps are taken. Obtain the sample standard deviation by computing:

$$s = \sqrt{\frac{\Sigma x^2}{N}}$$

where

$\quad$ s = sample standard deviation

$$x^2 = X^2 - \frac{(\Sigma X)^2}{N}$$

$\quad$ N = sample size

Then: substitute the sample standard deviation into the correction formula. The most common formula for this purpose is:

$$S_{\bar{x}} = \frac{s}{\sqrt{N}}$$

where

$\quad$ $S_{\bar{x}}$ = standard error of the mean
$\quad$ s = sample standard deviation
$\quad$ N = size of the sample

If the sample standard deviation of 16.8 was determined from an N of 200, the standard error of the mean would be determined in the following manner.

$$\begin{aligned} S_{\bar{x}} &= \frac{s}{\sqrt{N}} \\ &= \frac{16.8}{\sqrt{200}} \\ &= \frac{16.8}{\sqrt{200}} \\ &= \frac{16.8}{14.14} \\ &= 1.19 \end{aligned}$$

A standard error of the mean of 1.19, in itself, has little meaning. The primary use for this value is in the actual estimation of the parameter value. This operation is described in the next section.

It is important to note from the standard error of the mean formula that the larger the sample, the smaller the size of the standard error. The smaller the standard error, the more accurate a parameter value can be predicted.

Estimating Parameter Values

The ultimate objective of sampling is to estimate a parameter value from a sample statistic. This is one form of statistical inference.

In a study concerned with college aptitude, a sample of 217 is drawn from a known population of 500. A test is administered to the sample and a mean and standard deviation of 72 and 16 respectively are computed. From this information derived from the sample, the object is to make inferences about the parameter value. That is to say, we want to generalize the sample mean of 72 to the population. To accomplish this task, we follow the procedure outlined below.

Compute the standard error of the mean:

$$S_{\bar{x}} = \frac{s}{\sqrt{N}}$$

$$= \frac{16}{\sqrt{217}}$$

$$= \frac{16}{14.73}$$

$$= 1.09$$

We know from the previous section that if we were to draw numerous samples of the same size from this population we would get a normal distribution. This distribution would be expected to have an estimated standard deviation of 1.09. In other words, we would expect the computed sample mean to fall within 1.09 points of the parameter mean. We arrive at this conclusion on the basis of our knowledge of the normal curve which indicates to us that approximately two-thirds of the samples drawn repeatedly with an N of 217 would fall within 1.09 points of the parameter mean. With this in mind, the next step in estimating the parameter value is to consult the z-score table (Appendix B) for information pertaining to areas under the normal curve corresponding to various z-score values. It can be noted from the z-score table that a z-score of 1.96 includes 95 percent of the sample means and a z-score of 2.58 includes 99

percent of the sample means. In terms of probability, we use this information to say that our sample mean will fall within a range 95 out of 100
times, or in the case of a z-score of 2.58, the sample mean will fall within
a certain range 99 out of 100 times. In other words, we have the option of
determining how much error we are willing to tolerate by the confidence
level we select. Although any level can be selected, the 95 percent level or
the 99 percent level are the most commonly used in behavioral science
research.

In the college aptitude example, we found a sample mean of 72, a sample standard deviation of 16, and a standard error of the mean of 1.09.
We employ this information in the following manner to establish a band
where we estimate the population mean will fall.

$$95 \text{ percent confidence level} = \bar{X} \pm (1.96) \ S_{\bar{x}}$$
$$= 72 \pm (1.96) \ 1.09$$
$$= 72 \pm 2.14$$
$$= 69.86 - 74.14$$

We can now state that the probability is .95 that the population mean
is between 69.86 and 74.14 in the parent population. In other words, 95
out of 100 samples of the same size drawn from the same population will
fall in this band and only 5 out of 100 times will it fall outside this band.

If we want to be more precise, the 99 percent level of confidence could
be used.

$$99 \text{ percent level of confidence} = \bar{X} \pm (2.58) \ S_{\bar{x}}$$
$$= 72 \pm (2.58) \ 1.09$$
$$= 72 \pm 2.81$$
$$= 69.19 - 74.81$$

The same conclusion would be drawn from this as the previous one except instead of the probability being .95 it is now .99. That is, the probability is .99 that the sample mean will fall within the established band. It
can be noted that the band for the 99 percent level is wider than for the
95 percent level.

What all this means is that we can now say that the college aptitude
mean for the defined population is within the band established. We can
make this statement with the degree of confidence selected to establish the
band.

RANDOM ASSIGNMENT

Another important use of sampling is random assignment. In this case we
are not interested in estimating parameter values, but rather we are inter-

ested in equating groups. In research work, a common experimental design used to assess the effects of various treatments is the pretest–posttest control group design. This can be illustrated as follows.

$$R \ 0_1 \ X \ 0_2$$
$$R \ 0_1 \quad \ 0_2$$

where

R = random assignment
0_1 = pretest
X = treatment
0_2 = posttest

The essence of this type of design is to determine the effects of the treatment while holding constant those factors outside the treatment that might influence the outcome. One of the most efficient ways of handling this is to assign subjects to groups at random, thereby equating the groups on these extraneous factors. Procedures for accomplishing random assignment are identical to the procedures for random sampling.

CASES FOR APPLICATION

1. A study by Dolores Durkin[8] sought to test Piaget's thesis that children's concepts of justice change with age, specifically that "children maintain with a conviction that grows with their years that it is strictly fair to give back the blows one has received." To test this thesis, a sample of children was drawn from a midwestern community with a population of about 1,000. All of the children were white and, with the exception of three Catholic families, all were Protestant. The primary income for the community was farming. All children in grades two, five, and eight were included in the study. They were grouped and classified economically as poor, average, or rich, with 68 to 80 percent of the children in each grade being classified as coming from average homes, economically speaking. The conclusion reached from the study was that the Piaget thesis was not confirmed.
   In relation to this study:

   1. Define the population of the study.
   2. Evaluate the sampling procedures according to:
      a. equal chance

---

8. Dolores Durkin, "Children's Concepts of Justice: A Comparison With the Piaget Data," *Child Development* 30 (1959): 59–67.

      b. independence

      c. sample size

      d. method of sampling.

    3. Evaluate the validity of the conclusions of the study in view of sampling principles.

2. An attempt to determine "the impact of differing parental educational level on the educational achievement, attitude, aspiration, and expectation of the child" utilized a procedure which gathered appropriate information from about 20,000 high school seniors. The students were divided into four groups according to the educational levels of their parents. A random sample was then drawn from each of these groups.[9]

    What method of sampling was this?

    Was the method of sampling utilized appropriate to the study?

3. To study the relationship between creativity and intelligence, a procedure was used whereby the population was designated as "Eastern," "Western," or "Irish." Members of the sample population were then grouped accordingly and conclusions from the study grouped in the same fashion.[10]

    What method of sampling was utilized in this study?

    What advantages would this method have in this case?

    What limitations on the conclusions from the study would this method incur?

4. Assume a study with a purpose to predict the yearly income of black adult males in a certain community whose parents were on welfare when the subjects were in the 9–12 age span. From a sample of 226 subjects, it was determined that the mean annual income was $4876, with a standard deviation of $493. With a 95 percent level of confidence, the subjects' salary range can be predicted to fall within what range?

---

9. Michael E. Osborn, "The Impact of Differing Parental Educational Level on the Educational Achievement, Attitude, Aspiration, and Expectation of the Child," *The Journal of Educational Research* 65:4 (December 1971): 163–67.

10. John S. Dacey and George F. Madaus, "An Analysis of Two Hypotheses Concerning the Relationship Between Creativity and Intelligence," *The Journal of Educational Research* 64:7 (January 1971): 213–16.

4

Hypotheses

The purpose of including a chapter of this nature in the text is to demonstrate the relationship between hypotheses and statistical analyses. In addition to the discussion of hypotheses, the related matters of statistical significance, degrees of freedom, one- and two-tailed tests, error, and power are presented.

NATURE OF HYPOTHESES

A hypothesis may be defined as a statement concerning the relationship between two or more variables and results from an analysis of the problem area under study.

For example, a researcher might be interested in the problem area of youth crime. Obviously, youth crime in itself cannot be researched but has to be defined in more specific terms. After analyzing the problem and the research that has been undertaken, the researcher might decide to define the problem in terms of the impact of family status on the occurrence of youth crime. Again, after analyzing the research available on this aspect of the problem, the researcher might pose a general question related to the impact of family status on youth crime.

This general question would then be followed by more specific questions such as the following.

Do youth from broken homes become involved in crime more than youth from intact homes?

If the researcher desires to use statistics as an aid in answering a question of this nature, the question must first be translated into a testable hypothesis. In this case, the hypothesis might take the form of assuming that no difference exists in youth crime between youth who come from broken homes and youth who come from intact homes. The hypothesis could also be stated in such a way as to assume that youth from broken homes are involved in more crime than youth from intact homes.

Statements of this kind are important to the researcher in that they allow certain propositions related to the problem under study to be tested by empirical means.

CONSTRUCTING HYPOTHESES

The primary purpose for inferential statistics is the testing of hypotheses. It follows, then, that hypotheses must be stated in such a manner as to be testable.

In general, behavioral science researchers make use of two types of hypotheses. For our purposes, we will label them the *research hypothesis* and the *null hypothesis*.

Research hypotheses, usually symbolized by H_1, are statements that make a prediction regarding the outcome of the study. The following is an example of a research hypothesis.

H_1 Married couples without children will have a significantly different attitude toward selected child-rearing practices than married couples with children.

The null hypothesis, usually symbolized by H_o, is a statement that assumes there is no relationship between the variables under study. The research hypothesis stated previously could be written in the null form in the following manner.

H_o There is no difference in attitudes toward selected child-rearing practices between married couples with children and married couples without children.

Mention should be made at this point regarding the use of the terms "relationship" and "difference." We noted earlier that a hypothesis is a statement regarding the relationship between variables. Although determining relationships is the ultimate goal of some types of research, it makes a difference in terms of the general statistical approach whether we use the term relationship or the word difference in our hypothesis. If a hypothesis uses the term relationship, it would normally call for some type of correlation technique. However, if the term difference appears in the hypothesis, some difference-testing technique would be appropriate.

There are different opinions regarding the way hypotheses should be written. However, regardless of how one writes the hypothesis, the null form is what is actually being tested since it constitutes the alternate proposition to the research hypothesis. As we will see in a later section of this chapter, the way a hypothesis is stated makes a difference in the way a statistical value is interpreted.

When we employ the null hypothesis there are two decisions that can be made. First, the null hypothesis can be accepted. This decision is made when the computed statistical value fails to reach or exceed the critical table value. Second, the null hypothesis can be rejected. This decision is made when the computed statistical value reaches or exceeds the critical table value. The critical table value represents a point along the baseline of the probability distribution that corresponds to the statistical test being employed.

It should be noted at this point that it has become fashionable for hypotheses not to be stated in some published research reports. From the purpose of the study or the questions asked, it is simply assumed that the reader of a research report will interpret a significant statistical value to mean that the null hypothesis has been rejected, or when the statistical value is not significant, the null hypothesis has been accepted.

STATISTICAL SIGNIFICANCE

After the hypothesis, or set of hypotheses, has been formulated, the task is then one of subjecting the hypothesis to a statistical test to determine if it should be accepted or rejected. This is accomplished by taking the computed statistical value to the appropriate probability table to determine its significance.

Statistical significance refers to a situation where an observed set of circumstances, the relationship between two or more variables or the difference between two or more variables, represents a significant departure from what might be expected by chance. Statistical significance, then, is simply the probability that a given occurrence, the difference between two means, for example, did not happen by chance alone. This probability is related to the area of the underlying distribution, the normal curve, for example, of the statistic and represents the point on this distribution that provides the basis for accepting or rejecting the hypothesis. The appendix contains a distribution corresponding to the various statistical techniques presented. In order to determine significance, we consult the appropriate probability table with the following information:

1. the computed statistical value
2. the degrees of freedom
3. the significance level.

After locating the table value that corresponds to the significance level and degrees of freedom, our object now is to make a decision on the hypothesis. In order to do this, we first must determine if the observed difference or relationship is due to chance. In essence, we determine statistical significance by using the following rule.

> If a computed value is greater than the table value, the statistic is considered significant and the null hypothesis is rejected. If the computed value is less than the table value, the null hypothesis is accepted.

Selecting a Significance Level

It has been said that one can prove anything with statistics. In part, this statement has some truth. One can almost always reject a null hypothesis at some significance level. For example, a certain company advertised that their product had been tested scientifically against three other leading brands and was found to be superior. After obtaining the "scientific report" the company said was available for the asking, the point of "proving anything with statistics" became apparent. The study followed appropriate procedures but contained an interesting footnote at the bottom of a table. The footnote read "difference was statistically significant at the .80 level."

The choice of the significance level to be used in making a decision on a hypothesis is made by the researcher. However, it is common practice in behavioral science research to use the .05 level of significance or below. Some areas of the behavioral sciences make use of the .10 as well. When a particular significance level is selected, say the .05, the purpose is to state the probability that a given outcome will occur repeatedly 95 out of 100 times and only 5 out of 100 times would the outcome vary. The same type of interpretation would be used if the .01 level of significance is selected except we would be allowing the outcome to vary only 1 out of 100 times. If we selected the .80 level of significance as the company did in reporting the results of the comparison of products, we could expect the outcome to remain stable only 20 out of 100 times.

The selection of a significance level depends, in part, upon the risk the researcher is willing to take in terms of making an error when a decision is made on the hypothesis. In essence, the consequences that will result from the decision help determine the level selected.

DEGREES OF FREEDOM

As we noted in the previous section on statistical significance, the computed value is taken to a probability table to determine significance. We also noted that, in addition to the desired probability level or significance level, the number of degrees of freedom must be determined.

The concept of degrees of freedom is fundamentally mathematical, therefore we will simply look at degrees of freedom as the number of observations free to vary around a constant parameter. We can briefly illustrate this point in the following manner.

If a person is asked to write down any five numbers without any restrictions, the person would have the freedom to make a choice of any five numbers. However, if we asked the person to choose five numbers, but to make sure that the mean of these is equal to a given number, the person then has the freedom to choose any four numbers but must choose the fifth that will make the appropriate total in order to arrive at the given mean.

This can be illustrated with the following formula:

$$\text{df} = n - 1$$

In a more practical sense, degrees of freedom are used to control for sample size in making a decision regarding the significance of a statistical value. You will note from the examination of some of the probability tables in the appendices (t, F, r, chi-square) that the size of the computed value needed to reject a null hypothesis becomes larger as the number of degrees of freedom decrease. For example, suppose we were working with a sample size of thirty and using a technique that called for degrees of freedom $N - 2$. We can note from any of the tables in the appendices that the critical table value corresponding to degrees of freedom equal to 28 is larger than a table value corresponding to degrees of freedom equal to, for example, 60. In general, then, the smaller the sample, the larger the computed value must be in order to be significant within a specified significance level.

Procedures for determining degrees of freedom vary with the particular kind of statistical technique being used. These procedures are presented in the appropriate place along with the presentation of the various techniques.

ONE- AND TWO-TAILED TESTS

Another consideration that must be taken into account when making a decision on a hypothesis is whether the value yielded from a statistical test will be interpreted on a one-tailed basis or on a two-tailed basis. In a purely practical sense, this simply means that you have the option, depending upon the way the hypothesis is stated, of interpreting the statistical value from one place in the probability table or another.

The distinction between a one-tailed test and a two-tailed test is made on the basis of the tails of the probability curve. Whether a test is to be interpreted on a one-tailed basis or a two-tailed basis is dependent upon the way in which the hypothesis is written. If the hypothesis is a directional one, a research hypothesis that makes a prediction regarding the outcome, then, the decision on the hypothesis is made on a one-tailed basis. If the hypothesis is nondirectional, the null hypothesis then assumes neutrality and allows for the possibility of either a positive or a negative outcome. When this is the case, the decision on the hypothesis is made on a two-tailed basis. Consider the following as illustrative of this point.

H_1 Group A will exceed Group B on a test of social values after being exposed to a cultural sensitivity training program.

The above hypothesis is a directional one in that it makes a prediction regarding the outcome. The value derived from the statistical test of this hypothesis would be interpreted on a one-tailed basis. However, if the hypothesis was stated in the null form as presented below:

H_o There will be no difference between Group A and Group B on a test of social values after being exposed to a cultural sensitivity training program,

then the value derived from the statistical test of the hypothesis would be interpreted on a two-tailed basis.

In our discussion of the normal curve, and again in the previous section on statistical significance, we noted that, in the case of the normal curve, a z value must be at least plus or minus 1.96 to be significant at the .05 level. This is based on the assumption that the hypothesis is nondirectional and should be interpreted on a two-tailed basis allowing for the value to be either positive or negative. This idea is presented in figure 4–1.

We note that, in order to reject a null hypothesis, the statistical value must fall within 2.5 percent of either end of the curve. In other words, the

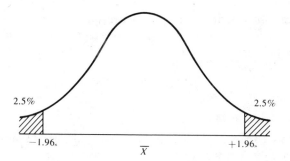

FIGURE 4–1.   Rejection Region for the Null Hypothesis Utilizing a Two-
              Tailed Test.

computed value of the statistical test must be plus or minus 1.96 or
greater in order to reject the null hypothesis.

If we employ a directional hypothesis, however, the size of our statistical value need not be as large to determine significance. This can be seen
in figure 4–2.

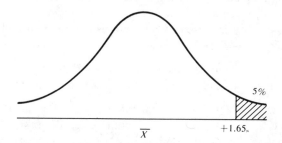

FIGURE 4–2.   Rejection Region for a Directional Hypothesis Utilizing a
              One-Tailed Test.

The decision to employ a one-tailed test or a two-tailed test is made on
the basis of the way in which the hypothesis is written. In essence, decisions on directional hypotheses should be made by interpreting the computed statistical value on a one-tailed basis. Decisions on null hypotheses
should be made on a two-tailed basis. For the most part, the difference is
simply where you locate the critical table value that corresponds to the
statistical technique you are using.

The decision to use a research hypothesis or a null hypothesis is one
the researcher must make. It should be mentioned, however, that if research hypotheses are used, a sound basis should precede their use since
a number of problems can occur in interpretation if the outcome is not in
the predicted direction.

In general, interpreting results on a two-tailed basis appears to have a number of advantages over one-tailed interpretation for behavioral science research. For this reason, the two-tailed test is usually used.

ERROR

Error, in this context, refers to the possibility of making an inaccurate decision on a hypothesis. In the previous section on statistical significance, we talked about the probability levels normally used in behavioral science research to make decisions on hypotheses. We also mentioned that these significance levels are used in order to minimize the danger of rejecting a true hypothesis or retaining a false hypothesis. If an error is made in either case, inaccurate conclusions will result.

If a researcher desires to be as accurate as possible when rejecting a null hypothesis, he selects a small significance level. On the other hand, a researcher increases the probability of rejecting a null hypothesis when it should be accepted by selecting a larger significance level.

In any event, when a decision is made on a hypothesis, the possibility of two kinds of error is present. Errors of this nature are usually described as Type I error and Type II error.

Type I Error: Rejecting a hypothesis when it is true.
Type II Error: Accepting a hypothesis when it is false.

In an effort to stay within a reasonable error band, it has become common practice to make decisions on hypotheses on the basis of .05 or beyond. Following this practice minimizes the possibility of committing a Type I error. There are many types of studies where the outcome will not result in a crucial decision and the consequences of making a Type I error are not great. In this type of situation, it is quite appropriate to use significance levels greater than .05.

POWER

In a statistical sense, power refers to the ability of a statistical test to detect the population differences that actually exist. Although a detailed explanation of the procedures for estimating the power of a statistical test is beyond the scope of this discussion, we will simply consider power as the probability of rejecting a null hypothesis that is false and should be rejected. When we select a statistical technique to analyze our data, we do so on the basis that the technique will give us the most accurate decision possible on the hypothesis under the circumstances.

The power of a statistical technique depends upon several factors. One of the most important is the difference between the true characteristics of the population as opposed to the hypothesized characteristics. The larger the difference, the more likely it is to be detected by the statistical test. The smaller the difference, the more likely it is to escape detection. With this in mind, we can state in general terms that any statistical test is more powerful when applied to a large population than it is when applied to a small population.

Two additional factors that influence the power of a statistical test are the size of the sample and the size of the significance level used to make a decision on a hypothesis. With respect to sample size, there is little doubt that a large sample has a better chance of reflecting the true population characteristics than does a small sample. Put another way, the closer the sample size is to the true population size, the more likely the statistical test will pick up the differences.

The size of the significance level chosen to test a hypothesis is also a factor in determining the power of a statistical test. This factor plays a crucial role regarding the likelihood of making Type I and Type II errors. You will recall in the previous section that a Type II error is committed when a false null hypothesis is accepted. Therefore, power can be further defined as the probability of avoiding a Type II error.

In practical research work, the matter of power is attended to by assuming that samples we choose to work with are representative of the population that has been defined. We accomplish this by determining sample size and the method of selection by the most appropriate means. In addition, we attend to the matter of power by utilizing the accepted levels of significance, or at least the levels that will minimize error, when making a decision on a hypothesis. Finally, we can minimize the risk of making an error by selecting the statistical technique that is most appropriate for the given situation.

SAMPLE STUDY

The study that follows will show how some of the concepts discussed in this chapter are used in an actual research situation.

You should not be concerned at this point with the statistical technique employed, but rather get a feel for the "flow" of events that occur during the research process. Pay particular attention to the hypotheses, the way they are stated, tested, and the conclusions that are drawn.

The study should not be taken as "ideal" in the sense that all studies should follow this format. The study does, however, illustrate the use of the major components of the research process found in any good study.

Idealization in Engaged Couples*

The problem of romanticism and idealization in our society has been a recurrent theme of family sociologists and marriage educators (e.g., Beigel, 1951; Burgess, 1926; Goode, 1959; Kephart, 1966; Kolb, 1950; Mowrer, 1939; Wallin, 1952). The usual rationale for investigating this subject is the concern that engaged couples imbued with fantasies about love and marriage, will project their fantasies upon their intended mates instead of seeing them as they really are. Furthermore, after marriage they will find out the truth and become disillusioned (Dean, 1962; Pineo, 1963; Winch, 1952). This process of idealization and disillusion is seen as a threat to the institution of marriage and the family insofar as it is held responsible for high divorce rates and one-parent families.

In addition to warning students and prospective couples of the pitfalls of idealization, tests have been developed to predict which couples would be more likely to be happily married and which would not (e.g., Burgess and Wallin, 1953). However, the items of these tests were transparent, i.e., vulnerable to a social desirability response set. Even the most naive respondent could tell when he or she was answering in a way that would justify or condemn the marriage. If we presume that engaged couples have a strong emotional investment in believing that their marriage will succeed, then it seems probable that they will be biased toward giving "socially desirable" responses and thus receive very high scores. In fact the scores on these tests are usually highly skewed toward the positive end (Edmonds, 1967). Therefore, those who are most likely to idealize their mates will be most likely to receive high scores on marriage prediction tests and will be encouraged to marry. Thus, the test system which was devised to screen out relationships that might end in disillusionment is actually fostering them.

The purpose of this investigation was to clarify the process of idealization between engaged couples both theoretically and operationally. A test was derived which is considered to be relatively free of social desirability and which is scored in a disguised manner. Comparison of scores on a standard engagement adjustment questionnaire with an empathy test suggested that idealization could be related to blocked communication in areas of potential conflict. Thus, couples with blocked communication could be identified as per-

*Marion L. Schulman, "Idealization in Engaged Couples," reprinted from Journal of Marriage and the Family 36 (February 1974): 139–47, by permission of the publisher and author.

ceiving idealistically and distinguished from those who were not distorting their perception. This test can differentiate couples on the basis of idealistic or realistic perception when these couples cannot be differentiated by a standard engagement adjustment questionnaire.

THEORETICAL RATIONALE

Stryker (1959) has emphasized the role-taking process as a variable for family research and the use of role-taking as an indicator of interpersonal competence. It is assumed that those who are able to accurately take the role of another can be more effective in their relationships with others. Since the role imputed to the other affects individual behavior in interactive situations, role-taking is highly relevant to the target population of this study, engaged couples. It is suggested that the role-taking process in idealizing couples is distorted in areas of potential conflicts so that consensus is perceived where it does not exist. In situations where rigid rules for collective action are not enforced and the actors want to coordinate their activity, Scheff (1967) proposes a model of social coordination in which communication is the precondition of consensus and consensus is the precondition of flexible behavior. He uses communication in Dewey's sense, which is defined as interpenetration of perspectives. If Scheff's model is applied to engaged couples, assuming that they are not subject to rigid rules and do want to coordinate their activity, it would be expected that the quality of their communication is important to their problem-solving ability. But what if communication in potential conflict areas is blocked? Where the quality of communication is poor, Turner (1956: 326) suggests that the accompanying behavior is the enactment of a "rigidly predetermined role" and "standardized responses." It seems plausible, therefore, that where communication is blocked, imputations to the other will not be accurate: thus idealized perception would be the "predetermined response" for the engaged person, since it is made available by the romantic attitudes of the society. Social coordination based on predetermined responses such as idealization rather than consensus will be inflexible and thus affect the couples' problem-solving ability.

Stryker (1963:290) attempts to account for blocked communication between parents and offspring by introducing an intervening variable of "vulnerability." His implied definition is that vulnerability of one or both partners in the relationship refers to the relatively greater importance of the relationship to "self-identification" and "respect." Where vulnerability could be assumed to enter into a relationship, it was found that blocked communication had cut off the tendency to empathize or had inhibited accurate role-taking.

If an engaged couple does not block communication in the areas of their difficulties, then they would be expected to either reach resolutions or terminate their relationship. They may also "agree to disagree" (Scheff, 1967:44), which implies awareness of conflict and at least temporary resolution. Where resolution of conflict can occur, it is expected that latent conflicts will not suddenly appear and create disillusionment after marriage. This study proposes to differentiate between those engaged couples who block communication and those who do not.

BACKGROUND

A summary of the empirical studies relevant to the theoretical position above and to the construction of the instrument is presented here. A more complete literature review can be found in Schulman (1971). Kirkpatrick and Hobart's (1954) results indicate lack of realism in all stages of courtship and early marriage, since the couples they studied actually disagreed with each other at a much higher rate than they estimated their number of disagreements to be. Parallel results were reported by Coe et al. (1969) in a study comparing the families of psychiatric inpatients and normal controls. The patient families admitted to 4 per cent disagreement with each other on a questionnaire concerning family interaction patterns, whereas control families admitted to 28 per cent disagreement. The actual percentage of disagreement was 38 to 40 per cent for the patient families and 32 per cent for the controls. Thus, the lack of realism seen in underestimating disagreements is also present in the families of psychiatric patients. Through further analysis of the divergence between disagreement and disagreement estimate scores on marital role opinions, Hobart (1958) found a narrowing of this gap or a "disillusion" effect in the transition from engagement to marriage. Using the third interview of Burgess' longitudinal sample, Pineo (1963) discovered a substantial decrease in marital adjustment scores made 20 years after the initial engagement interviews. He attributes this "disenchantment" to a regression effect from the couple's period of maximum satisfaction and to unforeseeable changes in situation, personality, and/or behavior. In comparing the mean adjustment scores at the time of engagement and early marriage for late-divorcing couples, he found divorced men to have had a higher adjustment at engagement than men still married. This finding is highly relevant to the results of the present study in which the same engagement adjustment questionnaire was used in order to show the effects of a transparent test assumed to be affected by social desirability. Divorced men having high scores on this test supports the author's contention that due to the social desirability component high scores can mean idealization which may lead to disillusionment after marriage. Dovetailing with this study is a recent investigation of the element of marital conventionalization within marital adjustment scales (Edmonds et al., 1972). Edmonds dealt with married couples and defined the tendency to distort answers on marital adjustment tests in a socially desirable direction as marital conventionalization. He showed that the positive relationship between conservatism and marital adjustment was erased when marital conventionalization was held constant; thus, the marital adjustment score is contaminated by conventionalization. Analogously, the present study concerns engaged couples; but it is assumed that the tendency to distort on engagement adjustment tests in a conventional (or a socially desirable) direction will take the form of idealized responses, since these responses are dictated by the romantic attitudes existing in society. The analogy between marital adjustment tests and engagement adjustment tests is based upon overlap in item content.

The following studies deal with the imputation of the partner's response, which has been called empathy, role-taking, understanding, co-orientation, etc., by various investigators. Essentially, the prediction of the other's response is used as an indicator of the amount of communication in the relationship. One of the original investigators to use this technique to measure "empathy" was Dymond (1954). Treating empathy as a trait, she found that happiness of married couples was significantly associated with accuracy of prediction scores. Stuckert (1963) studied marital satisfaction in terms of similarity of role expectations and accuracy of perception of other's role expectations. He found role similarity to be most important in the satisfaction of husbands, and accuracy of the wife's perception to be most important in the satisfaction of wives. Where the role similarity is low and his perception of his wife is accurate, the husband is often dissatisfied. However, husbands are satisfied when their role expectations are different from their wives, but they do not perceive this. Stryker's (1959) study, referred to above, supports Stuckert's findings; but it was done on a sample of young married couples and their parents. Contrary to what one might expect, Stryker did not find that high accuracy of prediction was always associated with a good relationship. Parents who were dependent on their children, highly traditional, or in low-agreement with their children had better relationships when they predicted with low accuracy. Laing et al. (1966) have developed a theory and test, which are discussed by Scheff (1967) in the context of consensus. Among their sample of twelve married couples seeking help and ten satisfied couples, they found fewer prediction errors in all phases of the interaction of satisfied couples. They also found that couples misunderstood more often on issues on which they disagreed. The authors ask, "Do people feel they agree, even when they do not because they never probe or make explicit issues where disagreement may exist?" (p.85).

From these studies comes the basic problem to be investigated in this paper, i.e., the relationship between potential conflict and perceptual distortion. Hypothesis I states: Where there is potential conflict in the engagement relationship, there will be distortion in perception of each other's views and feelings in the conflict area. The work on lack of realism in courtship and the use of questionnaires with large components of "social desirability" suggest hypotheses II and III. *Hypothesis II:* Those who idealize will receive high scores on tests of engagement adjustment. Those who are in fact "adjusted" should also receive high scores, and thus the two groups could not be separated from one another using only an engagement adjustment questionnaire. *Hypothesis III:* Those who idealize will perceive their relationship as running smoothly and free of conflict, even if latent disagreement is present. These hypotheses will be tested using objective criteria of potential conflict as well as of realism or distortion of perception.

METHOD

The sample consisted of 98 couples, who were either engaged or who were thinking seriously about marriage with each other. They were obtained from a random sample of undergraduate classes from a private university drawing students of a higher than average socioeconomic status. Fifty-three randomly chosen classes were contacted, the request for couples was made, and 125 premarital subjects volunteered. The subjects averaged 20 years of age and knew each other for an average length of 32 months. The long acquaintance time might be due to self-selection of unsure couples or to the decrease in the number of people thinking about engagement or marriage.

Each couple was contacted by phone and an appointment was made to take the questionnaire. Couples were not allowed to see each other's answers until both were completed. Of the 125 volunteers, 27 cases were lost. These were due to refusal of the fiance(e) (three), inability to contact (three), relationship breaking up before contact (eight), falsified names (five), failure to return questionnaires (six), inability to arrange a time (two).

A 37-item instrument was constructed to cover a wide range of marital and premarital issues. Most of the item concepts were taken from traditional tests and inventories, but they were worded in a concrete and neutral manner. The areas of coverage are religion, sexual relations, role relations, economic matters, parents and in-laws, and political position. The new instrument was pretested on a sample of 20 couples and rated by a group of marriage counselors for relevance and social desirability. It was revised to include only those questions rated as relevant and not eliciting socially desirable answers. The validity of the test does not reside in the answers to the questions per se, but in the description of the individual or couple obtained after scoring the responses; in other words, if a couple score in the idealist range, they should actually be undergoing a process of perceptual distortion. One would not expect reliability over time, as Hobart's (1960) use of empathy tests with couples in different stages of courtship and marriage indicated that marital role opinions change.

Each subject completes the questionnaire three times: (1) giving his own views, (2) giving his predictions of his partner's views, and (3) predicting his partner's predictions of him. Several scores are derived from this instrument including: (1) the number of disagreements between partners, (2) the accuracy of prediction of the partner's responses, (3) the number of disagreements with partner that are predicted (i.e., "disagreement estimate"). Scoring is as follows: where the disagreement estimate is in line with the number of disagreements, the person is considered to be "realistic" in his knowledge of the potential conflict in the relationship. Where the disagreement estimate is higher than the number of disagreements, the person is considered to be "pessimistic," because he overestimates the amount of disagreement. However, the focus in this research is where the disagreement estimate is lower than the number of disagreements; then the person is considered to be "idealistic" or unable to perceive where his partner is unlike himself. These three categories of perception were constructed by subtracting the disagreement estimate from the number of disagreements yielding an "accuracy estimate" in which the zero point indicates "realistic" perception, positive scores are in the "idealist" direction and negative scores are in the "pessimist" direction. For purposes of comparison, couples were divided at the median into high and low disagreers. Table 1 shows the distribution of couples in the sample, and also their distribution as individuals within the six categories of accuracy estimate by disagreements.

In addition to the empathy questionnaire, a standard engagement adjustment test (Burgess and Wallin, 1953:306–309) was administered. This inventory contains 24 items consisting of subjective estimations of the relationship.

TABLE 1.   Distribution of the Sample into Six Categories of Couples.

		Accuracy Estimate[1]					
		Pessimists (—5.5 to —1.5)		Realists (—1.0 to 2.5)		Idealists (3.0 to 12.0)	
	High	Couples	2	Couples	10	Couples	38
		Females	2	Females	7	Females	41	50
		Males	4	Males	12	Males	34	
Number of Disagreements[2]							
	Low	Couples	6	Couples	24	Couples	18
		Females	7	Females	15	Females	26	48
		Males	7	Males	26	Males	15	
		Couples	8	Couples	34	Couples	56	
		Females	9	Females	22	Females	67	
		Males	11	Males	38	Males	49	

1. A couple's accuracy estimate is constructed by subtracting their disagreement estimate from their number of disagreements.

2. Couples were assigned to the high or low categories based upon a cutting point at the median number of disagreements.

A casual reading of the questionnaire suggests that there is a large "social desirability" factor which appears to be involved, since the questions and the scoring are transparent. Furthermore, there is a large overlap between these items and at least 11 items of the 15-item Locke-Wallace (1959) Marital Adjustment Scale which has been shown to be contaminated by social desirability (Edmonds, 1972).

Finally, two Likert-type questions were asked concerning the happiness of the engagement and the amount of conflict in the engagement. These questions were also intended to elicit subjective estimations of the relationship.

FINDINGS

The first hypothesis states that *where there is potential conflict in the engagement relationship, there will be distortion in perception of each other's views and feelings in the conflict area.* This hypothesis was tested by the prediction that the greater the number of disagreements with partner, the greater the number of inaccurate perceptions of the partner's responses. The hypothesis was supported by a significant correlation of $r = 0.70$. This correlation supports the theoretical statement that avoidance of conflict is a factor which can block communication. It is also consistent with Laing *et al.* (1966) who found that couples misunderstood more often on issues on which they disagree. An item analysis of the questionnaire gives additional support to this hypothesis by revealing that the number of inaccurate predictions for any question closely parallels the number of disagreements on the question.

The second hypothesis states that *those who idealize will receive high scores on tests of engagement adjustment. Those who are in fact "adjusted" should also receive high scores and thus the two groups could not be separated from one another using only an engagement adjustment questionnaire.*

Prediction 1. Those couples who idealize (operationally defined as having an accuracy estimate of 3.0 or over) will receive as high a score on the engagement adjustment questionnaire as those who are realistic (operationally defined as having an accuracy estimate of −1.0 to +2.5). Not only did the idealizers receive as high a score as the realistic couples on the engagement adjustment questionnaire, but they actually received a significantly higher engagement adjustment score. In order to be sure that the idealizers did not receive higher scores than the realistic couples due to a single cell, a separate comparison was made between the cells of high disagreers and low disagreers. Logically, the high disagreers should have lower engagement adjustment scores than the low disagreers, but when the high disagreers are also idealizers, this does not occur and the engagement adjustment scores are not different.

Prediction 2. Those couples who idealize and are high in disagreements will receive as high a score on an engagement adjustment questionnaire as

those who are realistic and low in disagreement. This prediction was supported with a nonsignificant *t* of 0.11. Thus, there seems to be little recogni-
tion by the high disagreement idealists of their higher number of disagreements. Since a high number of disagreements is not indicative of engagement
adjustment, it would seem that these subjects have arrived at their high scores
by being unaware of areas where they disagreed and/or by giving socially
desirable answers (see Table 2).

TABLE 2.   Mean Engagement Adjustment Score as a Function of Perceptual
           Category and High or Low Number of Disagreements.

		Realistic	Idealistic	
Number of Disagreements	High	121.20	133.75	
		(n = 10)	(n = 36)	
	Low	134.13	145.67	
		(n = 24)	(n = 18)	
	Total	130.32	137.54	2.29*

*p < .05.
Note: *t* = 0.11 between the idealists with high number of disagreements and the realists
with low number of disagreements.

Additional evidence that a high score on engagement adjustment can be
an indication of nonrecognition of conflict rather than its absence is shown by
relating the disagreement estimate to engagement adjustment.

Prediction 3. The lower the disagreement estimate, the higher the score on
engagement adjustment. This prediction is supported with an $r = -0.49$. This
finding suggests that where disagreements are not detected, as well as not
present, the engagement will appear to be harmonious.

The third hypothesis states that *those who idealize will perceive their relationship as running smoothly and free of conflict, even if latent disagreement
is present.* Two Likert questions, one rating the amount of happiness in the
engagement and the other rating the amount of conflict, were used as the
dependent variables.

Prediction 1. Those who idealize and are high on number of disagreements
will be more likely to rate the course of their engagement as happy than
others with a high number of disagreements. Although in the predicted direction, the happiness scores of idealists with a high number of disagreements
were not significantly higher than realists and pessimists with a high number
of disagreements. However, the happiness scores showed very little variability
and thus cannot be expected to discriminate between variables. It is con-

cluded that the happiness score as used here is not a good measure, since in a sample of premarital couples, the level of subjective happiness is uniformly very high.

Prediction 2. Those who idealize and are high on number of disagreements will be more likely to rate the course of their engagement as conflict-free than others with a high number of disagreements. The conflict scores of idealists with a high number of disagreements were not significantly lower than realists and pessimists with a high number of disagreements, although they do show a trend in the predicted direction. However, this prediction was supported significantly in the case of females (see Table 3).

TABLE 3.   *t*-Tests between Mean Conflict Scores[1] for Those Couples Who Are High in Number of Disagreements.

	High Number of Disagreements		
	Idealistic Couples	All Other Couples	*t*
Total conflict	4.33	5.00	1.06
Female conflict	2.03	2.89	2.33*
Male conflict	2.22	2.53	0.93

*$p < .05$.
1. "Check the degree to which your relationship has been: Conflict free_____full of conflict."

Prediction 3. For those with a high number of disagreements, the greater the number of prediction errors, the less the subjective conflict of the engagement. No relationship was found between prediction errors and conflict scores for couples with a high number of disagreements. However, this appears to be due to the opposition of the results for males and females: $r = -0.39$ for females, but $r = +0.30$ for males. In terms of the theory, females who were not communicating effectively in problem areas were protecting themselves from seeing these conflicts and thus not predicting their partners' responses accurately or perceiving their conflicts (see Table 4). It appears that the males were more likely to perceive conflict where there were numerous problem areas even if they could not predict their partner's responses accurately. Thus, the males in this sample appear to be less idealistic than the females; this is also supported by the distribution of individuals shown in Table 1. However, the limitations due to the sample characteristics must be kept in mind, as other studies may be interpreted to have found more idealization occurring in men (e.g., Pineo, 1963; and Stuckert, 1963).

TABLE 4.   Correlations of Prediction Errors by Conflict Scores for Couples
with a High Number of Disagreements.

| | Subjects with a high number of disagreements | | |
	Couples	Females	Males
Prediction errors × conflict score	$r = +0.14$	$r = -0.39**$	$r = +0.30*$
	($n = 46$)	($n = 48$)	($n = 46$)

$*p < .05$
$**p < .01$

A comparison of the accuracy of prediction between men and women
failed to reveal any significant differences, suggesting that the men and
women in this sample tended to be equally accurate in predicting the responses of their fiance(e). This finding is inconsistent with those of Stryker
(1962) and of Stuckert (1963) who found women to be better predictors than
men. However, their results may have been due to the greater tendency of
women to say that their partners think just like they do. Thus on any questionnaire with a high degree of social desirability affecting the results, women
would be better predictors. But on this questionnaire, the relative absence of
social desirability could not guarantee accuracy for predicting one's partner
to be like oneself. Laing et al. (1966) found no difference in prediction ability
between men and women.

DISCUSSION

The findings of this study appear to bear out the theoretical statement that
communication can be blocked in relation to potential conflict and thus the
"other person" of a dyad is not perceived accurately. Not being able to predict a partner's response may be overlooked during engagement if the conflict area can be avoided, but with the day-to-day intimacy of married life,
the exposure of many differences is inevitable. Thus, those who have not
communicated about their differences may be surprised to find out about
them after marriage and also may not know how to deal with them (see
Hobart, 1958; Pineo, 1963).

In this research, idealistic, realistic, and pessimistic couples were operationally defined in order to refine our knowledge in the area of engagement. Of
particular interest in this study were the differences and similarities between
idealistic and realistic couples. Idealization was related to social desirability
in response and this was tested by giving the subjects an engagement adjustment questionnaire which is presumed to be high in this factor. The results

indicate that the idealistic and realistic couple cannot be distinguished from each other through the use of a standard engagement adjustment questionnaire. In fact, among couples who are all high in number of disagreements, the idealizers are significantly higher on the engagement adjustment questionnaire than realists and/or pessimists. In other words, the realists and pessimists seem to recognize their conflict areas while the idealists do not. These findings suggest that it is worthwhile to categorize couples according to their perception and communication dynamics rather than to treat them as all alike. The differentiation of the way in which couples experience the engagement process represents a refinement in our knowledge of developmental life stages. It also implies a differential diagnosis and treatment in the clinical area of counseling premarital couples. Since this sample contained only eight pessimist couples, this group could not be analyzed separately. However, a larger group of pessimist couples were found in the pilot sample, suggesting that there is a type of premarital couple who see more conflict in their relationship than actually exists.

Two more subjective items which were asked were (1) degree of happiness during engagement and (2) degree of conflict during engagement. The happiness item received such consistently high scores that it could not be analyzed. However, the conflict score did show that among those high in disagreement, female idealists perceived significantly less conflict in their engagement than realists and pessimists. The male conflict scores were in the same direction but were not significant. In addition, the relationship between inaccuracy of prediction and perception of conflict was $r = -0.39$ for females with a high number of disagreements suggesting that there is a relationship between inadequate communication and unawareness of disagreements which have been shown to exist. For males, no such distortion in perception of conflict was found, i.e., $r = +0.30$ between inaccuracy of prediction and perception of conflict for males with a high number of disagreements. Thus, it would seem that the males and females in this sample do differ in the extent of their idealization.

Among the limitations of this study is the sample. People planning to be married while undergraduates in college may be an anachronism today and perhaps marriage is no longer seen as an inevitable developmental step. In other words, the people who volunteered for this study may be atypical. However, the author considered it to be more advantageous to obtain a homogeneous sample in order to study the process of communication and perception. Another limitation of the study is that it was conducted on the basis of one testing session. Thus, nothing is known about the outcome of the categories of couples. A follow-up study is needed to be able to give prediction for these categories based on evidence other than theoretical rationale.

CONCLUSIONS

In the theory of marriage and family, idealism has been held responsible for disillusionment after marriage, yet no satisfactory way of identifying it premaritally had been found. This study has offered an operational definition of idealization, realism, and pessimism. The adding of a third possibility, pessimism, has given another dimension to the theoretical context. Using interaction theory, the high relationship between disagreements and errors in prediction supports the notion that potential conflict can block communication so that it cannot be recognized and resolved. Couples appear to differ in the vulnerability of their self-identification within the relationship, which affects the communication exchanged in problem areas, and thus, the consensus achieved. In particular, it can be seen that where conflict is not perceived the romantic ideal becomes the predetermined response, i.e., couples who are unaware that they disagree obtain high scores on transparent questionnaires having a great deal of social desirability. The results are consistent with the viewpoint that it is most profitable to view all couples in this society as affected by romanticism but not all as idealistic in their perception.

IMPLICATIONS

The implications of this theoretical position for marriage counseling and marriage education are obvious. The most important implication is that the use of standard engagement tests to predict happy marriages may not only be misleading but may actually encourage the marriage of idealizing couples. Empathy tests without social desirability appear to be more practical in detecting distorted perception; plus, they are able to reveal the areas in which the couple have not been communicating. Counselors and educators may be able to therapeutically induce communication in these areas, so that potential conflicts can be brought out, dealt with, and eventually resolved.

REFERENCES

Beigel, H. G.
   1951   "Romantic love." American Sociological Review 16 (Part 1):326–334.
Burgess, E. W.
   1926   "The romantic impulse and family disorganization." Survey 57:290–294.
Coe, W. C., A. E. Curry, and D. R. Kessler
   1969   "Family interactions of psychiatric inpatients." Family Process 8 (March): 119–130.

Dean, E. S.
   1962   "Psychotherapy and romantic love." American Journal of Psychotherapy 16
          (Part 2):441–451.
Dymond, Rosalind F.
   1954   "Interpersonal perception and marital happiness." Canadian Journal of
          Psychology 8 (September):164–171.
Edmonds, V. H.
   1967   "Marital conventionalization: definition and measurement." Journal of
          Marriage and the Family 29 (November):681–688.
Edmonds, V. H., G. Withers, and B. Dibatista
   1972   "Adjustment, conservatism, and marital conventionalization." Journal of
          Marriage and the Family 34 (February):96–103.
Goode, W. J.
   1959   "The theoretical importance of love." American Sociological Review 24
          (February):38–47.
Hobart, C. W.
   1958   "Disillusionment in marriage and romanticism." Marriage and Family
          Living 20 (February):156–162.
   1960   "Attitude changes during courtship and marriage." Marriage and Family
          Living 22 (November):352–359.
Kephart, W. M.
   1966   The Family, Society, and the Individual. Boston:Houghton Mifflin.
Kirkpatrick, C. and C. W. Hobart
   1954   "Disagreement, disagreement estimate, and non-empathetic imputations for
          intimacy groups varying from favorite date to married." American Socio-
          logical Review 19 (February):10–19.
Kolb, W. L.
   1950- "Family sociology, marriage education, and romantic complex: a critique."
   1951   Social Forces 29 (September):65–72.
Laing, R. D., H. Phillipson, and A. R. Lee
   1966   Interpersonal perception, a Theory and a Method of Research. New York:
          Springer.
Locke, H. J. and K. M. Wallace
   1959   "Short marital adjustment and prediction tests; their reliability and
          validity." Marriage and Family Living 21 (August):251–255.
Mowrer, E.
   1939   Family Disorganization: An Introduction to a Sociological Analysis. Chicago:
          University of Chicago Press.
Pineo, P .C.
   1963   "Disenchantment in the later years of marriage." Pp. 393–402 in M. B.
          Sussman (ed.), Sourcebook in Marriage and the Family. Boston:Houghton
          Mifflin.
Scheff, T. J.
   1967   "Toward a sociological model of consensus." American Sociological Re-
          view 32 (February):32–46.

Schulman, M. L.
1971 "Communication between engaged couples." Unpublished Ph.D. thesis, University of Southern California.

Stryker, S.
1959 "Symbolic interaction as an approach to family research." Marriage and Family Living 21 (February):111–119.
1962 "Conditions of accurate role-taking: a test of Mead's theory." Pp. 41–62 in A. M. Rose (ed.), Human Behavior and Social Processes: An Interactionist Approach. Boston:Houghton Mifflin.
1963 "Role-taking accuracy and adjustment." Pp. 385–393 in M. B. Sussman (ed.), Source-book in Marriage and the Family. Boston:Houghton Mifflin.

FOR REVIEW AND FURTHER STUDY

Using the above study on idealization in engaged couples, consider the following:

1. Was the research or null form of hypothesis used? Why do you think this form of hypothesis was chosen for this study? Restate the hypotheses in the other form. Would the conclusions be the same if the hypotheses were stated in the other way?
2. What conclusions were drawn relative to each hypothesis? Considering levels of significance and other pertinent factors, were the conclusions justified by the evidence?
3. For each of the stated hypotheses, should a one- or two-tailed test have been used?
4. For each stated hypothesis, what would have been the results of a Type I error? a Type II error?
5. On the basis of information given on this study, what conclusions seem warranted concerning the power of the tests used?

5

The Concept of Correlation

One of the most widely used statistical techniques in behavioral science research is correlation. In a statistical sense, correlation is a technique that measures the degree of relationship between variables. It can be used either to describe the degree of relationship that exists between variables or to test hypotheses regarding the relationship between variables. Depending upon the purpose of a given study, correlation can be considered a descriptive technique in one sense and an inferential technique in another.

For example, if we simply wanted to know the degree of relationship that exists between Graduate Record Examination scores and GPA at the end of the first year of graduate study, the result of this analysis would be descriptive of the degree of relationship that exists between these two variables. However, if we desire to find out whether or not the correlation is significant we would be operating in an inferential realm.

TYPES OF RELATIONSHIPS

The degree of relationship that exists between variables is measured by an index known as a correlation coefficient. A correlation coefficient is a numerical value that exists at some point on a line between zero and plus one and zero and minus one. In its simplest form, we can interpret any correlation coefficient by where it falls on the following line:

$$-1 \underline{\hspace{3cm}} 0 \underline{\hspace{3cm}} +1$$

By inspecting the line, we can see that a possibility exists for three types of relationships to occur with regard to the relationship between variables. These are a positive relationship, a negative relationship, and a zero relationship. It is also possible for a fourth type of relationship to occur, and this will be presented later in this chapter.

A Positive Relationship

When two variables are positively related it means that as one variable increases the second variable increases somewhat in proportion. For example, if we say that ability and performance are related in a positive way, we would note that the data on performance parallel the data on ability to some degree. If this were the case, we would note that those with higher ability scores would tend to score high on performance and those with low ability scores would tend to score low on performance. If the second variable increased in exact proportion to the first variable, the relationship would be a perfect positive 1.00.

For example, suppose we had two sets of scores, IQ and achievement, on ten subjects (table 5–1). Inspection of the table will show that the subject that has the highest IQ also made the highest score on the achievement test. You will also note that this pattern is held constant throughout. Figure 5–1 illustrates this perfect relationship in graphical form.

In actual practice it is rare for a perfect relationship to occur between variables. When a positive relationship does occur, it will be something

TABLE 5–1.

Subject	IQ	Achievement
1	130	100
2	125	95
3	120	90
4	115	85
5	110	80
6	105	75
7	100	70
8	95	65
9	90	60
10	85	55

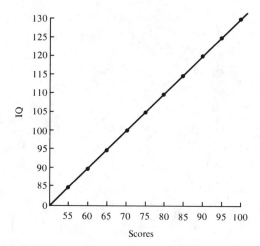

FIGURE 5-1. A Perfect Positive Relationship.

less than plus one. For example, if we change the achievement test scores so they do not match perfectly with IQ, we no longer have a perfect relationship (table 5-2). Figure 5-2 illustrates how this less than perfect relationship would look when plotted on a graph.

TABLE 5-2.

Subject	IQ	Achievement
1	130	95
2	125	100
3	120	90
4	115	80
5	110	85
6	105	70
7	100	75
8	95	65
9	90	60
10	85	55

A Negative Relationship

A negative relationship occurs when the scores for the second variable decrease as the scores for the first variable increase. For example, we know that used automobiles, in most instances, have less monetary value than new automobiles. Put another way, as the automobile gets older, or increases in age, the monetary value goes down. A perfect negative rela-

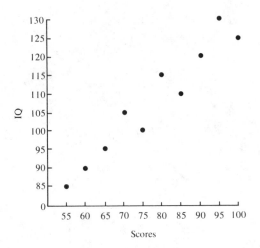

FIGURE 5–2. A Highly Positive Relationship.

tionship is one where the second variable decreases in exact proportion as
the first variable increases, or the other way around. As with the case of a
positive relationship, the more realistic outcome would be something between zero and minus one. Figure 5–3 illustrates a perfect negative correlation using the same data as figure 5–1 except the second variable,
achievement, has been reversed.

A Zero Relationship

Although it is possible to obtain a zero correlation between two variables,
it would be a rare event. When no relationship exists between variables,
the coefficient will be near zero, but not absolute zero. Figure 5–4 illustrates a situation where the degree of relationship is small.

A Curvilinear Relationship

A fourth kind of relationship that can exist between two variables is a
curvilinear relationship. This type of relationship occurs when the second
variable follows the pattern of the first variable to a point and then re-
verses its direction. For example, the relationship between age and some
physical task, say speed, usually produces a curvilinear relationship. Take
a situation where a small child is timed on the one hundred yard dash and
timed at later points in his life. What we might have is a person running
the dash as a child in about forty seconds, improving his time to about

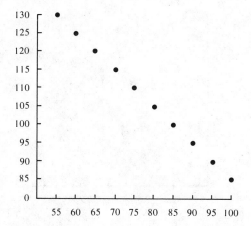

FIGURE 5–3.   A Perfect Negative Relationship.

eleven seconds at age eighteen, leveling off at about age twenty-five, and decreasing to a point, say at age eighty, where his time may be similar to his time as a child. Figure 5–5 illustrates a plot of a curvilinear relationship.

The following are familiar examples of the different types of relationships that can occur between variables.

Variables that are normally positively correlated are those such as:

Ability and Academic Performance

Parental Attitudes toward School and Student Achievement

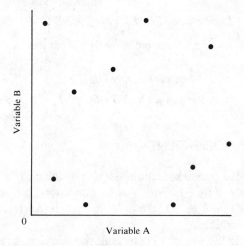

FIGURE 5–4.   A Low Positive Relationship.

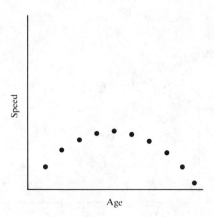

FIGURE 5–5.   A Curvilinear Relationship.

Amount of Exercise and Aerobic Capacity

Opinions of Parents and Opinions of Small Children

Variables that are normally negatively correlated are those such as:

World Crisis and Stock Market Prices

Cost of Living and Excess Money in the Family Budget

Age of Automobile and Trade-In Value

Supply of Food and Cost of Food

Variables that are normally not correlated at all are those such as:

Size of Feet and Achievement in School

Typing Speed and Writing Ability

Variables that may be correlated in a curvilinear manner are those such as:

Age and Some Physical Task

Rain and Crop Yield

SIZE OF THE COEFFICIENT

As we noted in the previous section, the size of the correlation coefficient will range from −1 to +1. With this in mind, we know that the closer the coefficient is to +1 or −1, the more the second variable is in proportion to the first variable.

With respect to the size of a coefficient, the question is raised regarding how close to +1 or −1 a coefficient must come to be considered "good."

In general, the size of a correlation coefficient is neither good nor bad. The size of the relationship between any two variables must be interpreted in terms of the variables involved. In some cases, a coefficient of .46 might be considered satisfactory, whereas a coefficient of .76 might be considered unsatisfactory in another situation.

In a purely descriptive sense, the size of the coefficient is not labeled at all but is simply taken as the degree that two variables are related.

INTERPRETATION OF THE COEFFICIENT

When we find the degree of relationship between two variables, we can use this information in the following ways.

1. Describe the degree of relationship that exists. For example, if we find that age is related to attitudes toward certain political issues, and the degree of relationship is +.62, we can stop at that point and simply describe the relationship in terms of the coefficient obtained.

2. Test a hypothesis. If we desire to determine if the observed relationship exceeds what chance would allow, we could take the coefficient to a probability table and determine its significance.

3. Predict one variable from the knowledge of the other. For example, once the relationship between two variables has been established, we can proceed to predict data for individuals within a specified degree of error. If we know the relationship between IQ and some kind of performance, we can use an individual's IQ to make a prediction regarding his performance. The accuracy of this prediction is based largely upon the degree of relationship that was found between IQ and performance.

An additional point regarding the interpretation of a correlation coefficient should be made at this time. When two variables are related to one another, it does not necessarily hold that one is the *cause* of the other. To illustrate this point, we will use a rather far-out example. Studies have shown that a positive relationship exists between the number of cigarettes smoked per day and the occurrence of lung cancer, and from this we get a popular conception that smoking causes cancer. Now, in fact, smoking may well cause lung cancer but the technique used to associate the two does not provide the basis for making cause and effect statements.

Let's take this known relationship and add a rather wild possibility. Suppose cancer is caused by the combination of nicotine and some element in the atmosphere and the impact of this combination on the human body produces the trouble. In other words, if we could isolate and control for the atmospheric variable, we could continue to smoke without fear of cancer.

The possibility of extraneous variables not accounted for when the degree of relationship between two variables is determined is the primary reason why cause and effect statements cannot be made from the results of correlation.

SIGNIFICANCE OF THE COEFFICIENT

If the purpose of determining the degree of relationship between variables is to generalize the relationship to a larger population, it becomes necessary to find out if the observed relationship could be attributed to chance or if the outcome is greater than pure chance would allow.

When we take this approach, we first assume a null hypothesis indicating that the relationship is zero. To make a decision on this hypothesis, we take our computed coefficient to the table located in appendix F. We enter the table with degrees of freedom equal to the number of pairs minus two ($n - 2$) and the desired probability level.

As with other techniques, if the computed coefficient is larger than the table value, the coefficient is considered significant. The significance of the coefficient would then be the basis for rejecting the null hypothesis.

FOR REVIEW AND FURTHER STUDY

1. Identify one or more possible research studies in your area of interest which would be likely to show a positive correlation between variables; a negative correlation; little if any correlation; a curvilinear correlation.
2. Identify one or more possible research studies in your area of interest which would be likely to show a high degree of relationship between variables; a low degree of relationship between variables.
3. Write a hypothesis for a research study which would be tested by determining a correlation.
4. Identify some situations in which a high correlation would be likely to exist between two variables, indicating a probable cause and effect relationship. Identify some situations in which a high correlation between two variables would probably not indicate a cause and effect relationship.
5. How would you determine if a certain correlation coefficient indicated a significant relationship between variables?
6. Identify some areas of concern in your field of study in which it would be useful to be able to predict one variable on the basis of knowledge of another variable. Approximately what degree of relationship would be necessary?

6

Techniques for
Determining
Relationships

You will recall from the previous chapter that correlation refers to the degree of relationship between two variables. You will also recall that we measure the degree of relationship between two variables with an index called a correlation coefficient. We can obtain this coefficient in a number of ways, but for the purposes of this book we will consider the following techniques.

The Pearson Product-Moment Correlation
The Point-Biserial Correlation
The Spearman Rank-Order Correlation
The Partial *r*

In addition to the specific techniques, we will look at how the correlation coefficient is used in prediction. Other techniques for determining the relationship between variables are available. However, those included in this chapter appear to be the ones most commonly used in behavioral science research.

THE PEARSON PRODUCT-MOMENT CORRELATION

Probably the most widely used relationship technique in behavioral science research is the Pearson Product-Moment technique. This relationship technique is appropriate to use when the following conditions are present.

1. The data are distributed in a linear fashion. This can be determined rather quickly by plotting the data on a graph and observing if the data can be represented by a straight line. If the plot shows a substantial departure from linearity, then the Pearson r should not be used. The alternative here would be the correlation ratio, or eta, discussed later in this chapter.

2. The variance between the two variables must be approximately equal. In other words, we must concern ourselves about the equality of spread or dispersion of data between the two variables. This is sometimes referred to as homoscedasticity, or equal scattering. This matter, too, can be checked by observing a scatter plot. In most instances, when the data are linear, the variances of the two variables will be approximately equal. Figure 6-1 shows a plot illustrating the lack of equal variance.

3. The data on both variables must be continuous. Although this is somewhat redundant to the first condition, it serves as an immediate check regarding the selection of the relationship technique to be used. By continuous data, we mean those data that can be measured on an interval scale, i.e., test scores, age, weight, etc.

Using the Pearson r on data that do not meet these conditions will result in a coefficient that is not reflective of the true relationship between two variables. Figure 6-2 illustrates a type of plot that would lead to the assumption that the conditions mentioned above have been met.

FIGURE 6–1.   A Plot Indicating the Lack of Equal Variance.

Computing the Pearson r

Once we have determined that the Pearson r is appropriate for the data we have, we proceed to obtain the coefficient. In keeping with our purpose of using the raw score approach, we compute the Pearson r with the following formula.

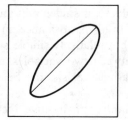

FIGURE 6–2.   A Plot Indicating the Data Are Linear and Have Approximately Equal Variance.

$$r = \frac{N\Sigma XY - (\Sigma X)(\Sigma Y)}{\sqrt{[N\Sigma X^2 - (\Sigma X)^2][N\Sigma Y^2 - (\Sigma Y)^2]}}$$

where

$$\Sigma XY = \text{sum of the cross products}$$
$$\Sigma X = \text{sum of the data (variable } X)$$
$$\Sigma Y = \text{sum of the data (variable } Y)$$
$$N = \text{number of subjects (number of pairs)}$$
$$N\Sigma X^2 - (\Sigma X)^2 = \text{sum of squares for } X$$
$$N\Sigma Y^2 - (\Sigma Y)^2 = \text{sum of squares for } Y$$

Before we look at a computational example, let's look at the formula for a moment. We have made the point several times that variance is the primary component in parametric statistical analyses. Whether we are concerned with determining relationships or differences, the variance that exists between groups or between sets of data determine to a great extent the size of the statistical value. We can note from the denominator of the formula the role that variance plays in determining the size of the coefficient.

A Computational Example

In many institutions the Graduate Record Examination is used to admit prospective graduate students to various degree programs. The accuracy of the decision to admit a student or not admit a student on the basis of the GRE is dependent upon the degree of relationship that exists between the GRE and some measure of success.

Concern has been voiced that GPA, the factor that is normally used as a success measure, is not the most reliable measure of graduate student success. In response to this concern, one institution made a request to explore the relationship between GRE and a preliminary examination given to all prospective doctoral students in an effort to see how a student's GRE score relates to his performance on this type of examination.

We are faced here with a relatively simple situation of computing the degree of relationship between two variables. Since the data are linear, continuous, and equal variance exists, the Pearson r is the appropriate technique to use.

Data were gathered on thirty prospective doctoral students. These data are presented in table 6–1. Using these data, we proceed with computing

TABLE 6–1. GRE and Preliminary Examination Scores on Thirty Prospective Doctoral Students.

Subject	GRE (X)	Exam (Y)	Subject	GRE (X)	Exam (Y)
1	1380	78	16	890	52
2	1310	68	17	890	52
3	1240	62	18	860	63
4	1120	60	19	840	51
5	1010	71	20	840	47
6	1000	60	21	800	50
7	1000	61	22	780	51
8	980	73	23	760	42
9	960	56	24	760	43
10	940	52	25	750	51
11	940	56	26	730	44
12	920	56	27	680	36
13	910	61	28	680	27
14	900	58	29	650	38
15	900	53	30	630	41

the Pearson r by obtaining values for the various components of the formula.

$$N = 30$$
$$\Sigma XY = 1,504,440$$
$$\Sigma X = 27,050$$
$$\Sigma Y = 1613$$
$$\Sigma X^2 = 25,354,500$$
$$\Sigma Y^2 = 90,437$$

We then substitute the values into the formula and complete the computation of r.

$$r = \frac{30(1,504,440) - (27,050)(1613)}{\sqrt{[30(25,334,500) - (27,050)^2][30(90,437) - (1613)^2]}}$$

$$= \frac{1,528,600}{\sqrt{[28,932,500][111,341]}}$$

$$= \frac{1,528,600}{1,794,818.50}$$
$$= .85$$

It is evident from the above computation that large numbers are involved when using the raw score approach. However, with machines available for use in this kind of work, the large numbers are manageable. We can simplify the process somewhat by subtracting a constant from our data in order to reduce the size of the numbers. For example, we could have subtracted 600 from all the scores on X and 27 from all the scores on Y. The outcome would have been identical.

Interpretation

As we have noted before, we can interpret a correlation coefficient in several ways. In this case, we were concerned with the relationship between scores made on the Graduate Record Examination and scores made on a preliminary examination. In a purely descriptive sense, we interpret this coefficient of .85 on the basis of where it falls on the line zero to plus one, and simply say that the degree of relationship between these two variables is a positive .85. A plot made prior to computation is shown in figure 6–3.

If we wish to determine the significance of this value, i.e., find if the degree of relationship is beyond what pure chance would allow, we would assume the null hypothesis of $r = 0$ and enter appendix F with $n - 2$, or

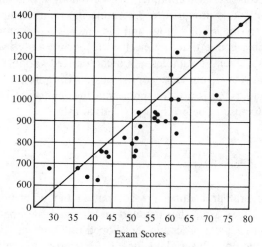

FIGURE 6–3.   A Plot Showing an r of .85 between GRE Scores and Preliminary Exam Scores.

28 degrees of freedom, and the desired probability level. Degrees of freedom for the Pearson are always determined by $n - 2$. If we selected the
.05 level of significance, we note from the table that our coefficient must
be .36 or larger in order to reject the null hypothesis. Since our value of
.85 is larger than the table value, we reject the null hypothesis and say
that the relationship obtained between these two variables is significant at
the .05 level. We note that the same decision on the hypothesis would be
made at the .01 level.

We will make the point here again regarding statistical significance and
practical significance. We have determined that the r of .85 between GRE
scores and preliminary examination scores is not due to chance. Put another way, there is a statistically significant relationship between the two
variables. The practicality of this information, however, is another matter.
For example, if the GRE is to be used as the sole basis for selecting ap-
plicants for a graduate program, the question regarding the amount of
error involved must be answered, and this is a practical matter, not a statistical one. Use of this relationship for prediction will be presented later
in this chapter.

THE POINT-BISERIAL CORRELATION

In order to use the Pearson r we must have two sets of continuous data.
There are situations in behavioral science research where this is not the
case. The point-biserial technique, symbolized by r_{pb}, is an extension of
the Pearson r and is designed to determine the relationship between two
variables when one is continuous and the other is a dichotomy. A dichotomized variable is one that is conceived to occupy only two points on a
scale of measurement. Examples of a dichotomized variable are sex, pass-
fail, yes or no, etc. If our data consist of one variable that is continuous
and one variable that is a true dichotomy, the point-biserial technique is
appropriate for use in determining the relationship.

Computation of Point-Biserial

There are several procedures for computing the point-biserial but, for
the most part, they are rather detailed and time consuming. For our purposes, we will follow a procedure developed by Dingman (figure 6–4) in
determining the point-biserial coefficient. This procedure involves the use
of a graph and is a quick and efficient way of estimating the point-biserial.
Comparisons of coefficients determined by the graph method and the

other computing procedures show only a slight difference in outcome. Therefore, we can rest assured that our estimate is accurate.

A Computational Example

For this example, we will use part of the data from the discussion of the Pearson r.

Let's assume that we would like to determine how much influence the method used for preparing for the preliminary examination had on the

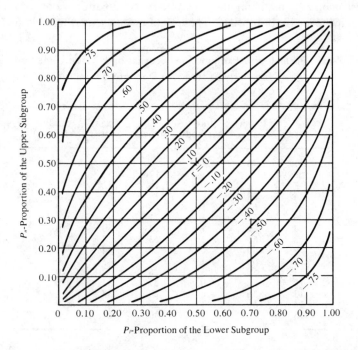

FIGURE 6–4. A Graph for Estimating the Point-Biserial Coefficient. (Prepared by Harvey F. Dingman) Source: J. P. Guilford, *Psychometric Methods* (New York: McGraw-Hill, 1954). Reprinted by permission of the publisher.

students' exam performance. In other words, what is the relationship between test performance and method of preparation? For the particular group of graduate students involved, two methods were used. First, some of the students organized study groups and devoted the majority of their study time to this group effort. Second, some of the students elected not to join a group and prepared for the examination on their own.

As we begin to look at our data for analysis, we note that two variables are involved, preliminary examination scores, a continuous variable, and method of preparation—in this case the students either studied with a group or they did not. This latter variable is dichotomized. We see, then, that the point-biserial technique is appropriate.

We turn now to the problem of quantifying the dichotomized variable. We can do this by using the numbers 1 and 0. We assign a 1 to those who participated in group study and a 0 to those who did not participate in group preparation.

We set up our data for this analysis in the same manner as we did for the Pearson *r* by matching the preliminary examination score with a 1 or a 0, whichever is appropriate. These data are presented in table 6–2.

TABLE 6–2. Preliminary Examination Scores and Coded Method of Study for Thirty Prospective Doctoral Students.

Subject	Exam Scores	Study Method	Subject	Exam Scores	Study Method
1	78	1	16	52	0
2	73	1	17	52	1
3	71	0	18	52	1
4	68	0	19	51	1
5	63	1	20	51	0
6	62	1	21	51	1
7	61	1	22	50	0
8	61	1	23	47	1
9	60	0	24	44	1
10	60	1	25	43	0
11	58	1	26	42	0
12	56	0	27	41	0
13	56	0	28	38	1
14	56	1	29	36	0
15	53	1	30	27	0

Using these data, we proceed to use the graph to determine the relationship between the two variables under study. The graph is used by dividing the continuous variable at the median and determining the proportion of subjects above the median and the proportion of subjects below the median. We take the proportion for the upper group and locate this point on the ordinate (on the left of the graph). We take the proportion for the subjects below the median and locate this point on the abscissa (across the bottom of the graph). The estimated point-biserial coefficient is located at the perpendicular intersection of these two points.

For our data, the point-biserial would be determined in the following manner.

1. Find the median of the examination scores. This is found to be approximately 52.5.
2. Count the number of subjects above the median who participated in group study (all subjects with a coded 1). The count here is 10 out of a total of 17.
3. Count the number of subjects below the median who participated in group study. The count here is 7 out of a total of 17.
4. Determine the proportion for each. For above the median, the proportion would be:

$$10/17 = .59$$

The proportion of subjects in the upper group who participated in group study is .59. This point is located on the ordinate.

For below the median, the proportion would be:

$$7/17 = .41$$

The proportion of subjects in the lower group who participated in group study is .41. This point is located on the abscissa.

The intersection of these two points gives us a point-biserial coefficient of about .23.

We can see that if the top seventeen subjects had participated in group study and the bottom seventeen subjects had not, we would get a proportion for the upper group of 1.00 and a proportion for the lower group of .00, therefore giving us a perfect positive 1.00.

Interpretation of r_{pb}

Since the point-biserial technique is an extension of the Pearson r, the outcome is interpreted in the same manner.

SPEARMAN RANK-ORDER CORRELATION

Another relationship technique that is useful in behavioral science research is the Spearman-Rank Order Correlation (*rho*). This technique is used when data are ranked and the number of subjects is small (less than thirty). For example, if we wish to determine the relationship between rank in high school and class rank at the end of the freshman year for fifteen subjects, this would be the appropriate technique. The Spearman Rank-Order is also an extension of the Pearson r and could be used with

the same type of data. However, with machines available for computation, the Pearson *r* is much more efficient with a large number of subjects.
There are occasions, however, where data in ranked form are all we have
to work with and we would need to use this method regardless of the size
of the sample.

Computation of *rho*

The basic formula for the computation of *rho* is:

$$\rho = 1 - \frac{6\Sigma D^2}{N(N^2 - 1)}$$

where

N = the number of pairs
ρ = rho
D^2 = difference, squared, between the ranks on the first variable and
the ranks on the second variable

Before we can make use of the formula, we must prepare our data for
analysis. One way of accomplishing this is to set up a worksheet similar
to that shown in table 6-3. To illustrate the computation of *rho,* we will

TABLE 6–3. Worksheet for Computation of *rho*.

Subject	GRE Score	Exam Score	Rank on GRE	Rank on Exam	D	D^2
1	1380	78	1	1	0	0
2	1310	68	2	4	2	4
3	1240	62	3	6	3	9
5	1010	71	5	3	2	4
6	1000	60	6.5	9.5	3	9
7	1000	61	6.5	7.5	1	1
8	980	73	8	2	6	36
9	960	56	9	12.5	3.5	12.5
18	860	63	18	5	13	169
21	800	50	21	22	1	1
23	760	42	23	26	3	9
27	680	36	27.5	29	1.5	2.25
28	680	27	27.5	30	2.5	6.25
29	650	38	29	28	1	1
30	630	41	30	27	3	9

$\Sigma D^2 = 273$

use the same data that we used in the computation of the Pearson r, but instead of using raw scores we will transform the raw scores for the GRE and the preliminary examination to ranks. For illustration purposes, we will shorten the example to fifteen subjects selected at random.

Before we move to computing, let's look at the table. You will note that the data on both variables are ranked on the basis of their standing from high to low. Since we are using only fifteen of the original subjects, the total rankings are not shown. The ranking process is accomplished by assigning a 1 to the highest score, a 2 to the next highest, and so on down the line. When tie scores are involved, we average the ranks and assign the average rank to both scores. For example, if the fourth and fifth scores are the same, we average the two and obtain 4.5. This rank, 4.5, would occupy both the fourth and fifth places in the rankings. We can note from the table that both the fifth and sixth subject made a score of 1000 on the GRE and a rank of 6.5 was assigned to each. Too many such ranks, however, will affect the size of *rho*. The object of this worksheet is simply to obtain a value for the expression ΣD^2 in order that we can proceed with the use of the formula.

We are ready now to solve for *rho*.

$$\rho = 1 - \frac{6\Sigma D^2}{N(N^2 - 1)}$$

$$= 1 - \frac{6(273)}{15(15^2 - 1)}$$

$$= 1 - \frac{1638}{3375}$$

$$= 1 - .4853$$

$$= .53$$

Interpretation of rho

Since the Spearman Rank-Order is another extension of the Pearson r, interpretation of the obtained value is made in the same manner. For example, we can simply say that the relationship between GRE score and examination score for the fifteen subjects is .53, and visualize where this value falls on the line from 0 to +1. We could also test the significance of *rho* by assuming a null hypothesis and taking our obtained value to appendix F, making the decision on the hypothesis in the same manner as we did when using values obtained by the Pearson r or point-biserial.

THE PARTIAL r

The three correlational techniques discussed so far in this chapter are designed to determine the relationship between *two* variables. The partial r is a technique designed to allow a third variable to be considered relative to how it might influence the relationship between the first two variables. For example, suppose we were interested in determining the relationship between the frequency of participation in an adult exercise program, measured by the number of days a person participates per week over a three-month period, and stamina, measured by the number of laps a person can run around a track in a specified period of time. To obtain a coefficient between these two variables would be relatively simple; however, the relationship obtained might be somewhat suspect due to lack of control over age. The partial r would allow this third variable, age, to be examined relative to its influence on the relationship between frequency of exercise and stamina. In other words, we can use this technique to "partial out" the effect of age and see what happens to the relationship between exercise and stamina.

Computation of the Partial r

The basic formula for the partial r is as follows.

$$r_{12.3} = \frac{r_{12} - (r_{13}r_{23})}{\sqrt{(1 - r_{13}{}^2)(1 - r_{23}{}^2)}}$$

where

$r_{12.3}$ = the correlation between variables one and two with the effects of variable three partialed out

The formula could be written with other combinations of variables if the situation required. For example, we could have $r_{13.2}$ or $r_{23.1}$. We would change the subscripts in the remainder of the formula accordingly.

A Computational Example

To illustrate the computation of the partial r we will use the same situation described in the introductory section. The three variables involved in this situation are these:

Variable 1 = exercise
Variable 2 = stamina
Variable 3 = age

After we obtain the data, we compute a Pearson r between each of the variables. For a sample size of 85, let's assume we obtained the following coefficients:

$r_{12} = .86$
$r_{23} = .91$
$r_{13} = .93$

As we look at these coefficients, we note that the relationship between exercise and stamina is .86. With a sample size of 85, this would be a significant relationship. We might even be tempted to conclude that the more you exercise, the more stamina you will have, at least in terms of running laps. However, when we look at the relationship between age and stamina, we should begin to question the conclusion.

Substituting the coefficients into the formula, we have:

$$r_{12.3} = \frac{.86 - (.93)(.91)}{\sqrt{(1 - .93^2)(1 - .91^2)}}$$

Completing the computation:

$$r_{12.3} = \frac{.01}{\sqrt{(.14)(.17)}}$$

$$= \frac{.01}{.15}$$

$$= .07$$

We can see that by removing the effect of age, the relationship between exercise and stamina has been substantially reduced from .86 to .07. The partial r is another extension of the Pearson r and can be interpreted in the same manner.

PREDICTION

We have noted in our discussion of the uses of correlation that predictions can be made from the knowledge of the relationship between two variables. If we know the relationship between two variables, we can use this knowledge to predict one variable from the knowledge of another. In determining relationships, we are dealing primarily with group data and in prediction, we are concerned about individual data. If we know the relationship between X and Y, for example, we can predict an individual's Y score from the knowledge of his X score.

To illustrate this point, recall the example used in the discussion of the Pearson *r*. We were concerned in this situation with the relationship between GRE score and preliminary examination score for thirty prospective doctoral students. From the information obtained about the relationship between these two variables, we are now in a position to use an individual's GRE score to predict how well he will do on the preliminary examination. This process is known as linear regression.

To make predictions, we need the following information:

1. the coefficient between the two variables being studied;
2. the raw score (X) which we will use to predict Y;
3. the standard error of estimate.

The Standard Error of Estimate

When we attempt to make a prediction, the predicted score is rarely exactly the same as the actual score. It would be a most unusual situation if we could take an individual's GRE score and predict precisely what his preliminary exam score would be. Our predictions are in error to some extent. We can, however, measure this error and use this information in making our predictions. If the error factor is large, our predictions will not be as accurate as if our error factor is relatively small. If the size of the coefficient is large, normally the error factor is small. Conversely, if the coefficient is small, the size of the error is large.

We measure the amount of error involved with a technique known as the standard error of estimate, which is similar to standard deviation. For example, if the variance, or standard deviation, between two variables is large, the correlation coefficient is usually small. Therefore, the standard error works the same way.

We obtain the standard error of estimate in the following manner:

$$s_{yx} = s_y \sqrt{1 - r_{xy}^2}$$

where

s_{yx} = standard error of estimate
s_y = standard deviation of the Y variable
r_{xy}^2 = coefficient, squared, between the variables X and Y

When our sample size is less than fifty, it becomes necessary to add an expression to the basic formula to correct for small sample bias. This correction is handled by multiplying the following expression by the results of the standard error of estimate formula:

$$\sqrt{\frac{N}{N-2}}$$

where

N = the number of subjects (number of pairs)

Using the data on GRE scores and preliminary examination scores from the first part of this chapter, the standard error of estimate would be:

$$
\begin{aligned}
s_{yx} &= s_y \sqrt{1 - r_{xy}^2} \\
&= 10.19 \sqrt{1 - .42} \\
&= 10.19 \sqrt{.58} \\
&= 10.19 \, (.76) \\
&= 7.74
\end{aligned}
$$

After multiplying 7.74 times correction for sample size, $\sqrt{(N/N-2)}$ = 1.03,

$$s_{yx} = 7.97$$

The Regression Equation

Before we see how the standard error of estimate is used in the prediction process, we will discuss the procedure for predicting one variable from the knowledge of another.

The basic regression equation for predicting the dependent variable from a single independent variable is presented below.

$$Y' = \bar{Y} + r_{xy} \left(\frac{s_y}{s_x}\right)(X - \bar{X})$$

where

Y' = dependent variable
$\bar{Y}$ = mean of the dependent variable
r_{xy} = correlation between variable X and variable Y
s_y = standard deviation of Y variable
s_x = standard deviation of X variable
X = individual X score
$\bar{X}$ = mean of X variable

In terms of our problem, we are concerned with predicting preliminary examination score (Y) from GRE score (X).

Given a GRE score of 980, we would compute Y' in the following manner:

$$Y' = 53.77 + .65\left(\frac{10.19}{170.71}\right)(980 - 901.67)$$

$$= 53.77 + .039\ (78.33)$$

$$= 53.77 + 3.05$$

$$= 56.82$$

We found the standard error of estimate to be 7.97. We use this value to set up a prediction band for our Y variable. We know that some error is involved which makes it unlikely that our individual with a GRE score of 980 would make exactly 56.82 on the preliminary examination. Therefore, the standard error of estimate is used to establish a range of preliminary examination scores into which we can say an individual with a GRE score of 980 would fall.

Using the standard error of estimate, we would say that a person with a GRE score of 980 would score on the preliminary examination:

$$56.82 + \text{or} - 7.97$$

or between

$$48.85 \text{ and } 64.79$$

We note that the larger the standard error, the more accurate our prediction. However, when the prediction band is too wide, the prediction has little practical effectiveness.

SAMPLE STUDY

The study presented here utilizes the technique of correlation in a variety of ways. By determining the variables involved, you should be able to identify the specific correlational technique employed.

Grading Standards: The Relation of Changes in Average Student Ability to the Average Grades Awarded*

The question of academic standards is a persistent theme in rhetoric about higher education. On the one hand we hear that yesterday's college student

*Leonard Baird and William J. Feister, "Grading Standards: The Relation of Changes in Average Student Ability to the Average Grades Awarded," reprinted from *American Educational Research Journal* 9, no. 3 (Summer 1972):431–42, by permission of the publisher.

could not compete academically with his peers of today and,
that "standards" are slipping badly. Constantly rising admissions s.
according to one view, are resulting in college freshman classes that u.
brighter than previous freshman classes and will cause many able students
to flunk out. According to another view, the floodgates have been opened to
masses of unqualified students who will make an "A" meaningless. In particular, this is the position taken by many critics of the "open admission" concept. They feel that lower admissions standards will produce lower levels of
achievement.

In this discussion it seems sensible to look at the college grades being
awarded to these students. One would expect higher grades to be awarded
to brighter students.[1] Thus, we should examine the stability or change in the
ability of incoming college students and the relation of average student ability to average college grades. We are then concerned with such questions as
the following: To what extent are college student bodies becoming more
able? When we describe the "academic pressure cooker" of rising standards
are we talking about 10 percent, 25 percent, 50 percent or 100 percent of
American colleges? When student ability rises, do college grades awarded
rise proportionately? And what happens when the ability level of a student
body decreases? How often does it happen? Do college grades tend to decrease too?

There are some related questions concerning the meaning of grades. Does
a grade represent the same level of performance, accomplishment and ability
from college to college, and from year to year at the same college? More
generally, is the variation of average student ability and grading patterns so
great that we know little about the meaning of a particular grade, or is there
some relation between grades awarded and some permanent or stable
standards?

These are important questions. This study was designed to try to find answers to them. The changes in academic ability in incoming students were
studied in several hundred colleges, and these changes were related to the
average grades these students received in their first year of college.

METHOD

Source of Information

The American College Testing Program's Research Services provide research
results and statistical summaries for colleges. The Standard and Basic Research Service provides data about the ability of freshmen, their overall

---

1. This expectation would be based on an assumption of fairly stable standards of performance, i.e., the level of performance required for a "B" would remain the same; when brighter
students entered, a larger proportion of students would obtain "Bs." Furthermore, one must
assume that motivation, interest and effort are stable at the various levels of "brightness"
defined by college admission tests.

grades in their first year of college, as well as equations for predicting grades. The Standard and Basic Research Service summary reports yielded the basic data used in this study. For each college, each year, data included the mean and standard deviation on the ACT Composite for the admitted freshmen, the means and standard deviation on the average of the student-reported high school grades, the mean and standard deviation of the freshman college grades awarded to these students, and the multiple correlation predicting grades from the ACT test scores and high school grades. These data were available for 284 colleges in 1964, 365 colleges in 1965, 469 colleges in 1966, 555 colleges in 1967, and 444 colleges in 1968.

Treatment of Data

The data for each college for each year were punched on cards. To normalize the distributions, the correlations were converted to Z scores, using Fisher's r to Z transformation. Then, using a missing data computer program, the difference scores between each set of data were computed. In this way, we derived difference scores for each statistic over one, two, three, and four years. Thus, for each statistic the following difference scores were computed:

One year: 1968–1967, 1967–1966, 1966–1965, 1965–1964
Two years: 1968–1966, 1967–1965, 1966–1964
Three years: 1968–1965, 1967–1964
Four years: 1968–1964

Correlational Studies

Using a missing data computer program, we computed the correlations between all means, standard deviations, multiple correlations and the difference scores. These correlations showed year-to-year relationships which will be presented below.[2]

Analysis of Changing Colleges

In order to study the effects of changing levels of academic aptitude over various periods of time, we first counted the number of colleges where the ACT Composite mean score had changed less than 1, 1 to 1.4, 1.5 to 1.9, and 2.0 or greater standard scores. Then we selected the colleges which changed most over the three and four year periods. The results for colleges whose mean ACT Composite score increased 2.0 or more points over four years and those whose means decreased 1.5 or more points over three years are reported.

---

2. The results for the size of the multiple correlations will be presented elsewhere.

RESULTS

The Question of "Standards"

The correlations between the mean ACT Composite scores and mean college grades awarded are shown in Table 1. There were low to moderate correlations between the average ability of incoming students and the average grades awarded to those students; colleges whose incoming students were bright *tended* to award higher average grades, and colleges whose incoming students were less able *tended* to award lower average grades. The correlations were moderate at best, however, and the unaccounted for variance suggested that many colleges with bright students *tended* to award low grades, and colleges with less able students *tended* to award high grades.

TABLE 1. Means, Standard Deviations, and Correlations between ACT Composite and College GPA Means and Standard Deviations.

A. ACT Composite Means and College GPA Means

Year	Mean of ACT-C Means	S.D. of ACT-C Means	Mean of CGPA Means	S.D. of CGPA Means	r-ACT-C and CGPA Means	Number of Colleges
1964	19.13	2.50	2.13	.24	.35*	282
1965	19.31	2.49	2.12	.26	.25*	361
1966	19.49	2.48	2.14	.26	.36*	465
1967	19.53	2.47	2.15	.25	.43*	551
1968	19.33	2.47	2.20	.35	.42*	440

B. ACT Composite Standard Deviations and College GPA Standard Deviations

Year	Mean of ACT-C S.D.'s	S.D. of ACT-C S.D.'s	Mean of CGPA S.D.'s	S.D. of CGPA S.D.'s	r-ACT-C and CGPA S.D.'s	Number of Colleges
1964	4.30	.46	.76	.11	.39*	282
1965	4.20	.50	.77	.11	.42*	361
1966	4.22	.53	.77	.12	.46*	465
1967	4.23	.55	.79	.12	.45*	551
1968	4.33	.53	.80	.12	.49*	440

*Significant at the .01 level.

Table 1 also shows the correlation between the ACT Composite standard deviation and the standard deviation of college grades awarded. These correlations were also moderate. They suggest that colleges whose students include a broad range of academic aptitude *tended* to award a wider range of grades than colleges with narrow ranges of student aptitude.

The results shown in Table 1 suggest that, taken as aggregate groups, faculties tended to have adjusted their grading practices to the characteristics of the students they teach. Where students were brighter they *tended* to award higher grades: where students represented a broader range of academic aptitude, they tended to award a broader range of grades. These tendencies were moderate, however. The size of these correlations suggests that much of the variance in the means and standard deviations of college grades from college to college remains to be explained and was not explained solely by the input of means and standard deviations of student talent. The results do not seem attributable to changes in the variances of the measures from year to year. The standard deviations of the means and standard deviations were generally also about the same size from year to year.

Apparently these tendencies are based on very stable student bodies, as can be seen in Table 2. The mean ability of students in 1964 correlated .93 with the mean ability of students in 1968 at 188 colleges. Over shorter periods the r was higher. The average ability of students at these various colleges was clearly very stable. The range of ability of the students enrolled was also stable, as shown by the correlations in Table 2. Thus, year to year both the average ability and distribution of ability were quite stable at the majority of colleges. As also shown in Table 2, the mean grades awarded to students were also fairly stable, but not as stable as the average and distribution of ability. Thus, year after year, the student input of colleges changed very little.

TABLE 2.   Stability of Mean ACT Composite, ACT Composite Standard Deviations, and Mean College GPA over Various Periods.[a]

| | | Correlations* | | | |
| | | | | | Number |
Time Periods		(1)	(2)	(3)	of Colleges
One Year	1964–1965	.96	.80	.64	218
	1965–1966	.97	.81	.74	281
	1966–1967	.96	.80	.73	345
	1967–1968	.96	.75	.78	362
Two Years	1964–1966	.95	.80	.68	235
	1965–1967	.96	.75	.58	271
	1966–1968	.95	.75	.70	298
Three Years	1964–1967	.95	.73	.57	214
	1965–1968	.94	.71	.66	221
Four Years	1964–1968	.93	.75	.61	188

[a]The mean means and standard deviations, and standard deviations of the means and standard deviations in each group of colleges used in these statistics are virtually identical to those reported in Table 1.

(1) Correlation between Mean ACT Composites
(2) Correlation between ACT Composite Standard Deviations
(3) Correlations between Mean College GPA's

*All correlations significant at .01 level.

The results in Table 2 also suggest that the correlations in Table 1 might have been higher, if grades had been more stable.

Changing Standards and Faculty Responses

As we have just seen, the student input at most colleges remained the same from year to year. But what happened when student input changed? Table 3 shows the correlations between the change scores for average student ability and the change scores for average grades awarded over various periods of

TABLE 3.   Correlations between Changes in Means and Standard Deviations of ACT Composite and College GPA.[a]

		Correlations		Number of Colleges
	Time Periods of Change Scores	(1)	(2)	
One Year	1964–1965 ACT Comp & 1964–1965 CGPA	.29*	.13	218
	1965–1966 ACT Comp & 1965–1966 CGPA	.31*	.26*	281
	1966–1967 ACT Comp & 1966–1967 CGPA	.25*	.23*	345
	1967–1968 ACT Comp & 1967–1968 CGPA	.32*	.33*	362
Two Years	1964–1966 ACT Comp & 1964–1966 CGPA	.26*	.18*	235
	1965–1967 ACT Comp & 1965–1967 CGPA	.16*	.14	271
	1966–1968 ACT Comp & 1966–1968 CGPA	.23*	.14	298
Three Years	1964–1967 ACT Comp & 1964–1967 CGPA	.19*	.08	214
	1965–1968 ACT Comp & 1965–1968 CGPA	.11	.20*	221
Four Years	1964–1968 ACT Comp & 1964–1968 CGPA	.30*	.05	188

[a]The mean means and mean standard deviations and standard deviations of the means and standard deviations for these colleges are virtually identical to those reported in Table 1.

(1) Correlations between changes in Means of ACT Composites and GPA's
(2) Correlations between changes in Standard Deviations of ACT Composites and GPA's

*Significant at the .01 level.

time. The correlations were generally low, indicating a slight trend for faculty members to award higher or lower grades when student ability increased or decreased. Thus, there seemed to be little tendency for faculty to "adapt" to change a year or so later. Table 3 also shows the correlations between change scores for the standard deviation of student ability and change scores for the standard deviation of college grades awarded. These correlations indicate a very slight tendency for a broader or narrower range of grades to be awarded when the range of student talent broadened or narrowed. There was almost no such tendency over the longest period of time.

The size of the correlations in Table 3 may be curtailed due to the high stability of student input described earlier and because of the use of change scores. Because most colleges seemed to remain the same, and in order to examine changes directly, we conducted the analyses described in the next section.

Analysis of Changing Colleges

In order to study the effect of changing levels of academic aptitude in more detail, we carried out the analyses described in the Methods section above.

As shown in Table 4, most colleges changed very little—less than one standard score on the ACT Composite—over any period of time. For example, from 1964 to 1965, 87.3 of the colleges changed their mean ACT Composite score by less than one standard score point. Very few colleges changed as much as two standard score points on the ACT Composite. This held true even over the period from 1964 to 1968, in which only about 5 percent of the colleges had changed student ability by as much as two standard scores—less than one-half a standard deviation on national college-bound student norms, or one standard deviation on norms based on college means. (Of course, a change of two standard score points would result from the presence of many more bright or dull students in a student body.)

TABLE 4.   The Degree of Change in ACT Composite Means.

	Percent Changing by Indicated Amount				
	Less than ±1.0	Between ±1.0 & 1.4	Between ±1.5 & 1.9	±2.0 & Greater	Number of Colleges
One Year Change					
1964–1965	87.3	8.2	2.2	1.3	219
1965–1966	83.8	10.9	3.9	1.4	284
1966–1967	87.4	8.9	1.7	2.0	348
1967–1968	87.7	9.3	1.9	1.1	365
Two Year Change					
1964–1966	74.6	13.6	8.5	3.4	236
1965–1967	72.6	19.3	5.8	2.2	274
1966–1968	85.0	9.0	4.0	2.0	301
Three Year Change					
1964–1967	60.9	24.2	9.8	5.1	215
1965–1968	76.3	15.6	6.3	1.8	224
Four Year Change					
1964–1968	64.0	20.1	10.6	5.3	189

As a next step in the analysis a series of figure was developed to portray graphically the analyses of the colleges changing most in student input. In these figures, ACT Composite and college grade means were graphed in equal standard deviation units, based on national student norms. In order to make the effects of changes clearer, ACT Composite means and college grade point average means (GPA) were shown at the *same* point for the first year in each figure by moving the left or right hand scale. This procedure showed most clearly the effects of changing student ability. If college grading standards were consistent from year to year, the mean GPA should have followed the changes in student ability from year to year.[3]

Figure 1 suggests that grades awarded by faculties also did not consistently

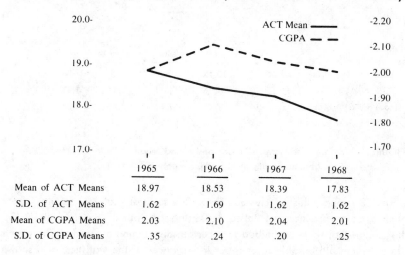

	1965	1966	1967	1968
Mean of ACT Means	18.97	18.53	18.39	17.83
S.D. of ACT Means	1.62	1.69	1.62	1.62
Mean of CGPA Means	2.03	2.10	2.04	2.01
S.D. of CGPA Means	.35	.24	.20	.25

FIGURE 1.   Relation of Mean ACT Composite and Mean College GPA for 12 Colleges Decreasing Most in ACT Mean 1965–1968.

follow declines in student ability in the twelve colleges where average student ability declined most, and that the average grades awarded were about the same in 1965 and 1968—a three year period—despite a drop in student ability.

The ten colleges where the mean ACT Composite rose by two or more scores over four years are shown in Figure 2. Again, the mean grades awarded by the faculty to freshmen in these colleges remained about the same, despite a marked increase in student ability. The change in mean grades in 1968 is relatively small, in comparison.[4]

In colleges with changing student input, faculties taken as a whole apparently awarded about the same grades from year to year whether their students were brighter or duller than the last year's students. The data in Figures

---

3. This statement makes the same assumptions mentioned in footnote 2.

4. The individual colleges which comprised the "changing" groups in these analyses were examined to see if they had any similarities. The colleges were of all types, levels, and control. Their enrollments, and changes in enrollments, were about average. They did not seem to have any common characteristics which would explain the changes in their student input. A number of analyses of colleges that changed over shorter periods show the same trends.

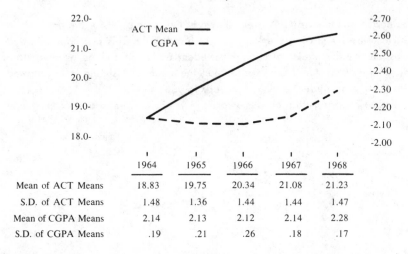

FIGURE 2.   Relation of Mean ACT Composite and Mean College GPA for 10
Colleges Increasing Most in ACT Mean 1964–1968.

1 and 2 support this conclusion. They also suggest that few faculties base
their grading practices on "absolute" standards, but rather, as Hills (1964)
has suggested, seem committed to a certain distribution of grades. The results
do not seem attributable to changes in variances of the statistics, also shown
in the figures. In short, most faculties, taken as an aggregate, award about
the same average grades each year, despite increases or decreases in student
academic aptitude.

DISCUSSION

This study confirms the earlier research of Aiken (1963), Hills (1964), Hills and
Gladney (1968), Webb (1963), Wilson (1970), and others which indicated
that faculty members, at least collectively, prefer or are committed to a certain distribution of grades. Thus, faculties show an "adaptation level" by
awarding, on the average, about the same average and distribution of
grades, whether their current students are brighter or duller than last year's.
Thus, following Helson (1964), we would surmise that faculty members "pool"
the stimuli in the "judgment series"—the performance of their *current* students
—and make judgments accordingly. (An interesting experiment could be done
to examine this idea further among a group of faculty members who are
faced with bright and dull students.)

     The correlational results suggested that college grades did tend to rise
slightly when student ability rose. (However, the largest correlation still accounted for only about 10 percent of the variance.) The analyses of colleges
which changed the most, however, suggested that, when student input
changes sharply, the average grades awarded do not change to correspond

to the increased (or decreased) ability of students. These two sets of results seem incompatible. However, as noted, the correlational results showed low correlations, which allow for great variation, including colleges at the extremes of change.

In sum, the present results provide little evidence that faculties will adjust grades to correspond to changes in average student ability after some time lapse. Thus, the results shown in the graphs and the correlational results provide little evidence that permanent or absolute standards are employed in evaluation or that faculty generally take the changing ability level of their student bodies into account when deciding how many A's, B's, etc., to award.

These considerations suggest a practical problem. Without some information about a college, admissions officers and counselors have no sure way of knowing what level of ability a grade on a transcript represents. This may represent a large problem for graduate schools or colleges which accept many transfer students. These groups of students may require testing to estimate their chances in the local setting.

Another practical implication is that colleges should not expect to raise admissions requirements and thereby obtain a group of students who will necessarily make markedly higher grades. More likely, the faculty will continue to award about the same grades.

Of course, there are possible explanations of these results other than those offered here, such as a tendency toward regression toward the mean among changing colleges, or questions about the extent to which "true" grades are a function of what the ACT tests measure. However, the consistency of the results over a number of years makes these alternative explanations seem implausible.

Finally, there remains a host of critical educational questions, such as those raised by Wilson (1970). When aptitude goes up or down, does the actual "quality" of student work in the classroom increase or decrease? If students are evaluated according to "class norms," what are the consequences for their attitudes toward the professor, the subject, and their own abilities? How do current college students feel about being "ranked" in a competitive system? All these issues appear to warrant further investigation.

These considerations, taken with the relative stability of mean grades and mean ACT Composite scores, suggest that any further increases in the level of prediction of grades may come from improvements in grading practices. We need to devote as much attention to understanding faculty grade-giving behavior as we have to student grade-getting behavior.

REFERENCES

Aiken, L. R. The grading behavior of a college faculty. *Educational and Psychological Measurement*, 1963, 23, 319–322.

Helson, H. *Adaptation-level theory.* New York: Harper & Row, 1964.

Hills, J. R. The effect of admissions policy on college grading standards. *Journal of Educational Measurement,* 1964, 2, 115–118.

Hills, J. R., and Gladney, M. B. Factors influencing college grading standards. *Journal of Educational Measurement,* 1968, 5, 31–39.

Webb, S. C. Increased selectivity and institutional standards. In K. M. Wilson (Ed.), *Research related to college admissions.* Atlanta, Ga.: Southern Regional Board, 1963.

Wilson, K. M. Increased selectivity and institutional grading standards. *College and University,* 1970, 46, 46–53.

FOR REVIEW AND FURTHER STUDY

1. For the sample study presented in this chapter, which correlation technique was used? Why was this the appropriate technique?
2. What changes in the data used in the sample study would have warranted the use of each of the other correlational techniques described in this chapter?
3. A study[1] was designed to determine if the nonauditory, nonverbal subtests of a psycholinguistics test for normal children could be validly used for individualized educational prescriptive purposes with deaf children. No test currently available for such use is designed for deaf children. It was assumed that if a close correlation existed between the psycholinguistic quotient derived from the visually oriented subtests of the Illinois Test of Psycholinguistic Abilities (which was developed for prescriptive use with normal children) and the intellectual quotient derived from the Leiter International Performance Scale (for deaf children), then the visually oriented subtests of the ITPA would be valid for prescriptive use with deaf children. The two tests were administered to a group of thirty-six deaf children and the scores from each test were then correlated.
   a. Which correlation technique should have been used for this study? What assumptions about the data must you make to justify the use of this technique?
   b. The ITPA scores correlated with the Leiter intelligence quotient with a coefficient of .93. At what probability level would this relationship be considered significant?
   c. Would it be possible to predict a Leiter intelligence quotient from an ITPA score with considerable accuracy?
   d. What conclusions could have been drawn from this study?
4. If fourteen individuals were administered inventories to determine their attitudes toward social mores and religious beliefs, yielding the following

1. Robert O. Taddonio, "Correlation of Leiter and the Visual Subtests of the Illinois Test of Psycholinguistic Abilities with Deaf Elementary School Children," *Journal of School Psychology* 11:1 (March 1973):30–35.

scores, would it be determined that a significant association existed between the two sets of scores? Would this mean that according to these measures there is a significant correlation between the social mores and the religious beliefs being determined? Use both the Pearson product-moment technique (r) and the Spearman rank-order technique (rho) to calculate this relationship, then compare and evaluate the results.

Individual	Attitudes Toward Social Mores	Attitudes Toward Religious Beliefs
1	24	27
2	22	23
3	33	40
4	25	28
5	15	19
6	33	40
7	20	21
8	34	28
9	33	32
10	21	22
11	25	36
12	25	29
13	19	26
14	28	31

5. A high school guidance counselor might administer an attitude scale to a group of high school students and wish to compare the scores of boys and girls. If the scores were as follows, determine the correlation of boys' and girls' scores.

    Boys: 5 2 1 9 4 8 5 9 4 3 5 7 9
    Girls: 10 7 6 8 11 8 11 5 8 6 4 2 12

6. A study[2] was designed to determine relationships of grade-point average, the Scott Motor Ability Test, and intellectual aptitude. With a group of female physical education students, the following intercorrelations were found:

    Grade-point average to motor ability test   .30
    Grade-point average to intellectual aptitude test   .22
    Motor ability test to intellectual aptitude test   −.04

    a. If intelligence is removed as a consideration, what is the correlation between grade-point average and motor ability test?
    b. If motor ability test is partialed out, what is the correlation between grade-point average and intellectual aptitude score?
    c. If grade-point average is partialed out, what is the correlation between intellectual aptitude score and motor ability test?

---

2. Laretha Leyman, "Prediction of Freshman and Sophomore Grade-point Averages of Women Physical Education Major Students," *Educational and Psychological Measurement* 27 (1967):1139–41.

   d. What other partial correlations are possible?
   e. Interpret the results of this study in the light of your calculations.
7. Describe hypothetical studies which would utilize each of the four correlational techniques described in this chapter. Show what kinds of data would
   be necessary. Also indicate assumptions and restrictions relative to conclusions which might be drawn.

7

Multiple
Correlation:
An Introduction

Multiple correlation, or multiple regression, is a technique designed to determine the relationship between more than one independent variable and a single dependent variable. In the last two chapters, we have been concerned with the relationship between one independent variable and a dependent variable. Many of the same principles are involved except we are now interested in looking at the relationship between a combination of variables and a dependent variable rather than a single independent variable.

In conducting research, we are guided by the basic function:

$$Y = f(X)$$

where

Y = dependent variable
f = function of
X = independent variable

In multiple correlation, this basic function can be written:

$$Y = f(X_1, X_2, X_3, \ldots \ldots X_n)$$

This function designs for us a situation where we are concerned with the function of a combination of independent variables on the dependent variable. More specifically, multiple correlation is designed to accomplish the following:

1. Determine the overall relationship between more than one independent variable and one dependent variable. There are many occasions in behavioral science research when it is more meaningful to consider the relationship between a combination of variables rather than a single variable. For example, instead of looking at the relationship between college success and high school rank, we can find out more information by looking at a combination of variables as they relate to college success.

2. Determine the interrelationships between the various independent variables. This information tells us which of the variables make the most unique contribution to the combined relationship. For example, suppose we were interested in discovering a combination of variables that would be helpful in predicting success in college. We might start with the following:

> College success (Y) = high school rank (X_1), high school GPA (X_2), high school honors (X_3), high school activities (X_4), SES (X_5), dominant language (X_6), education of parents (X_7), and whatever else we might want to include.

If we should find that any of these variables are significantly related to each other, then one would be as good as the other in making a contribution to the overall relationship. With the variables listed above, we could expect some of them to be related to each other, such as X_1 and X_2. We will see how to handle this situation later on in the chapter.

3. Determine the relationship between each independent variable and the dependent variable. What is happening here is simple correlation or the relationship between one independent variable and the dependent variable.

4. Determine the combination of variables that can be used to predict most accurately the dependent variable. The multiple correlation analysis results in an equation that can be used, if the situation warrants, to predict the dependent variable for individual subjects. Like prediction that stems from simple correlation, the prediction equation is based on group data. Individual data are then used in the equation to predict the dependent variable.

For the college success illustration, for example, the analysis of the named independent variables would yield an equation that could be used to predict college success.

We are going to approach this chapter a little differently from the others in that our emphasis is on use and interpretation rather than computational procedures. The reason for this is that the computational procedures for this technique are complicated and are normally done by computer.

A SAMPLE STUDY

A sample study is included at this point to show one of the uses of multiple correlation. The problem here is one of determining the relationship between three independent variables and one dependent variable with the goal of determining the effectiveness of these three variables in predicting performance of teachers.

Effectiveness of Three Selective Admissions Criteria in Predicting Performance of First-Year Teachers*

In recent years emphasis has been placed on requiring separate standards for students who seek to prepare themselves as teachers. This emphasis has resulted in influencing many institutions that train teachers to establish formal selection procedures for prospective teachers. These selection procedures are designed with the intent of allowing only those who meet certain standards admittance to a teacher education curriculum. The idea of high standards for teachers is generally accepted, but there appears to be wide disagreement as to what standards should be used to select students.

In the area of selection of students to pursue a teacher preparation program, the major emphasis of previous investigations has centered around determining the extent of such programs and investigating the validity of certain criteria for selecting students.

In a study of selection procedures, Edson and Davis (1) obtained information concerning the changes taking place in selection procedures in Minnesota colleges and universities. They found that there was an increase in the use of measures of academic achievement and in employment of indexes of competency in English usage as a basis for selection.

Another study concerned with what colleges and universities are doing to select students was conducted by Magee (3). This study addressed itself to surveying forty-eight universities and 132 colleges as to the type and place in the students' program of the use of selective devices. The results indicated that most institutions selected students at the beginning of the upper division or at the entrance into student teaching. This study also reported that 92 per-

---

*Joe D. Cornett, "The Effectiveness of Three Selective Admissions Criteria in Predicting Performance of First-Year Teachers," reprinted from The Journal of Educational Research 62, no. 6 (February 1969): 247–50, by permission of the publisher.

cent of the institutions imposed some additional standard for entry into a teacher preparation program in addition to the normal college requirements. These additional standards, the study noted, were of the nature of grade requirements imposed upon total work, professional courses, and major courses.

Numerous studies concerned with the criteria for selection have been reported in recent years but reveal very little agreement as to what criteria should be used. One such study, conducted by Simon and Asher (5), studied the relationship of selected undergraduate factors and school administrators' ratings of first-year teachers. They concluded that the best single predictors of ratings were student teaching grades, academic average, and faculty rating.

THE PROBLEM

Southeastern Louisiana College is one of the institutions that impose additional standards, above the normal college requirements, for admittance into the teacher education program. The requirements are these:

(1) An overall grade point average of C (2.0) at the time of application.

(2) A grade of C in second semester freshman English.

(3) A grade of C in the introductory course in education.

Students registered in the Division of Education normally make application for admission by the end of their fourth regular semester in college, or as students in the introductory course in education. Students who fail to meet the above criteria are not allowed to pursue the teacher preparation program until one or more of the deficiencies are removed. If the principle purpose of formally selecting students in teacher education is to accept only those who show promise of performing well as teachers, then the following question needs to be answered. How effective are these criteria in predicting teaching performance?

Rabinowitz and Mitzel (4) stated that if the combined predictors used to select students for a teacher preparation program resulted in a multiple R no higher than .40 with a reliable measure of teaching success, one was screening out too many potentially successful teachers. The intent of this investigation was to determine the relationship between the three selective admissions criteria: grade point average, grade in second-semester freshman English, grade in introductory course in education, and performance of first-year teachers as measured by principals' ratings. Also, an effort was made to determine if the prediction efficiency of the admissions criteria was different for elementary teachers and secondary teachers.

PROCEDURE

In the spring of 1967 the Office of Teacher Placement of Southeastern Louisiana College made available the confidential principals' ratings of graduates who had completed their first year of teaching. A total of sixty-eight ratings were received constituting thirty-one elementary teachers and thirty-seven secondary teachers. All of the subjects included in the study had been selected for the teacher preparation program, while some were admitted only after repeated application due to a deficiency in one or more of the selection criteria.

Data were gathered on the variables from records kept by the Selective Admissions and Retention Committee and recorded at the time of first application. A description of the variables is as follows:

(1) Grade point average. (X_2) The GPA used for this study represented the students' standing at the time of application.

(2) Grade in introductory education courses. (X_3) A grade of C is considered the minimum grade in this course for admittance. It is a course designed to acquaint the students with the opportunities, requirements, ethics, and foundations of the teaching profession.

(3) Grade in second semester freshman English. (X_4) A grade of C or better is required for acceptance. It is a freshman composition course concentrating on expository writing, the research paper, factual reports, business correspondence, and the finer qualities of style.

The rationale for acceptance or rejection, then, is knowledge of the teaching profession, demonstrated academic ability, and performance in English composition.

(4) Principals' rating. (X_1) The criterion measure used in the present study was a composite rating achieved by each graduate after their first year of teaching. The scale, completed by the school principal, consisted of thirty-six factors rated on a 5-point scale.

Means and standard deviations of the criterion measure and the three independent variables are presented in Table 1.

TABLE 1.   Means and Standard Deviations of Principals' Ratings and Three Selective Admissions Criteria.

Variable	Secondary and Elementary Combined (N = 68)		Elementary (N = 31)		Secondary (N = 37)	
	Mean	S. D.	Mean	S. D.	Mean	S. D.
Principals' Ratings*	134.35	24.18	136.94	23.38	132.19	24.98
Grade Point Average	2.28	.48	2.22	.50	2.32	.47
Grade in Introduction to Education	2.56	.72	2.58	.81	2.54	.65
Grade in Second-Semester Freshman English	1.81	.76	1.71	.64	1.89	.81

*The thirty-six factors rated on a 5-point scale would yield a perfect Score of 180.

TABLE 2.   Intercorrelations among Principals' Ratings of Elementary Teachers
and Three Selective Admissions Criteria ($N = 31$).

	X_1 Principals' Ratings	X_2 Grade Point Average	X_3 Grade in Introduction to Education	X_4 Grade in Second-Semester Freshman English
X_1	1.00	—.04	—.20	—.09
X_2		1.00	—.04	.21
X_3			1.00	.72**
X_4				1.00

**Significant at the .01 level.

A set of multiple regression equations was developed using the three selective admissions criteria for 1) elementary and secondary teachers combined,
2) elementary teachers, and 3) secondary teachers. The contribution of each
variable was determined by computing the difference between the R^2 for the
regression equation with the variable in it and the multiple correlation coefficient with that variable not in it. The difference, expressed as a percent, was
used to indicate the contribution that a variable made to the prediction equation. The intercorrelations for each of these equations are present in Tables
2, 3, and 4.

Following the initial development of the equations further analyses were
completed. The resulting betas from each of the analyses were tested for
significance in predicting the criterion. The multiple R_s and beta weights are
summarized in Table 5. A correction formula devised by Guilford (2) was

TABLE 3.   Intercorrelations among Principals' Ratings of Secondary Teachers
and Three Selective Admissions Criteria ($N = 37$).

	X_1 Principals' Ratings	X_2 Grade Point Average	X_3 Grade in Introduction to Education	X_4 Grade in Second-Semester Freshman English
X_1	1.00	.37*	.01	.26
X_2		1.00	.31	.65**
X_3			1.00	.43**
X_4				1.00

*Significant at the .05 level.
**Significant at the .01 level.

TABLE 4. Intercorrelations among Principals' Ratings of Elementary and Secondary Teachers and Three Selective Admissions Criteria.

	X_1 Principals' Ratings	X_2 Grade Point Average	X_3 Grade in Introduction to Education	X_4 Grade in Second-Semester Freshman English
X_1	1.00	.17	—.09	.11
X_2		1.00	.12	.47**
X_3			1.00	.54**
X_4				1.00

**Significant at the .01 level.

TABLE 5. Summary of the Multiple R_s and Beta Weights for Initial Equations in Predicting Teaching Performance of First-Year Teaching.

Groups	Multiple R	Beta Weights X_2	X_3	X_4
Elementary and Secondary Combined	.20	.15	—.10	.04
Elementary	.27	.08	—.18	—.09
Secondary	.38	.35	.01	.03

applied to each equation for purposes of adjustment due to small sample sizes.

DATA ANALYSIS

The correlations between principals' ratings of elementary teachers and the three selective admissions criteria were —.04, —.20, —.09 with a resulting multiple of R of .27. It is obvious from these data that the criteria used for selection are ineffective in predicting teaching performance of elementary teachers. The fact that the results were negative sheds further doubt on the effectiveness of the admissions criteria. Also, the substantial correlation (.72) between grade in introductory course in education and grade in second semester freshman English indicates that neither factor makes a unique contribution to the prediction equation.

For secondary teachers, the data revealed a somewhat different situation. The correlations between the criterion and the independent variables were

.37, .01, and .26 with a multiple R of .38. The significant correlation between principals' ratings and GPA is somewhat obscured by the substantial correlation between grade in introduction to education and grade in second semester freshman English with an additional moderate correlation between GPA and grade in second semester freshman English. Thus, for secondary teachers, 36 percent of the variability in teaching performance is accounted for by the admissions criteria.

When the equation was run for both elementary and secondary teachers, the correlations were .17, −.09, and .11 with a multiple R of .20. Again, the independent variables were not found to be independent as revealed by the moderate correlations between the independent variables.

CONCLUSIONS

(1) The present program of selecting prospective teachers on the basis of a 2.0 average at the time of application, a C or better in the introductory course in education, and a C or better in second semester freshman English is judged to be ineffective in predicting teaching performance of elementary and secondary teachers. It is possible, then that the present program is screening out too many potentially successful teachers. When principals' ratings were correlated with the three admissions criteria, the resulting multiple R was .20.

(2) A difference was noted in the predictive efficiency of the admissions criteria for elementary teachers and secondary teachers. When viewed separately the criteria for selecting prospective teachers was found to be ineffective in predicting teaching performance for elementary teachers. The negative trend of the correlations between principals' ratings and the admissions criteria violates the logic of selective admissions.

The relationship between principals' ratings and the admissions criteria for secondary teachers revealed a somewhat different situation. The best single predictor of teaching performance for secondary teachers was found to be GPA. This resulted in a low, but significant relationship. But when the other variables were added, a multiple R of .38 was obtained. Therefore, the prediction efficiency of the equation was not improved with the addition of grade in introductory education course and grade in second semester freshman English.

The obvious limitation of this study is the use of principals' ratings as a measure of teaching performance. Although this is a questionable means of evaluating teaching performance, it appeared to be the only practical way of obtaining data for the dependent variable. Since this study represents the evaluation of only one selective admissions program, generalizations can at best be tentative.

REFERENCES

1. Edson, William H. and Davies, Don. "Selectivity in Teacher Education," *Journal of Teacher Education,* XI (September, 1960), pp. 306–312.
2. Guilbord, J. B. *Fundamental Statistics in Psychology and Education* (New York: McGraw-Hill Book Company, Inc., 1956).
3. Magee, Robert M. "Admission-Retention in Teacher Education," *Journal of Teacher Education,* XII (March, 1961), pp. 81–85.
4. Rabinowitz, William and Mitzel, Harrold E. "Some Observations on the Selection of Students for Teacher Education Programs." *Journal of Teacher Education,* XII (June, 1961), pp. 157–64.
5. Siman, Patricia and Asher, John W. "The Relationship of Variables in Undergraduate School and School Administrators' Ratings of First-Year Teachers," *Journal of Teacher Education,* XV (September, 1964), pp. 293–302.

MULTIPLE CORRELATION AND REGRESSION

Thus far we have used the terms "multiple correlation" and "multiple regression" in the same way. Although this is done to some extent, they are actually two separate processes. You will recall in the discussion of simple correlation that we were concerned with establishing the degree of relationship between two variables and, if the situation required, using this information for prediction purposes. The same situation applies with this technique. Multiple correlation is the process of establishing the degree of relationship that exists between a combination of independent variables and a dependent variable. Multiple regression is the process of establishing a prediction equation based on the information obtained through multiple correlation. Whether or not a researcher uses one or both of these techniques depends upon the nature of the study. The sample study of the admissions criteria utilized multiple correlation but information is provided to set up a prediction equation. From the data in the sample study, however, we can see that a prediction equation would be of little value.

Basic Procedure for Multiple Correlation

When a number of independent variables are involved, the computation of multiple correlation is a job for the computer, but we want you to see how the multiple R is obtained using just two independent variables. The procedure is basically the same when additional variables are included.

The formula for obtaining the multiple correlation coefficient for two independent variables is as follows.

$$R_{1.23} = \sqrt{\frac{r_{12}^2 + r_{13}^2 - 2r_{12}\,r_{13}\,r_{23}}{1 - r_{23}^2}}$$

where

     R = multiple correlation coefficient

     r = correlation between each independent variable and the dependent variable. Subscripts indicate the various combinations.

This formula may also be written:

$$R_{1.23}^2 = \frac{r_{12}^2 + r_{13}^2 - 2r_{12}\,r_{13}\,r_{23}}{1 - r_{23}^2}$$

The difference between the two formulas is that R is the square root of R^2. We interpret R as the degree of relationship that exists between the independent variables, in combination, and the dependent variable. We interpret R^2 as the proportion of criterion (dependent variable) variance accounted for by knowledge of the independent variables with the regression weights used.

When additional independent variables are included the procedure for obtaining the multiple R is basically the same as the procedure described above. However, the computation becomes quite difficult when attempted by hand or desk calculator and will not be described here since a computer can handle a rather complicated problem with ease.

When using a computer, procedures are provided for determining the combination of variables that make the highest contribution to the dependent variable. One of the ways this is accomplished is by "dropping out" single predictors or combinations of predictors and calculating the effect that the absence of these variables has on the overall relationship.

Basic Procedures for Multiple Regression

After the multiple R has been obtained, we are now in a position to formulate a prediction equation. The procedure here is not totally different from prediction when only two variables are involved. Using two independent variables again, the basic equation takes the following form:

$$X'_1 = a + b_{12.3}X_2 + b_{13.2}X_3$$

where

X'_1 = dependent variable
a = constant
b = partial regression coefficient
X = independent variables

The object of this equation is to predict the dependent variable given the data for the independent variables. To employ this equation to predict the dependent variable, we need to obtain from the computer the partial regression coefficients and the constant. The general procedure used to obtain these values is:

$$b_{12.3} = \left(\frac{\sigma_1}{\sigma_2}\right) B_{12.3}$$

$$b_{13.2} = \left(\frac{\sigma_1}{\sigma_3}\right) B_{13.2}$$

where

b = partial regression coefficient
σ = standard deviation
B = beta weights

Before the regression coefficients can be obtained, the beta weights are computed. Beta weights for a two independent variable problem are obtained in the following manner.

$$B_{12.3} = \frac{r_{12} - r_{13}r_{23}}{1 - r_{23}^2}$$

$$B_{13.2} = \frac{r_{13} - r_{12}r_{23}}{1 - r_{23}^2}$$

After the beta weights have been obtained, the b formulas can be solved.

The final bit of information that is needed to complete the prediction equation is the constant. The constant is obtained in the following manner.

$$a = \bar{X}_1 - b_{12.3}\bar{X}_2 - b_{13.2}\bar{X}_3$$

The equation now has all the necessary elements to make a prediction about the dependent variable.

To illustrate briefly how this prediction equation could be used, let's assume we have a problem involving the following variables:

X'_1 = undergraduate peer rating
X_2 = SES
X_3 = High school GPA

For these variables, we have the following values:

$R = .53$
$b_{12.3} = .31$
$b_{13.2} = .21$
$a = 47.13$

The regression equation would then be:

$$X'_1 = 47.13 + .31X_2 + .21X_3$$

For an individual who had a socioeconomic score of 20 and a high school GPA of 2.50, the predicted undergraduate peer rating would be:

$$X'_1 = 47.13 + .31(20) + .21(2.50)$$
$$= 53.85$$

This value would be used, along with the standard error of estimate which is provided in the analysis and used in the same manner as with simple prediction, as the predicted value of the dependent variable.

There are a number of computer programs available for this technique and anyone interested in using multiple correlation and regression should become familiar with them. One of the most popular is known as "stepwise" regression. Briefly, this program involves setting criteria, usually a probability level, for entry of variables into the equation. The end product of the analysis is an equation where only those variables that make a significant contribution to the prediction are included. This is an extremely efficient and valuable program for behavioral science researchers. Other programs utilize a "dropping out" procedure which involves starting with a full model of the equation, dropping out various combinations of variables, and calculating the difference between the full and restricted models of the equation in terms of prediction efficiency.

INTERPRETATION

Although the computation of multiple correlation and regression is rather complicated, the interpretation of the results of this technique is not.

For illustration purposes, let's use the study presented in the first part of this chapter. After reading it again, we note that the purpose of the study was to determine the relationship between three selective admissions criteria: grade point average, grade in second semester freshman English, grade in an introductory course in education, and performance of first-year teachers as measured by principals' ratings. Look at table 3 on page 122 and table 5 on page 123.

From the data in these tables, we can make the following interpretations relative to the secondary teachers:

1. The overall relationship between the three admissions criteria and principals' ratings is .38. A multiple R of .38 may be interpreted in a descriptive sense the same way as an r.

2. An R^2 of .38, which would be .14, tells us that approximately 14 percent of the variance of principals' ratings is accounted for by the three criteria.

3. The beta weights are provided to serve as the basis for formulating a prediction equation. They represent the weighted relationship between the various combinations of variables. The beta weights may be used directly in a regression equation, as provided for by one procedure, or they can be transformed into regression coefficients, as we briefly described earlier, and used in the regression equation.

4. Table 3 gives us two kinds of information. First, we have the relationship between each independent variable and the dependent. We see that the relationship between principals' ratings and GPA is .37 and is significant at the .05 level. We could look at it in terms of r^2 and say that approximately 14 percent of the variance on principals' ratings can be accounted for by grade point average.

The second bit of information that can be gained from the table is the intercorrelations among variables X_2, X_3, and X_4. We can note that X_2 and X_4 are significantly related as are X_3 and X_4. When two independent variables are significantly related it means that they are measuring much the same thing. In terms of prediction, this tells us that we are not gaining anything by using both. We can see that none of the independent variables is making much of a contribution toward predicting the dependent variable.

Regardless of the number of independent variables employed, the interpretation of multiple correlation and regression is basically the same.

FOR REVIEW AND FURTHER STUDY

1. Consider once again the study by Leyman which was included in the review exercises of chapter 6. Intercorrelations between motor ability test

scores, intellectual aptitudes test scores, and physical education grade-point averages were:

Grade-point average to motor ability test   .30
Grade-point average to intellectual aptitude test   .22
Motor ability test to intellectual aptitude test   −.04

In tabular form, this information may be shown as follows, with grade-point average X, motor ability test Y, and intellectual aptitude test Z.

	X	Y	Z
X	1.00	.30	.22
Y		1.00	−.04
Z			1.00

a. Write the formula for obtaining the multiple correlation coefficient for the dependent variable (grade-point average) and the two independent variables in this study. If R were determined to be .27, what proportion of the grade-point average variance could be accounted for by knowledge of the intellectual aptitude and motor ability test scores?

b. Write the prediction equation for obtaining X from Y and Z. After X is obtained, how is the standard error of estimate used?

c. Is there a significant advantage to using both motor ability test scores and intellectual aptitude test scores to predict grade-point average, rather than just one or the other?

8

Techniques for Determining Differences

The previous three chapters dealt with techniques designed to determine the relationship between variables. Chapters 8 and 9 present parametric techniques designed to determine differences between means.

It may be recalled from a previous comment that the two main functions of applied statistics are to produce indicators of relationship and indicators of difference. The direction one selects depends upon the hypotheses to be tested and the nature of the data. For example, if we wish to determine the predictive effectiveness of a given test, some relationship technique would be appropriate to provide the information. However, if our goal is to determine the difference between groups regarding the effect of a certain kind of propaganda, some difference-testing technique would be in order.

Techniques presented in the next two chapters include the t-test analysis of variance–single classification, analysis of variance–multiple classification, and analysis of covariance. Sample studies illustrating the use of each are also included.

THE t-TEST

The purpose of the t-test is to determine the significance of difference between *two* means, i.e., is the observed difference between the two means greater than pure chance would allow? For example, suppose we were interested in determining the effects of an organized exercise program on selected measures of the physical fitness of middle-aged men. An objective might be to compare a group of men who had participated in an organized program with men who had not participated in such a program. The basic design for such a comparison might look like the data in table 8–1. The design described calls for a straight comparison between two means on the three measures selected to represent physical. fitness. What remains to be done is to submit the data that produced these means to a *t*-test to determine if the observed difference is greater than pure chance would allow. The procedure is essentially one of adjusting the observed difference between the means on the basis of sample size and the variability present within the data. Procedures for accomplishing this task are described in the sections that follow.

Selecting the Appropriate *t* Technique

When it is determined that a *t*-test is the proper type of analysis for a given problem, several questions regarding the nature of data to be analyzed must be answered in order to select the most appropriate technique, because there exists more than one way of determining the significance of difference between two means.

1. Is there a positive correlation between data contained in the two groups? Data are considered correlated when a comparison is made between two sets of data derived from matched pairs or when comparisons are made from data taken on the same subjects. An example of data taken from the same subjects would be testing significance of pre and post gains for the same group of subjects. If our data are not derived from matched pairs or derived from the same subjects, we can consider it uncorrelated.

TABLE 8–1. Comparison of Exercise Participants and Nonparticipants on Selected Measures of Physical Fitness.

Variable	Group	N	Mean	s	t	p
Aerobic count	P NP		$\bar{X}$ $\bar{X}$			
Push-ups	P NP		$\bar{X}$ $\bar{X}$			
Quarter mile	P NP		$\bar{X}$ $\bar{X}$			

2. Is there a significant difference between the variances of the two groups? Because this is a parametric test, we are concerned about the homogeneity of variance in the population and being able to account for this in the technique we select. To determine this, we assume a null hypothesis of no difference between variances and submit the sample variances s_1^2 and s_2^2 to a test of significance. The significance test appropriate for this situation is the F ratio. The F-test is described below.

$$F = \frac{s_1^2}{s_2^2}$$

where

    s_1^2 = the greater variance of the two groups
    s_2^2 = the lesser variance of the two groups

We complete this operation by dividing the greater variance by the lesser variance to obtain the F ratio. We then take the resulting F value to the F table (Appendix F) to determine significance. When using the Table of F to determine significance, we first must determine the degrees of freedom for each variance. Degrees of freedom for the F-test are obtained by subtracting one from the n of each group $(n - 1)$. We enter the table by locating the degrees of freedom for the greater mean square (variance) at the top of the table and the degrees of freedom for the lesser mean square (variance) at the left side of the table. The intersecting point is the value used to determine significance, i.e., if the computed value is larger than the table value the null hypothesis is rejected, or if the computed value is smaller than the table value the null hypothesis is accepted.

For instance, suppose we had data from two samples and we wish to test the null hypothesis regarding the significance of difference between the variances. We would proceed in the following manner.

$$n_1 = 32 \qquad n_2 = 28$$
$$s_1^2 = 20.8 \qquad s_2^2 = 18.5$$
$$\mathrm{df} = 31 \qquad \mathrm{df} = 27$$

$$F = \frac{20.8}{18.5}$$
$$= 1.12$$

Entering the F table with degrees of freedom 31 and 27, we note that the intersecting value is 1.88 (.05). Since our computed value of 1.12 is less than the table value we will accept our null hypothesis and conclude that no significant difference exists between the variances of the two groups.

3. Are the two groups equal in size? Since simple observation provides the answer to this question nothing else needs to be said.

After the three questions presented above have been answered, we proceed to selecting the appropriate t technique.

The Pooled Variance Technique.   This approach to determining the significance of difference between two means is employed when:

1. the two sample sizes are equal and no significant difference exists between the two sample variances; or
2. the two sample sizes are not equal and no significant difference exists between the two sample variances; or
3. the data are uncorrelated.

The pooled variance formula is presented and described below.

$$t = \frac{\bar{X}_1 - \bar{X}_2}{\sqrt{\frac{\Sigma x_1{}^2 + \Sigma x_2{}^2}{n_1 + n_2 - 2}\left(\frac{1}{n_1} + \frac{1}{n_2}\right)}}$$

where

$\bar{X}_1 =$ mean of the first sample
$\bar{X}_2 =$ mean of the second sample
$\Sigma x_{1,2}{}^2 = \Sigma X^2 - \dfrac{(\Sigma X)^2}{N}$
$n_{1,2} =$ sample size

It can be noted from the formula that three factors are considered in determining the significance of difference between two means. First, the observed difference between the two means is considered. The magnitude of the difference plays a crucial role in determining the size of t. Second, the amount of variability found in the two groups is considered. Group variability is considered in the formula by $\Sigma x_1{}^2$ and $\Sigma x_2{}^2$. Third, the size of the two samples plays an important role, as represented in the formula by n_1 and n_2.

In essence, the size of the t value, and the resulting decision made on the null hypothesis, depend on the combined effects of mean difference, group variability, and sample size. In general, the size of t increases when the total denominator decreases in size and the opposite will occur when the denominator increases in size. This depends, of course, on the numerator remaining constant.

To illustrate the use of the pooled variance technique, suppose we wish to test the following null hypothesis.

H_{o1} There will be no significant difference in attitudes toward product X between subjects who have been exposed to a "hard sell" advertising approach and subjects exposed to a "soft sell" approach.

Assuming we have met the conditions for using the pooled variance technique, we proceed with the computation.

Given the following data extracted from the two groups:

$$N = 100 \qquad\qquad N = 89$$
$$\bar{X} = 15.50 \qquad\qquad \bar{X} = 21.63$$
$$\Sigma x^2 = 1950.16 \qquad \Sigma x^2 = 1563.36$$

We substitute these data into the pooled variance formula:

$$t = \frac{15.50 - 21.63}{\sqrt{\dfrac{1950.16 + 1563.36}{100 + 89 - 2}\left(\dfrac{1}{100} + \dfrac{1}{89}\right)}}$$

Complete the computation:

$$t = \frac{6.13}{.628}$$
$$= -9.761$$

We note that the formula has yielded a t value of 9.761. To use this value in making a decision on our hypothesis, we take this value to the appropriate table. For the t-test, we consult the distribution of t probability (Appendix E). Before entering the table we first determine the degrees of freedom for this problem and decide upon the probability level we wish to use. For this problem, the degree of freedom is $n_1 + n_2 - 2$ or 187 and for purposes of illustration let's use the .05 level.

The decision to accept or reject the null hypothesis is determined in the following manner.

> With degrees of freedom infinity (df of 187 is read in this case as infinity), the intersecting value at the .05 level is 1.960. Following the rule—if our computed value is larger than the table value we reject the null hypothesis—H_{o1} would be rejected.

We conclude that the two groups did differ significantly in terms of attitude toward the product as a result of the type of advertising approach employed. We can also say that the probability is .95 that this same type of outcome would occur in repeated testing, i.e., we could expect this outcome to occur 95 out of every 100 times the study was run.

The Separate Variance Technique.   This approach to determining the significance of difference between two means is employed when:

1. the two sample sizes are equal and a significant difference exists between the two sample variances, or
2. the two sample sizes are not equal and a significant difference exists between the two sample variances, or
3. the data are uncorrelated.

The separate variance formula is presented and described below:

$$t = \frac{\bar{X}_1 - \bar{X}_2}{\sqrt{\dfrac{s_1^2}{n_1} + \dfrac{s_2^2}{n_2}}}$$

where

$\bar{X}_1, \bar{X}_2$ = mean of each group

s_1^2, s_2^2 = variance of each group

n_1, n_2 = sample size of each group

We can note from the above formula that the determination of t is affected by the same three factors as it is in the pooled variance technique, i.e., mean difference, variance, and sample size. The difference between the two techniques is the way variance is utilized. The pooled technique combines the variances while the separate variance technique deals with the variance of each sample independently.

For example, if we had a situation where the variances were not homogeneous, we would proceed in the following manner.

Given the data:

	Group 1	*Group 2*
	$\bar{X} = 62.43$	$\bar{X} = 49.51$
	$n_1 = 36$	$n_2 = 24$
	$s_1^2 = 148.16$	$s_1^2 = 51.16$

Substituting in the separate variance formula:

$$t = \frac{62.43 - 49.51}{\sqrt{\dfrac{148.16}{36} + \dfrac{51.16}{24}}}$$

$$= \frac{12.92}{\sqrt{4.12 + 2.13}}$$
$$= 5.168$$

To determine the significance of t produced by the separate variance technique, the usual procedure is followed except for degrees of freedom. In this case we use $n_1 - 1$ instead of $n_1 + n_2 - 2$. Entering the table, then, with 35 degrees of freedom at the .05 level of significance, we find our t value to be significant. Therefore, we would reject the null hypothesis related to our data.

It should be noted here that when $n_1 = n_2$ we can use the pooled variance technique and enter the table with half the usual degrees of freedom.

Correlated Data Technique. In situations where two groups have been matched or in situations where two measures have been taken from the same individuals, the data are considered correlated. A common example of correlated data is that produced as a result of pre- and posttesting on the same subjects. When these kinds of data are to be analyzed, the correlated data technique must be used. The procedure for using the correlated data technique is presented below.

Calculate the degree of relationship that exists between the two sets of data. This is accomplished by employing the Pearson r.

$$r = \frac{N\Sigma XY - [(\Sigma X)(\Sigma Y)]}{\sqrt{[N\Sigma X^2 - (\Sigma X)^2][N\Sigma Y^2 - (\Sigma Y)^2]}}$$

Since this technique is described in an earlier chapter, we will simply present the solution of $r = .81$.

We now proceed to the computation of t utilizing the correlated data formula.

$$t = \frac{\bar{X}_1 - \bar{X}_2}{\sqrt{\frac{s_1^2}{n_1} + \frac{s_2^2}{n_2} - 2r\left(\frac{s_1}{\sqrt{n_1}}\right)\left(\frac{s_2}{\sqrt{n_2}}\right)}}$$

We note that this formula contains the basic elements of the earlier formulas, especially that of the separate variance technique, with some additions. The primary addition is the inclusion of r. Since there is a tendency of correlated scores to be more similar than scores from uncorrelated groups, means from correlated data are less likely to be significantly different than are means taken from uncorrelated data. To compensate for this, the value of t is adjusted upward by including r in the formula. The degree of adjustment is a function of the magnitude of r.

We also note, again, that the size of t is determined by the interrelationship of the mean difference, variance, and sample size with an additional element, r, added for this purpose.

The procedure for determining the significance of t is the same for this technique as it is for the others with the exception of degrees of freedom. In this case, df is determined by the number of pairs minus one.

ANALYSIS OF VARIANCE: SINGLE CLASSIFICATION

As we noted in the previous section, the t-test is confined to determining the significance of difference between two means. When our concern is expanded beyond two means, the t-test is not appropriate.

For situations where more than two means are to be compared, analysis of variance is the appropriate technique. By single classification, we are talking about a situation where our concern is to make a straight comparison between more than two means on a single factor. For instance, suppose we desire to compare the effects of three methods of teaching introductory psychology, and our primary factor for determining effect is an achievement test. Table 8–2 illustrates this.

The difference between single classification and multiple classification (described in chapter 9) can be seen in table 8–3.

In table 8–2, it can be noted that the analysis is confined to a straight comparison of performance between subjects exposed to the three instructional methods, while the multiple classification scheme allows the option of comparing performance on the basis of ability level or on any other factor or combination of factors.

Concept of Analysis of Variance

The name of this technique, analysis of variance, denotes the process this technique employs in arriving at data regarding the differences between

TABLE 8–2.   Effect of Three Methods of Teaching Introductory Psychology on Achievement.

Group 1 Lecture	Group 2 Independent Study	Group 3 Combination
$\bar{X}*$	$\bar{X}$	$\bar{X}$

*Represents the mean achievement of subjects in group 1. The means of group 2 and group 3 also represent mean achievement.

TABLE 8–3. Effect of Three Methods of Teaching Introductory Psychology on Achievement When Factored on the Basis of Ability.

| | Instructional Method | | |
Ability Level	Lecture	Independent Study	Combination
Middle	$\bar{X}$	$\bar{X}$	$\bar{X}$
High	$\bar{X}$	$\bar{X}$	$\bar{X}$
Low	$\bar{X}$	$\bar{X}$	$\bar{X}$

means. Since $\bar{X}_1 - \bar{X}_2 - \bar{X}_3 \ldots - n$ is not feasible, it becomes necessary to analyze the variance that produced the means rather than working with the means directly. In other words, since we cannot compare means directly, we must use an indirect approach by analyzing the variance. The end product of this analysis is the F − ratio defined by the following formula.

$$F = \frac{\text{MS}_{\text{between}}}{\text{MS}_{\text{within}}}$$

where

F = value to be used in making a decision on the hypothesis
$\text{MS}_{\text{between}}$ = mean square between groups
$\text{MS}_{\text{within}}$ = mean square within groups

When the F value has been determined, a decision on the hypothesis regarding the significance of difference between the groups is made in the usual manner by entering the table of F with the computed value, the appropriate degrees of freedom, and the desired significance level. In order to produce this F value, a mean square for the between variance and a mean square for the within variance must be computed. In essence, we must analyze the amount of variance that exists within each group and the amount of variance that exists between each group. These variances are measured by a value called mean square. We use the term "mean square" in conjunction with analysis of variance to represent variance. You will recall that variance has been defined as s^2, or the standard deviation squared, and we are now simply referring to this statistic as mean square.

Before we continue, let's look at the end product of analysis of variance. You will note that in order to produce the desired F value we must

TABLE 8–4. Summary of Analysis of Variance on Three Groups Exposed to Three Treatments.

Source of Variation	SS	df	MS	F
Between Groups	300	1	300	
				6.00
Within Groups	2000	40	50	
Total	2300	41		

first determine the sum of squares for each source of variation, degrees of freedom, and mean square.

We note from table 8–4 that once the SS and df have been established, MS and F are produced by simple division. The primary computation task, then, is the sum of squares. It should be noted that we do not use SS as the primary index of variability because the size of SS is greatly affected by the size of N. When we employ df to convert SS to MS, we have a much better measure of variability.

Sum of Squares (SS)

We encounter a new symbol here but we shall soon discover that the symbol is all that is really new. The sum of squares is the measure, Σx^2, something we have worked with throughout the text. You will recall that $\Sigma x^2 = \sqrt{\Sigma X^2 - [(\Sigma X)^2/N]}$. The only departure from this is that we are now concerned with variance instead of standard deviation, so we will work without the square root sign: $\Sigma^2 = \Sigma X^2 - [(\Sigma X)^2/N]$.

Although we need only compute two of the SS values and obtain the other by either adding or subtracting, it is desirable to compute all three due to the possibility of computation error. Since we are dealing with two sources of variation, between groups and within groups, we will need to determine a sum of squares for each source of variation. Therefore, we will be working with:

$SS_{between}$
SS_{within}
SS_{total}

To facilitate the description of how these three sums of squares are obtained, we will work from the data provided in table 8-5.

TABLE 8–5.   Raw Scores Derived from Three Groups of Subjects.

Group 1	Group 2	Group 3
3	5	2
6	5	2
6	7	4
8	8	5

SS_{total}.   We compute SS_{total} by use of the following formula.

$$SS_{total} = \Sigma X^2 - \frac{(\Sigma X)^2}{N}$$

Employing the raw scores from the above table:

$$SS_{total} = 357 - \frac{(61)^2}{12}$$

$$= 357 - 310.08$$

$$= 46.92$$

SS_{within}.   To determine the SS_{within}, we calculate the variance for each group separately and then sum the variance for each group. The SS_{within} is obtained in the following manner.

$$SS_{within} = \sum X^2 - \frac{(\Sigma X)^2}{n}$$

Utilizing the example data again, we compute the variance for each group.

$$GROUP\ 1 = \Sigma X^2 - \frac{(\Sigma X)^2}{n}$$

$$= 145 - \frac{(23)^2}{4}$$

$$= 145 - 132.25$$

$$= 12.75$$

$$GROUP\ 2 = \Sigma X^2 - \frac{(\Sigma X)^2}{n}$$

$$= 163 - \frac{(25)^2}{4}$$

$$= 163 - 156.25$$
$$= 6.75$$

$$\text{GROUP } 3 = \Sigma X^2 - \frac{(\Sigma X)^2}{n}$$
$$= 49 - \frac{(13)^2}{4}$$
$$= 49 - 42.25$$
$$= 6.75$$

The sum of squares for each group added together yields a within SS of $12.75 + 6.75 + 6.75 = 26.25$.

$SS_{between}$.   We obtain $SS_{between}$ in the following manner.

$$\text{SS}_{\text{between}} = \sum \frac{(\Sigma X)^2}{n_a} - \frac{(\Sigma X)^2}{n_t}$$

where

$\dfrac{(\Sigma X)^2}{n_a}$ = square total of each group's sum of raw scores divided by the number in each group (n_a)

$\dfrac{(\Sigma X)^2}{n_t}$ = the sum of all raw scores squared and divided by the total number of observations (n_t)

Substituting the data from the table again, we compute SS between in the following manner.

$$\text{SS}_{\text{between}} = \frac{(23)^2}{4} + \frac{(25)^2}{4} + \frac{(13)^2}{4} - \frac{(61)^2}{12}$$
$$= 132.25 + 156.25 + 42.25 - 310.08$$
$$= 330.75 - 310.08$$
$$= 20.67$$

We now have the three values needed to construct our summary table. However, before constructing the table, we must first determine the appropriate degrees of freedom. This is accomplished in the following manner:

$SS_{\text{total}} = n - 1$ or number of observations less one
$SS_{\text{between}} = K - 1$ or number of groups (K) less one
$SS_{\text{within}} = n - K$ or number of observations less the number of groups

TABLE 8–6. Summary of Analysis of Variance.

Source of Variation	SS	df	MS	F
Between Groups	20.67	2	10.34	
				3.54
Within Groups	26.25	9	2.92	
Total	46.92	11		

Summarizing the Analysis of Variance

We now have the necessary information to construct a summary table (table 8–6) and complete the work toward the desired F value. We note from the table that once the SS for between, within, total, and the degrees of freedom have been established, the mean square for the two sources of variation is obtained by dividing the SS by the appropriate degree of freedom. The F value is then obtained by dividing the between mean square by the within mean square. The example data yielded a mean square for between of 10.34, a mean square for within of 2.92, and an F value of 3.54.

Interpretation of F

You will recall from earlier discussions that the object of obtaining a statistical value such as the F is to be able to make a decision on the null hypothesis, i.e., to accept it or to reject it at the desired probability level. To accomplish this task we enter the F table (Appendix F) with the number of degrees of freedom for the greater mean square across the top and with the number of degrees of freedom for the lesser mean square on the side. If the computed F value is larger than the table value (at the desired probability level) a decision to reject the null hypothesis is made. If the computed value is smaller than the table value, the decision to accept the null hypothesis is made.

To determine significance of our example value, $F = 3.54$, we enter the F table with 2 degrees of freedom at the top and 9 degrees of freedom at the side. The intersecting value at the .05 level is 4.26. Therefore, we would accept our null hypothesis regarding the significance of difference between the three means.

Additional Analysis

There are several ways of making internal comparisons of means after the overall analysis of variance has been completed. In most instances, internal comparisons would be most meaningful if the initial F value was found to be significant. The Scheffé test will be presented here as one method for accomplishing this task. Regardless of the number of means involved, the Scheffé method provides a means for making comparisons of all possible combinations utilizing two means at a time. For example, if three means were involved, the following comparisons would be possible.

A vs. B
A vs. C
B vs. C

For each pair of means, we compute an F value in the following manner.

$$F = \frac{(\bar{X}_1 - \bar{X}_2)^2}{S_w^2(N_1 + N_2)/N_1N_2}$$

where

$\bar{X}_{1,2}$ = means of any two pairs
S_w^2 = mean square for within
$N_{1,2}$ = number of observations

To determine significance for these internal comparisons we follow the procedure described below.

Locate the intersecting F value in the table corresponding to the degrees of freedom for the greater mean square across the top and the degrees of freedom for the lesser mean square on the side. Multiply this value by $K - 1$, where K is the number of groups. Compare each of the computed Fs with the result. If the computed F exceeds the $K - 1$ product, the two groups are said to be significantly different.

SAMPLE STUDIES

The two studies that follow were selected for the purpose of illustrating the use of the t-test and single classification analysis of variance in actual research efforts.

The Quality of Students Who Transfer to and from Teacher Education*

The decision to become a teacher does not occur at the same time for all people. For some, the decision to become a teacher occurs in high school, while others decide to become teachers after they have entered college. Ford found that approximately one half of the prospective teachers included in his study decided to become teachers when they were either in high school or during their first year of college. A similar study by Fox found that 80 percent of female elementary majors decided to become teachers in high school. Another study by Tink further indicates the variation concerning when a prospective teacher decided to pursue teacher education.

A change in the decision to become a teacher or not to become a teacher makes it necessary for the student to transfer to his chosen field. From this situation arises a question concerning quality. Is there any difference in the quality of students who transfer to teacher education after entering college and students who select teacher education upon entering college and then transfer to another field?

No studies relating specifically to this problem were located, but related studies concerning the quality of prospective teachers serve as a meaningful yardstick. Mitzel and Dubnick[1] found no difference in quality when comparing academic excellence of prospective teachers with other groups of students. Similar findings were reported by Snider and Long[2] and Cummings.[3] A contrasting view was presented by Vertin[4] indicating that students preparing to teach at Wisconsin State College and Institute of Technology were below other students in academic aptitude.

The purpose of this study was to ascertain if there is a difference in the quality of students transferring to and from teacher education. The basic hypothesis tested is that there is no difference in the quality of students who leave teacher education to pursue another field of study and those who decide to become teachers after entering college.

---

*Joe D. Cornett and Eunice Magee, "The Quality of Students Who Transfer to and from Teacher Education," reprinted from *The Southern Journal of Educational Research* 11, no. 4 (1968): 301–4, by permission of the publisher and authors.

1. Harold E. Mitzel and Lester Dubnick, "The Relative Scholastic Ability of Prospective Teachers," *Journal of Teacher Education*, XII (March, 1961), 73–80.

2. Glenn R. Snider and Delbert Long, "Are Teacher Education Programs Attracting Academically Able Students," *Journal of Teacher Education*, XII (December, 1961), 407–11.

3. James Cummings, "A Study of Certain Characteristics of the Student Body in the College of Education at the University of Alabama," (unpublished doctoral dissertation, University of Alabama, 1960).

4. Lester D. Vertin, "A Study of Regional, Social, and Intellective Characteristics of a Group of State College Students Preparing to Teach," *Journal of Experimental Education*, XXX (December, 1961), 159–62.

PROCEDURE

Names of students transferring during a four-year period were selected from the files of the registrar at Southeastern Louisiana College. Of the total number of students transferring, only those remaining in college after transferring were included in this study. Students transferring from teacher education were classified as Group A and those transferring to education were classified as Group B.

The variables used in determining quality were these: ACE scores, math placement scores, English placement scores, and cumulative grade-point average. The first three were selected to represent ability and the last to represent performance. Therefore, quality was defined as ability plus performance as measured on selected variables.

Data for these variables were obtained from the following sources:

1. *American Council on Education Psychological Examination 1949 College Edition*—This scale of mental ability and general scholastic aptitude yields three scores: the linguistic score (L), the quantitative score (Q), and the combined L and Q scores produce the total score (T).

2. *Cooperative Mathematics Pre-Test for College Students*—Items on this 40 minute test are heavily concentrated in algebra basic to the study of college mathematics, with plane and solid geometry and trigonometry topics included.

3. *Southeastern Louisiana College English Department's Departmental Placement Test*—This is a placement test constructed by the English department for local use. It is concerned with basic concepts of English grammar.

4. *Cumulative Grade-Point Average*—Grade-point average was used to determine quality regardless of the student's standing at the time he transferred.

The statistical technique used in testing the hypothesis was the *t* test. The .05 level of significance was used in determining acceptance or rejection of the null hypothesis.

RESULTS

Table 1 indicates the number of students transferring to and from teacher education during the four-year period covered by this study. During this time, teacher education lost 224 students and gained 137. It can be noted that 54 percent of the students in Group B withdrew from college as compared with 48 percent for Group A.

In comparing the means of the four variables used to indicate quality, students who transferred from teacher education were not significantly different from students who transferred to teacher education (Table 2). Therefore, the null hypothesis was accepted.

TABLE 1. Number of Students Transferring to and from Teacher Education during a Four-Year Period.

Group	Total Number Transferring	Number Withdrawn	Number Remaining
A. From Education	224	108	116
B. To Education	137	74	63
Total	361	182	179

TABLE 2. Comparison of Means of Group A and B on Variables Selected to Represent Quality of Students Who Transferred to and from Teacher Education.

Variables	Group	N	Mean	t
ACE Test	A	116	96.63	−1.6241*
	B	63	105.60	
Math Placement Test	A	116	14.30	− .6313
	B	63	15.37	
English Placement Test	A	116	61.07	−1.2937
	B	63	67.37	
GPA	A	116	2.2479	.7348
	B	63	2.3714	

*All of the t ratios failed to reach the .05 level of significance.

DISCUSSION

This research was intended to yield data pertaining to the quality of students transferring to and from teacher education. Within the limitations of this study, it seems reasonable to conclude that students who change their minds about becoming teachers and transfer to other fields are not significantly different on the measured variables from students who decide to become teachers after entering college.

The Relative Effectiveness of Discovery and Expository Strategies in Teaching Toward Economic Concepts with First Grade Students*

A major characteristic of newer social studies programs is an organization of instructional content around key concepts from the social sciences which are

*Frank L. Ryan and Myrtle A. Carlson, "The Relative Effectiveness of Discovery and Expository Strategies in Teaching Toward Economic Concepts with First Grade Students," reprinted from The Journal of Educational Research 66, no. 10 (1973): 446–50, by permission of the publisher.

introduced in the students' early formal educational experiences and spiraled upon in succeeding instructional encounters (11, 12). Indeed, some evidence has accrued that students at the earliest grade levels are capable of learning key concepts from the social sciences (e.g., 4, 6, 10). A parallel and relevant development to the conceptual-spiraling curriculum approach in organizing instructional content has been the advocacy of active student involvement in the generation of their own learnings. Teachers are being urged to actively involve students by allowing them to "discover" knowledge and its related-ness, rather than relegate students to the role of passive receptors of the ex-position of others, on the assumption that student learnings, including concep-tual learnings, will thereby be enhanced (1).

However, educators have sometimes tended to treat discovery as a "grand strategy" which is appropriate for all learners in all instructional situations, although Kagan (8) has wondered whether younger learners (i.e., 5–7 years of age) who can easily experience difficulty in comprehending the nuances of a "problem situation," can benefit from discovery strategies.

Therefore, the problem of this investigation was to ascertain the relative effects of two teaching strategies, discovery and expository (telling), on the learning of economic concepts by first grade students, as measured by a cri-terion test instrument. For purposes of this study the term "discovery teaching strategy" includes those instructional procedures which have students gener-ate (versus receive) knowledge, whether it be through an inductive or deduc-tive mode (12:28–29, 15).

PROCEDURES

Sample. All students (N = 77) from the three first grade classrooms of an ele-mentary school located in a St. Paul, Minnesota, suburb were included in the investigation. For purposes of identifying several of the characteristics of the Ss, reading readiness grade placements, and intelligence test scores collected prior to the study's inception, were utilized. Scores on the Lorge–Thorndike Intelligence Test (x = 102.71; SD = 10.97) and reading readiness grade placements using the Lee–Clark Reading Readiness tests (x = 1.74; SD = .34) were similar to the average, using national norms.

The school from which the Ss were chosen is estimated by the investigators as serving an average socioeconomic level.

Experimental Design. Three groups were utilized: discovery (D), expository (E), and control (C). Specific characteristics of D and E are given in a succeed-ing section.

Utilized was a posttest only control group experimental design as described by Campbell and Stanley (2). Its form as applied to the present study was as follows:

Group D: R X_1 O_1
Group E: R X_2 O_2
Group C: R O_3

Where R stands for random assignment of Ss to groups, X denotes the treatment, and O a posttest administration.

The assumption is made in employing this design that because of the random assignment of Ss to the groups there is a lack of initial bias between groups, thus eliminating the necessity for pretesting (2:25). Campbell and Stanley have also discussed the suitability of using this design for studies involving primary grade students with new subject matter and for controlling any possible interaction effects between testing and a study's treatments (2:25).

Instructional Program. Utilized in the present investigation was Senesh's primary grade economics program, *Families at Work* (14). The program is based on what Senesh calls an organic curriculum in which basic ideas and generalizations from the social sciences are introduced in the earliest lessons and built upon in succeeding lessons. The first grade program is almost entirely oriented toward the discipline of economics. A teacher resource book and a set of twenty-eight phonograph records are available for implementing the program. The main ideas for the lessons are presented primarily in an expository manner on 15-minute recordings, and the basic continuity of the program is achieved through the records. Materials also include an illustrated textbook which students view as they listen to the recordings.

Specific lesson plans developed by the investigators were based on the first twenty of the twenty-eight lessons in Senesh's program (14). The first twenty lessons presented the following main economic concepts that were to be tested: producers, consumers, goods, services, division of labor, specialization, and interdependence. The lesson plans utilized with D and E were constructed according to a slightly modified version of an instructional model developed by Ryan (12:54). In Ryan's model, daily planning is carried out within a consideration of six major elements for any lesson: review, lead-in, investigation, evaluation, summary, and future. In writing lesson plans for the present study, the evaluation and summary elements were combined. The lesson plans for Groups D and E were similar insofar as the plans for both groups contained the same five instructional elements taken from the model (i.e., review, lead-in, investigation, summary, future). The materials used in the instruction of Groups D and E were identical, i.e., the recordings were played for both groups and the program's textbook was used in both treatment groups.

A description of the investigation element of the daily lesson plans will be developed in detail since (a) two different instructional strategies (discovery, expository) were employed during this main segment of each day's lesson, and (b) the procedure contained in the daily lessons for the other instructional element were identical for both D and E.

For Group E, the recording for each lesson was played in its entirety without interruption. The only opportunities for student involvement during the investigation were through the questions asked in the recording. As the recording was not interrupted, however, there was no opportunity for the Ss to make overt individual responses to the questions. Thus, the instructional strategy for Group E during the investigation was exposition.

In contrast to Group E, Ss in Group D were provided with numerous opportunities to "discover" understandings. For example, the recordings were interrupted in each lesson to give Ss an opportunity to make educated guesses to the questions posed either by the recording or the classroom teacher. In addition, learner involvement was provided for Group D by using selected activity sheets included in Senesh's program (14). Selected supplemental lessons included in the second part of the textbook also formed a part of the discovery activity for Group D. As was the case with the E group, Ss of the D group were allowed to pose questions about the content of the recordings, although the teacher did not systematically solicit such questions.

Lesson 5, which was developed according to the main economic concepts of division of labor, specialization, and interdependence, can serve as an example of how a daily lesson plan was constituted.

For Group E, teacher's instructions for the investigation element of the lesson were to play the entire record without stopping for discussion. Thus, the economic concepts were learned by exposition. However, specific learner involvement was planned for Group D in this section of the lesson. For this group the instructor was directed to play the record to the end of the first section of the story about a little boy named Pelle and how he was involved in various experiences that led to the production of a new set of clothes. Inductive teaching was employed when the children were asked to proceed from these steps of production and guess what the process was called when the work was divided. Student responses were listed on the chalkboard, and the record was played to the next section. After listening to this section of the record, students were asked what the recorded voice called it when the work was divided. The students' responses were listed next to the responses that were made before the record was played. The instructor then read the two lists so students could compare their ideas for the questions that were asked before the record was played and the ideas that they had after the record was played. No specific answers were given to the students.

From this point on, the lesson was taught deductively, for the Ss were asked to make an application of the general concept "division of labor" to specific examples at school and neighborhood. The S's responses as to how they could divide the labor in their classroom and neighborhood were listed on the chalkboard. After listening to the next section of the record, the students were asked what the record told them about dividing the labor in the classroom and neighborhood. The students' responses were listed next to the responses that were made before the record was played. The teacher read the lists so that Ss could compare their ideas about division of labor in the classroom before and after listening to the record.

One teacher, with a total of 17 years teaching experience, volunteered to teach both the D and E groups. Also, she had taught the Senesh economics program for first grade for several years and was well acquainted with it. The teacher was enthused about the study and diligently studied the lesson plans before she taught them. Her background was supplemented with a series of orientation meetings with the investigators during which the philosophy of the Senesh program was reviewed, the purposes of the study and the implementation of the lesson plans were discussed, and the study's schedule was agreed upon. A planned schedule for balancing the order of lesson presentations for D and E was devised and instructionally implemented during the latter part of the school year. A daily log kept by the teacher was used to record any deviations from the lesson plans written by the investigators. Weekly conferences were held in which an investigator and the teacher met to discuss the daily logs, the lesson plans, problems that had occurred during the week, and the most recent classroom observation made by an investigator or the school's principal.

While the D and E groups received social studies instruction, the C group was involved in a series of language arts lessons which lasted for the length of the study.

Criterion Instrument. Used as a criterion instrument was one of the Primary Tests for Grade One (PET—1) developed by Larkins and Shaver (10) for assessing a student's conceptual understandings after using Senesh's economic materials. Larkins (9) reports a reliability of .85 for the matched-pairs test selected for usage in the present investigation and describes his procedures for establishing the instrument's content validity. Seventy-six Ss were administered the criterion test simultaneously in one setting at the conclusion of the seventh week of the study. Due to an extended illness, one S was dropped from the study. Although differential treatment mortality may be a threat to a study's internal validity (2), the loss of just one S as compared to the initial $N = 77$ was judged as insufficient in size to serve as a plausible rival explanation to any findings that might emanate from the study.

RESULTS AND DISCUSSION

The analysis of the data summarized in Tables 1 and 2, indicated a significant F ratio ($F = 3.20$; $p < .05$). *Post hoc* comparisons after the method of Neuman–Keuls (16) revealed a significant contrast at the .05 level of E over C.

An argument ordinarily advanced as supportive of utilizing a discovery strategy is that active student involvement in the learning situation facilitates the acquisition of new learnings (1), as opposed to the "passive" listening to the exposition of someone else (i.e., use of recordings in this study). However, the reverse was the outcome in this investigation—children learned at a significant level listening to the records, but the discovery strategies were less successful.

TABLE 1.   Posttest Means and Standard Deviations.

Group	N	Mean	SD
D	26	12.50	4.92
E	24	14.38	4.75
C	26	10.88	4.33

Possibly it is time for investigators to identify those requisite conditions which serve to set the stage for learners to thrive in discovery situations. For example, one can wonder if the students in the D group had learned how to cope with the discovery situations they were placed into during their social studies instruction. For example, if the questions which were posed to establish an environment of involvement for the learner, were instead perceived by the students as mere impediments to "getting the answers," then the students may have even resented the "discovery-involvement" situations, and, therefore, failed to see them as learning experiences. Indeed, the teacher responsible for instruction in the two experimental treatments reported, in the log she was asked to maintain during the experimental period, that on several occasions students in the D group openly expressed a desire to listen to the rest of the recording, rather than first respond to some questions. Possibly the students didn't assimilate that a problem situation was before them, or at least any need for it, and therefore, behaved as though no cognitive reorderings or accommodations were required (5, 12:26–28). Kagan has even

TABLE 2.   One-Way Analysis of Variance for Posttest Results.

Source	df	SS	MS	F
Between	2	139.61	69.80	3.20*
Within	73	1592.77	21.80	
Total	75	1732.38		

$p < .05.$

maintained that "young children 5 to 7 years of age do not have a sufficient appreciation of what a problem or what a solution is, and therefore, the incentive value attached to discovery is fragile" (7:159–60). A possible corollary to Kagan's statement is that without having learned to be "discoverers," students will fail to assume the role of involvement required for a "discovery situation" to be instructionally profitable.

Ordinarily, discovery strategies have been associated with such overt manifestations of learner involvement as, manipulating concrete instructional objects, verbally answering a teacher's or student's questions, or jointly solving a problem with others. However, involvement might also be considered in terms of how well a student is *attending* to the objectives of a learning environment (7, 8). Certainly students in the E group were "attending" and, therefore, "involved" in the instructional program. The instructional implication could be that to equate overt manifestations of student involvement with student learning is to overly restrict a definition of involvement, as well as to run the risk of incorrectly assuming that student learning will automatically be the by-product of such "discovery" activity. One can easily observe, for example, that many of those children who are learning from such a television program as Sesame Street are viewing in a manner that suggests little overt activity (e.g., sitting in front of a television set) but nevertheless are involved as they attend to the presentation.

It should be remembered that this investigation was only concerned with the relative effects of two instructional strategies in moving learners toward conceptual understandings. However, a social studies program has additional objectives, including the involvement of students in the methods and techniques of inquiry of the social scientist, the formulation of values and attitudes, and the use of various thinking processes (12:1–17). The implication is that instructional strategies must be assessed in terms of their effectiveness to move a learner toward several objectives concurrently. The present investigative design does not accommodate such an assessment of teaching strategies and thus, further research is required.

Furthermore, educators must move toward a selection of strategies in terms of not only the objectives of instruction but also the characteristics and background experiences of the individual for whom the teaching strategy is intended (3, 13). For example, using the median IQ the Ss in the present study were divided into high and low groups (high: $x = 11.49$, $SD = 7.68$; low: $x = 9.00$, $SD = 5.29$). An examination of Table 3 suggests the possibility that low IQ Ss of the D group were not thriving as well as their counterparts in the E group, although the high IQ Ss in both D and E showed some signs of learning progress.

Such interpretations are of course tenuous but nevertheless tend to support the notion that an examination of the instructional impact of a teaching strategy may reveal differentiated outcomes when specific learner characteristics are taken into account.

TABLE 3.   Posttest Means and Standard Deviations for High and Low IQ Ss
           in Each Group.

	High IQ			Low IQ		
Group	Mean	SD	N	Mean	SD	N
D	14.36	5.33	11	11.13	4.25	15
E	15.08	4.60	12	13.66	4.99	12
C	11.50	4.51	14	10.72	3.87	11

In a spirit of such interpretation one might infer from the results of this study that expository teaching was effective for certain individuals, as was discovery teaching, a finding which might be more important than the one which indicates that one of the experimental groups produced superior learning results over the other.

Therefore, in a similar vein, future investigations might include an examination of the relationship between such learner variables as anxiety, locus of control, dogmatism, age, sex, previous achievement levels, need for achievement, and the effectiveness of various teaching strategies in helping the learner attain multiple social studies objectives.

REFERENCES

1. Bruner, Jerome S., The Process of Education, Vintage Books, New York, 1960.
2. Campbell, Donald T.; Stanley, Julian C., Experimental and Quasiexperimental Designs for Research, Rand McNally, Chicago, 1966.
3. Carlson, Jerry S.; Ryan, Frank L., "Levels of Cognitive Functioning as Related to Anxiety," Journal of Experimental Education, 37:17–20, 1969.
4. Derosier, R. R.; Schuck, R. F., "A Comparison of the Effectiveness of Two Social Studies Instructional Programs upon First Grade Level Pupil Achievement in Economics," Educational Leadership, 27:815–824, 1970.
5. Furth, Hans G., Piaget for Teachers, Prentice–Hall, Englewood Cliffs, NJ, 1970, pp. 11–19; 77–79.
6. Jefferds, William J., "A Comparison of Two Methods of Teaching Economics in Grade One," unpublished doctoral dissertation, University of California, Berkeley, 1966.
7. Kagan, Jerome, "Learning, Attention, and the Issue of Discovery," in Shulman, Lee S.; Keislar, Evan R. (eds.), Learning by Discovery, Rand McNally, Chicago, 1966.
8. Kagan, Jerome, "Personality and the Learning Process," Daedalus, 90:553–563, 1965.
9. Larkins, A. Guy, "Assessing Achievement on a First Grade Economics Course of Study," unpublished doctoral dessertation, University Microfilms, Ann Arbor, MI, 1968, no. 68–13, 752.

10. Larkins, A. Guy; Shaver, James P., "Economics Learning in Grade One: The USU Assessment Studies," *Social Education*, 33:958–963, 1969.

11. Morrissett, Irving, *Concepts and Structure in the New Social Science Curricula*, Holt, Rinehart, and Winston, New York, 1967.

12. Ryan, Frank L., *Exemplars for the New Social Studies*, Prentice–Hall, Englewood Cliffs, NJ, 1971.

13. Ryan, Frank L.; MacMillan, Donald L., "Effects of Interruption During Social Studies Instruction on Learning Effectiveness and Efficiency," *Journal of Educational Psychology*, 34:27–32, 1970.

14. Senesh, Lawrence, *Our Working World: Families at Work*, Science Research Associates, Chicago, 1963.

15. Shulman, Lee S.; Keislar, Evan R. (eds.), *Learning by Discovery*, Rand McNally, Chicago, 1966, p. 27.

16. Winer, B. J., *Statistical Principles in Experimental Design*, McGraw–Hill, New York, 1962.

FOR REVIEW AND FURTHER STUDY

1. Teaching language as communication has become an accepted aim of foreign language teachers. Consequently, evaluation of student progress in foreign language courses requires examinations based on listening. Listening is usually tested by aural stimuli broadcast from an audio-tape. This study[1] examined the idea that testing listening comprehension might be improved by using television to offer nonverbal cues in addition to aural stimuli. A video-tape was made from the script of the Form MB Modern Language Association (MLA) French Listening Examination. An audio-tape was recorded from the video-tape. Subjects were randomly assigned to be tested by television or by audio-tape. Comparison of audio and video listening examination scores at the end of the semester were as follows.

		Mean	SD	N
Group A	Audio	21.16	6.32	107
	Video	20.59	5.77	108
Group B	Audio	15.70	4.25	113
	Video	16.22	5.34	73
Group C	Audio	25.06	4.40	33
	Video	24.46	4.74	48

---

1. William M. Stallings, "A Comparison of Television and Audio Presentations of the MLA French Listening Examination," *The Journal of Educational Research* 65:10 (July-August 1972): 472–74.

    a. Word a null hypothesis to test the significance of differences in examination scores using the two different examination techniques.

    b. Which t-test technique should be used with each group?

    c. Did a significant difference exist in the examination scores for Group B resulting from the use of the two different examination procedures?

2. A study[2] was made of differences between eighth-grade girls in 1934 and 1958 by comparing various data from a group in 1934 and a comparable group in 1958. It was assumed that the two groups were comparable because they were taken from the same schools, and the school communities had remained fairly stable over the 24-year period. Another study had compared the 1958 population of the school with the 1934 population and found them similar on the basis of IQ, socioeconomic status, and other characteristics.

    Data from the study yielded the following weights of the girls in the two groups:

1934 Group $n = 47$ $\bar{X} = 104.9$ lbs.		1958 Group $n = 45$ $\bar{X} = 110.8$ lbs.	
Weights:		Weights:	
94.9	130.4	94.4	120.1
92.3	107.2	98.5	136.4
107.5	109.9	109.6	85.6
89.5	95.6	113.4	113.2
93.6	99.3	100.5	115.9
110.8	81.4	110.9	123.2
112.2	131.2	107.6	111.7
101.6	120.5	103.0	118.2
114.2	110.3	108.2	113.6
79.6	87.8	131.7	107.6
109.9	90.9	97.4	104.4
88.4	114.3	113.1	101.6
103.6	125.4	99.4	122.9
107.1	98.6	116.8	105.3
96.5	103.2	115.9	127.4
97.6	88.4	102.5	87.4
88.4	115.6	137.2	126.5
116.9	105.3	109.2	107.7
121.4	89.6	131.4	120.3
105.7	97.0	94.4	116.3
117.2	92.5	104.6	121.6
94.5	144.0	111.3	93.8
101.6	121.2	95.3	
125.7			

    a. State a null hypothesis to test the significance of weight differences of girls in 1934 and in 1958.

    b. Which t-test technique should be used?

    c. Did a significant difference exist in the weight of eighth-grade girls in 1934 and 1958?

---

2. Adapted from Anna S. Espenschade and Helen E. Meleney, "Motor Performances of Adolescent Boys and Girls of Today in Comparison with Those of 24 Years Ago," *AAHPER Research Quarterly* 32 (May 1961): 186–89.

3. A study[3] in sociology examined the effects of military service on current income of clerical personnel for three ethnic groups (Mexican Americans, blacks, and Anglos) in five southwestern states. On the basis of data given from a small sample, test the hypotheses at the .05 level of significance. The sample was adjusted to compensate for level of education and geographical area.

Yearly Incomes of Subjects

Mexican-American		Black		Anglo	
Veteran	Nonvet	Veteran	Nonvet	Veteran	Nonvet
$5340	$3964	$5034	$4793	$5740	$6721
3365	4309	4762	4561	7632	5964
4876	4628	4914	5139	4315	5832
3860	4026	5414	4411	6214	6509
4320	5103	4423	5062	6132	6123
4930	4474	4617	4673	4148	7092
5010	4019	3998	4918	4763	5421
5228	3762	4916	4382	6421	4963
6120	3840	5248	3140	6186	6741
7340	4449	4962	5142	5870	6504
4673	4701	4804	3861	6942	6197
4924	5119	4269	5114	5761	5764
4602	4302	3742	3605	4324	5538
5416	3964	4294	4772	5762	4914
5923	3605	5861	4914	5941	4728
6204	4163	6033	5132	6397	6592
5210	4496	4291	5260	6104	6473
5060	4017	4462	4675	6029	6219
4230	3779	3749	4549	5871	6014
6020	3994	4704	4785	4962	7021
5114	4629	4673	4917	5144	6841
4016	4244	4966	4867	5767	5714
5277	4463	5102	4114	5901	5235
6013	3972	5419	6019	6027	5150
4977	3744	4791	3514	6451	5962
4623	4105	4421	4438	6872	6341
4704	4269	4683	4724	7943	6512
5096	4377	5174	5150	6094	7044
4293	4144	5062	4447	6621	5744
5906	5259	6142	4872	6346	5987

a. There is no significant difference in clerical personnel income of Mexican Americans, blacks, and Anglos who are not veterans of military service.

b. There is no significant difference in clerical personnel income of Mexican Americans, blacks, and Anglos who are veterans of military service.

c. There is no significant difference in clerical personnel income of Mexican Americans and blacks who are veterans of military service.

d. There is no significant difference in clerical personnel income of Mexican Americans and Anglos who are veterans of military service.

---

3. Adapted from Harley F. Browning, Sally C. Lopreato and Dudley L. Poston, Jr., "Income and Veteran Status Variations Among Mexican Americans, Blacks and Anglos," *American Sociological Review* 38, No. 1 (February 1973): 74–85.

e. There is no significant difference in clerical personnel income of Mexican American veterans and nonveterans.

f. There is no significant difference in clerical personnel income of black veterans and nonveterans.

g. There is no significant difference in clerical personnel income of Anglo veterans and nonveterans.

4. Assume that the purpose of a study on relative effectiveness of grouping procedures was to determine if homogeneous ability grouping, heterogeneous ability grouping, or a flexible, "open-concept" type procedure was more effective in teaching mathematic concepts. Such a study might compare the mathematics achievement scores of similar students grouped in the three different ways. The mathematics achievement scores of students in the three groups might be as follows.

Heterogeneous	Homogeneous	Flexible
76	86	68
84	82	72
62	73	88
91	61	89
73	90	84
82	85	86
54	71	90
93	64	89
79	56	87
87	51	90
68	92	86
59	84	86
87	77	67
90	71	87
81	91	89
89	67	93
71	68	74
68	72	85
59	88	81
62	92	77
77	67	69
85	70	85
84	71	79
71	62	88
	81	79
	75	91
	94	

a. Make the necessary calculations to construct a summary table for analysis of variance in the study.

b. Did the study indicate a significant difference in the effectiveness of the three grouping procedures for developing mathematics concepts?

c. Using the Scheffé test, compare the effectiveness of homogeneous grouping to heterogeneous grouping, homogeneous grouping to flexible grouping, heterogeneous grouping to flexible grouping.

d. In this hypothetical study, what should be done in designing and conducting the study to help assure its validity?

e. What reservations concerning conclusions might be appropriate in this case?

9

Other Techniques
Used in Determining
Differences

Chapter 8 presented two techniques designed to determine differences between means—the t-test when two means are involved, and single classification analysis of variance when more than two means are involved. This chapter presents two additional techniques for determining differences between means—multiple classification analysis of variance and analysis of covariance.

MULTIPLE CLASSIFICATION ANALYSIS OF VARIANCE

We employ single classification analysis of variance when determining differences between more than two means and when only one independent variable is involved. Testing a null hypothesis regarding the effect of three counseling approaches on the self-concept of adult unemployed males is an example of the type of problem where single classification would be appropriate. In this case, single classification tests the hypothesis of no difference between the mean self-concept scores. Table 9–1 shows this single classification analysis.

There may, however, be reason to believe that the outcome of this type of analysis might not be taking into account a variable, or variables, that might be contaminating the self-concept score. It could be, for example,

TABLE 9–1.   Comparison of Three Counseling Approaches on the Self-Concept Scores of Unemployed Males.

Approach 1	Approach 2	Approach 3
$\bar{X}$*	$\bar{X}$	$\bar{X}$

*Mean score on self-concept scale.

that the length of time a subject has been unemployed might be affecting the response on the self-concept scale. In other words, the differences noted between groups might not be attributable in total to the type of counseling that was received. If we consider the factor of length of unemployment, we are adding a second independent variable. When a second independent variable is added, we turn to the technique of multiple classification analysis of variance for the solution to this type of problem. Table 9–2 shows this type of analysis.

TABLE 9–2.   Comparison of Three Counseling Approaches on Self-Concept Scores of Unemployed Males Classified According to Length of Unemployment.

Length of Unemployment	Counseling Approaches 1	2	3
Less than one year	$\bar{X}$	$\bar{X}$	$\bar{X}$
One to three years	$\bar{X}$	$\bar{X}$	$\bar{X}$
More than three years	$\bar{X}$	$\bar{X}$	$\bar{X}$

Multiple classification analysis of variance is based on the same rationale as single classification. Since differences of more than two means cannot be measured directly, the variance is used to make this determination. However, when we add a second independent variable we have the ability to test three hypotheses instead of one. With the unemployment example, we can test hypotheses regarding the counseling approach used, the length of unemployment, and interaction of counseling approach and length of unemployment. Stated in the null form, the hypotheses would read:

H_{o1} There will be no significant difference between the three counseling groups on the score obtained from the self-concept scale.

H_{o2} There will be no significant difference between the three length-of-unemployment groups on the score obtained from the self-concept scale.

H_{o3} There will be no significant interaction between the two independent variables on the score obtained from the self-concept scale.

Two-Way Classification Analysis

The hypotheses stated above lend themselves to what is called a two-way classification analysis, i.e., one dependent variable (self-concept) and two independent variables (counseling approach and length of unemployment).

Our goal with this type of analysis is to obtain an F value for each hypothesis. To obtain the desired F values, we first must determine values for the sources of variation, degrees of freedom, and mean square. Table 9–3 will contain this information when the analysis is complete.

TABLE 9–3.   Analysis of Variance of Self-Concept Scores for Unemployed Males Classified by Counseling Approach and Length of Unemployment.

Source of Variation	Sum of Squares	Degrees of Freedom	Mean Square	F
Approach				
Length of Unemployment				
Approach × Length				
Within				
Total				

Source of Variation.   When two independent variables are employed, multiple classification allows us to determine the amount of variation that can be attributed to each main effect (independent variable). This is accomplished by determining the between sum of squares for each subgroup representing each independent variable. With two independent variables, the two-way analysis yields a between sum of squares for each independent variable.

With our illustration problem in mind, we note that, with regard to main effects, two possibilities exist for explaining the differences between means—counseling approach and length of unemployment. In other words, we are interested in determining if either main effect is responsible for the mean differences. As with single classification, the end product of this analysis is an F value derived from the sum of squares for each main effect.

In addition to the sum of square for main effects, a sum of squares for *interaction* must be obtained. A unique factor in multiple classification analysis of variance is the interaction effect. Briefly, interaction refers to the relationship between the dependent variable and the combined effects of the independent variables. As we have noted in the illustration problem, the differences between self-concept scores can be attributed to three sources: (1) the counseling approach used, (2) the length of unemployment, and (3) the combination of counseling approach and length of unemployment.

A possibility exists, then, that neither the counseling approach nor the length of unemployment is singularly responsible for the differences in self-concept scores. Rather, the differences might be attributable to a combination of both factors. When a significant F is obtained for interaction, it tells us that neither main effect is the primary cause of the differences in means.

A final sum of squares, called the *within* sum of squares, must be obtained before we can proceed with the analysis. We will simply say at this point that the within sum of squares is the "error factor" and is used in the calculation of F.

A Computational Example

To illustrate the computational procedure for a two-way analysis of variance, we will continue with the unemployment example, supply some hypothetical data, and test the three hypotheses stated previously. It should be noted that this type of analysis is usually not amenable to hand calculation and should be done on a computer whenever possible. We should, however, be aware of what is taking place in an analysis of this nature.

The data presented in table 9–4 are hypothetical and consist of only 24 scores. In an actual study more subjects would be needed, but for ease of presentation and clarity, we will illustrate the computation with an N of 24. Also included in the table are the basic calculations that will be needed.

Table 9–4 contains the raw scores (X) of 24 subjects classified on two independent variables, the square of the raw scores (X^2), the subtotals for each classification, the mean for each classification, the totals for each

TABLE 9–4. Self-Concept Scores of 24 Unemployed Males Classified according to Counseling Approach and Length of Unemployment

| Length of Unemployment | Counseling Approach | | | | | | Total | |
| | 1 | | 2 | | 3 | | | |
	X	X^2	X	X^2	X	X^2	X	X^2
Less than one year	62	3844	57	3249	50	2500		
	60	3600	60	3600	47	2209		
	63	3969	36	1296	61	3721		
	51	2601	52	2704	54	2916		
Subtotal	236		205		212		653	36,209
	$\bar{X} = 59.00$		$\bar{X} = 51.25$		$\bar{X} = 53.00$			
More than one year	50	2500	43	1849	38	1444		
	47	2209	45	2025	36	1296		
	49	2401	50	2500	27	729		
	51	2601	42	1764	33	1089		
Subtotal	197		180		134		511	22,407
	$\bar{X} = 49.25$		$\bar{X} = 45.00$		$\bar{X} = 33.50$			
Total	433	23,725	385	18,987	346	15,904	1164	58,616

row and each column, and the grand total for X and X^2. We can note from the table that the grand total for X and X^2 is the sum of both the row totals and the column totals.

Before we proceed with our analysis, we should check to see that the basic assumptions for this technique can be met. These are: (1) the data should approximate samples drawn at random, and (2) the variances should be homogeneous. You will recall that these are the same assumptions for single classification analysis of variance.

When we are working with data such as that presented in table 9–4, we can usually meet the first assumption without much difficulty and, due to the power of multiple classification analysis of variance, it can withstand some departures from homogeneity without substantially affecting F. Data should be inspected and if doubt exists regarding the homogeneity of variance, the test described in chapter 8, p. 133, should be applied. When applying the homogeneity test on a two-way classification problem, two F values are obtained. In our example problem, an F value would be produced for both counseling approach and length of unemployment. The variances would be calculated for each classification and F values obtained in the following manner:

$$F = \frac{\text{largest variance}}{\text{smallest variance}}$$

The F value is then tested in the usual way.

Computing the Sums of Squares

We are now ready to compute the sum of squares for each source of variation. For our two-way classification problem, we need to compute a sum of squares for total, for both main effects, for interaction, and for within.

Sum of Squares for Total. The sum of squares for total is determined by subtracting the squared raw score total divided by N from the grand total (total X^2 for rows and columns). For our problem, the total sum of squares would be:

$$SS_{total} = \Sigma X^2{}_{total} - \frac{(\Sigma X_{total})^2}{N}$$
$$= 58,616 - \frac{(1164)^2}{24}$$
$$= 58,616 - 56,454$$
$$= 2162$$

This value is interpreted as the total variance of all the scores without regard to classification. You will recall that this is the identical procedure for determining variance that was presented in chapter 2.

Sum of Squares for Main Effects. In our two-way classification problem, we have two main effects. You will note in table 9–4 that the data for counseling approach are presented in *columns* and the data for length of unemployment are presented in *rows*. In determining the sum of squares for main effects, we will compute the sum of squares for approach from column data and the sum of squares for length of unemployment from row data.

We compute the sum of squares for columns with the following formula.

$$SS_{columns} = \sum \frac{(\Sigma X)^2}{N_{groups}} - \frac{(\Sigma X)^2}{N_{total}}$$

This formula directs us to take each column total (ΣX), square it, and divide the results by the total number of scores in the column. We do this for each column and add them together. Then, we square the total X, divide this value by the total N, and subtract it from the first operation.

For our problem, the sum of squares for columns would be:

$$SS_{columns} = \frac{(433)^2}{8} + \frac{(385)^2}{8} + \frac{(346)^2}{8} - \frac{(1164)^2}{24}$$
$$= 23{,}436.13 + 18{,}528.13 + 14{,}964.50 - 56{,}454.00$$
$$= 56{,}928.76 - 56{,}454.00$$
$$= 474.76$$

At this point, the value 474.76 is interpreted as the amount of the total sum of squares (variance) that is due to differences between means of the three counseling approaches.

We compute a sum of squares for rows in the same manner, except we now use row data instead of column data. The sum of squares for rows would be:

$$SS_{rows} = \frac{(653)^2}{12} + \frac{(511)^2}{12} - \frac{(1164)^2}{24}$$
$$= 35{,}534.08 + 21{,}760.08 - 56{,}454.00$$
$$= 57{,}294.16 - 56{,}454.00$$
$$= 840.16$$

The sum of squares for rows is interpreted as the amount of the total sum of squares that is due to the differences between means of the two length of unemployment groups.

Sum of Squares for Interaction. We now must compute a sum of squares for interaction. In computing the sums of squares for total and the two main effects, we used total data only. In the case of interaction, our computation must also include subtotals. The sum of squares for interaction is obtained with the following formula.

$$SS_{interaction} = SS_{subgroups} - (SS_{columns} + SS_{rows})$$

In order to use this formula, we first must compute a sum of squares for subgroups.

$$SS_{subgroups} = \frac{(236)^2}{4} + \frac{(205)^2}{4} + \frac{(212)^2}{4} + \frac{(197)^2}{4}$$
$$+ \frac{(180)^2}{4} + \frac{(134)^2}{4} - \frac{(1164)^2}{24}$$
$$= 13{,}924.00 + 10{,}506.25 + 11{,}236.00 + 9702.25$$
$$+ 8100.00 + 4489.00 - 56{,}454.00$$
$$= 57{,}957.50 - 56{,}454.00$$
$$= 1503.50$$

We can now determine the sum of squares for interaction.

$$SS_{interaction} = 1503.50 - (474.76 + 840.16)$$
$$= 1503.50 - 1314.92$$
$$= 188.58$$

This value is interpreted as the part of the total sum of squares that is due to the relationship between the dependent variables (in this case, the self-concept scores) and the combination of the two independent variables.

Sum of Squares for Within. A final sum of squares is obtained for within.

$$SS_{within} = SS_{total} - (SS_{columns} + SS_{rows} + SS_{interaction})$$
$$= 2162.00 - (474.76 + 840.16 + 188.58)$$
$$= 2162.00 - 1503.50$$
$$= 658.50$$

The sums of squares for all sources of variation have now been obtained.

$$SS_{total} = 2162.00$$
$$SS_{columns} = 474.76$$
$$SS_{rows} = 840.16$$
$$SS_{interaction} = 188.58$$
$$SS_{within} = 658.50$$

Degrees of Freedom

After the sums of squares for each source of variation have been obtained, the next step is to determine the degrees of freedom.

In a two-way classification problem such as ours, degrees of freedom may be obtained by the following procedure.

Source of Variation	Degrees of Freedom
Columns	Number of columns $- 1$ $(c - 1)$
Rows	Number of rows $- 1$ $(r - 1)$
Interaction	Columns $- 1$ times rows $- 1$ $(c - 1)(r - 1)$
Within	Number in the sample $-$ columns times rows $(N - cr)$
Total	Number in the same $- 1$ $(N - 1)$

For our problem, degrees of freedom would be:

Columns $\quad c - 1 = 2$
Rows $\qquad r - 1 = 1$
Interaction $\quad (c - 1)(r - 1) = 2$
Within $\qquad N - cr = 18$
Total $\qquad N - 1 = 23$

Mean Squares

The final computation that must be done before the F values can be obtained is that of determining a mean square for each source of variation, with the exception of total. Mean squares are obtained by dividing each sum of squares by the corresponding degrees of freedom.

For our problem, the mean squares are computed in the following manner:

$$\text{Mean square for columns} \quad = \frac{474.76}{2} = 237.38$$

$$\text{Mean square for rows} \quad = \frac{840.16}{1} = 840.16$$

$$\text{Mean square for interaction} = \frac{188}{2} = 94.29$$

$$\text{Mean square for within} \quad = \frac{658.50}{18} = 36.58$$

F Values

You will recall that, in our example problem, we are dealing with three sources of variation: counseling approach, length of unemployment, and interaction. To test hypotheses relating to these three sources, we must obtain an F value for each. F values are obtained in the following manner:

$$F \text{ for counseling approach} = \frac{\text{Mean square for columns}}{\text{Mean square for within}}$$

$$\begin{matrix} F \text{ for length of} \\ \text{unemployment} \end{matrix} = \frac{\text{Mean square for rows}}{\text{Mean square for within}}$$

$$F \text{ for interaction} \quad = \frac{\text{Mean square for interaction}}{\text{Mean square for within}}$$

You will note that the denominator for each of these operations is the mean square for within. As we have mentioned, this is the error term, or residual factor, that is unaccounted for in the other sources of variation.

In other words, this is the portion of the variance that cannot be attributed to either main effects or interaction.

For our problem, the F values for each source of variation would be:

$$F \text{ for counseling approach} = \frac{237.38}{36.58} = 6.489$$

$$F \text{ for length of unemployment} = \frac{840.16}{36.58} = 22.967$$

$$F \text{ for interaction} = \frac{94.58}{36.58} = 2.585$$

Table 9–5 summarizes the data.

TABLE 9–5.   Summary of Analysis of Variance of Self-Concept Scores of 24 Unemployed Males Classified by Counseling Approach and Length of Unemployment.

Source of Variation	Sum of Squares	Degrees of Freedom	Mean Square	F
Counseling approach	474.76	2	237.38	6.459
Length of unemployment	840.16	1	840.16	22.967
Interaction	188.58	2	94.58	2.585
Within	658.50	18	36.58	
Total	2162.00	23		

Interpretation of F

After the F values have been computed, we are now in a position to make decisions on the three hypotheses stated for our example problem.

H_{o1} stated that no significant difference would result between the three counseling groups on the score obtained from the self-concept scale. To make a decision on this hypothesis, we take our computed F value of 6.489 for counseling approach to the F distribution table (Appendix F). Testing this hypothesis at the .05 level, we enter the table with 2 and 18 degrees of freedom. Degrees of freedom for the greater mean square are found across the top of the table and the degrees of freedom for the lesser mean square are found down the side of the table. With 2 and 18 degrees of freedom, the table value at the .05 level is 3.55. Since our computed value of 6.489 is greater than the table value, we reject H_{o1}.

Since the F for counseling approach was significant, we conclude that counseling approach did have a significant effect on the subjects' performance on the self-concept scale.

H_{o2} stated that there would be no significant difference between the length of unemployment groups on the score obtained from the self-concept scale. To make a decision on this hypothesis, we take our computed F value of 22.967 for length of unemployment to the table with 1 and 18 degrees of freedom. Testing again at the .05 level, we note the table value of 4.41 is less than the computed F of 22.967. This hypothesis, therefore, is rejected.

Since this F value is significant, we conclude that length of unemployment *did* make a difference in the way the subjects performed on the self-concept scale.

H_{o3} stated that there would be no significant interaction between the two independent variables and the score obtained on the self-concept scale. Following the same procedure, we enter the table with our F value of 2.585 at 2 and 18 degrees of freedom. We note that the table value of 3.55 is greater than our computed value of 2.585. Therefore, we accept H_{o3}.

Three-Way Classification Analysis

When a third main effect (independent variable) is added to a multiple classification problem, the analysis is referred to as a three-way classification analysis. Since the computation of this type of analysis is rather lengthy, we highly recommend that a computer be used if at all possible.

For our purposes, we will simply employ a brief narrative to explain the procedure of a three-way analysis. We should keep in mind that all the considerations and procedures for a three-way analysis are the same as used in a two-way problem. The only difference is the addition of a third independent variable. In more complex problems, more than three independent variables can be used.

To illustrate this procedure, we will continue with our example problem. Suppose we added a third independent variable, such as age, to our problem. With the third variable, we would have seven possible sources of variation instead of three. Table 9–6 (p. 170) illustrates the different sums of squares that must be computed in a three-way analysis of variance problem.

After the sums of squares, degrees of freedom, and mean squares have been obtained, an F value for each source of variation is computed. Decisions are then made in the usual way on the seven hypotheses. We note that by adding the third independent variable we now have four possible sources of interaction, all possible combinations of main effects (referred to as first-order interactions) and one involving all three main effects (referred to as third-order interactions).

Remember that when multiple classification analysis of variance is employed, the size of N should be large enough to insure an adequate num-

TABLE 9–6. Analysis of Variance of Self-Concept Scores of 24 Unemployed Males Classified according to Counseling Approach, Length of Unemployment, and Age.

Source of Variation	SS	df	MS	F
Counseling Approach				
Length of Unemployment				
Age				
Approach × Length				
Approach × Age				
Length × Age				
Approach × Length × Age				
Within				
Total				

ber in each classification. Each classification does not have to have an equal number of observations; however, when the number of observations in each classification differs greatly, some action should be taken to equalize it. One method for accomplishing this is to eliminate observations randomly from the disproportionate classifications. We can minimize this problem, though, by making sure N is large enough to accommodate the number of classifications found in the problem.

SAMPLE STUDY

The following study illustrates the use of the technique of multiple classification of variance. The study utilizes a two-way classification analysis to test the stated hypotheses.

The Influence of Test Difficulty upon Study Efforts and Achievement*

Educators appear to be confronted with a dilemma concerning appropriate test difficulty level when constructing classroom examinations. Test constructors have provided both theoretical and empirical evidence which indicates that tests have maximum reliability and validity when item difficulty is near 50 percent (Guilford, 1954), but classroom educators believe that difficult examinations decrease student motivation and consequently achievement (Wood,

*Ronald N. Marso, "The Influence of Test Difficulty upon Study Efforts and Achievement," reprinted from *American Educational Research Journal* 6, no. 4 (November 1969): 621–32, by permission of the author and publisher.

1961). Thus the goals of maximizing student achievement and of maximizing test reliability seem to be in conflict when considering the appropriate difficulty level for classroom examinations. If an actual discrepancy exists in the attainment of these two classroom goals, it seems plausible to assume that learning efforts and outcomes are potentially more important criteria in classroom test construction than are statistical criteria. However, little empirical evidence appears to exist regarding the relationship between test difficulty and student motivation or achievement.

A survey of the research literature resulted in the location of a single study pertaining to the relationship between test difficulty and achievement, Sax and Reade (1964); this study indicates that more difficult unit examinations actually result in greater student achievement. These researchers administered two unit examinations to a group of college students enrolled in an introductory educational measurements course. One-half of the students took "easy" forms of the unit exams, and the other one-half took "hard" forms of the exams. The mean difficulty level of the two "easy" unit exams was approximately 68 percent of the total number of items, and the mean difficulty of the two "hard" unit examinations was approximately 39 percent of the total number of items. The dependent variable in the study was a final examination administered to all of the students and having a mean difficulty level for the total group of approximately 48 percent (51 percent for those students having taken the "hard" unit exams and 45 percent for those students having taken the "easy" unit examinations). To this writer, however, it seems that three characteristics of this study make the generalization of its findings to the classroom questionable. First, the unit exams and the final examination were more difficult than commonly used in the typical classroom (Wood, 1961). Second, different test items appeared on the two test forms administered during the course thus allowing the possibility of one form favoring the final examination. And third, following the administration of each of the unit exams, the researchers combined the two raw score distributions resulting from the two test forms and presented them as a single distribution to the students. This latter factor may have caused the students whose scores appeared at the lower end of the single distribution (in this particular situation those students taking the more difficult test form) to study more as a reaction to their comparatively poor performance and anticipated low grade. A student reaction of this nature to an anticipated low earned grade would seem feasible as some research data exists which indicate that college student achievement is influenced by varying grade assignments (Fay, 1937).

EXPERIMENT I

Procedure. This study was designed to test two hypotheses. First, students achieve significantly more after experiencing less difficult unit examinations. And second, students with high test anxiety profit significantly more from experiencing easy unit examinations than do students with low test anxiety.

The sample consisted of 155 students enrolled in four sections of an introductory educational psychology course at the University of Nebraska during the Spring semester of 1967. The students were randomly assigned to either the group taking form W (difficult) unit examinations or to the group taking form G (easy) unit exams and were given three regularly scheduled hour examinations during the course. In addition each student completed the Quick Word Test (QWT) developed by Borgatta and Corsini (1960) and a combination of test anxiety scales identified by Carrier and Jewell (1966). Two levels of test difficulty for the unit examinations were maintained by varying the distractors on the multiple-choice test items. The test difficulty level for form W was held near the statistically desirable 50 percent level while the test difficulty level for form G was held near 70 percent of the total number of test items which is considered to be more representative of typical classroom practice (Wood, 1961). Each form of the unit examinations consisted of 35–40 four alternative multiple-choice items with identical stem and correct response. Only the item distractors of the multiple-choice questions were varied on the forms to establish the desired levels of test difficulty. This was done through the selection of test items from previously used items with a difficulty level near 50 percent and with an acceptable index of discrimination. The latter criterion was included to ensure the validity or equality of the items and to alleviate the danger that the more difficult items were not simply more confusing. The second form, the less difficult form, for each of these selected items was then constructed by retaining the original stem and correct response while making one or more of the item distractors less plausible (Wood, 1961, p. 60). This procedure was followed, rather than the utilization of parallel test forms, to ensure that the items on one test form did not favor the final examination items and as it is considered normal procedure to modify items in this manner in efforts to maximize test reliability (Wood, 1961).

Although the test items were randomly arranged on each form of the unit examinations, the students were informed that the experiment was being conducted to determine the effect of varying the arrangement of the test items on the unit examination and that in other respects the two test forms were identical. To further prevent knowledge of the true nature of the study, the two groups met separately to discuss the unit test items the class period following the administration of the exams; and standard scores within each group were reported to the students rather than raw scores so that the students would not be aware of the discrepancy in the performance between the two groups. Equal letter grade assignment frequencies were also maintained across the two groups so that any "motivation for grade improvement" would be constant in the two groups. In addition the procedures were designed such that influence of instructor, student group interaction, and content presentation were constant across the two experimental groups as each group was randomly selected from within each of the four class sections all taught by the investigator. And in an effort to check student reaction to the experimental conditions, questionnaires were administered to the students to determine if changes in study habits occurred and if the students suspected the true nature of the investigation.

The 123 four alternative multiple-choice item final examination taken in common by the two experimental groups was designed to cover the objectives of the entire course and to be of a difficulty level half-way between the difficulty levels of the two forms of the unit examinations. The items for the final examination were selected from a recently developed departmental examination for the course for which item analysis data had been derived from administrations of the exam to two large groups of students having completed the same course taught by the investigator. The items were selected on the basis of biserial correlations (the majority were +.25 or higher) with the total test score and on the basis of content validity charts designed to ensure representation of the material covered and appropriate cognitive levels of knowledge required by the items (Bloom, 1956). In general the final examination was composed of items involving responses of somewhat higher cognitive levels as compared to the unit exams, but this is usually considered to be desirable for course final examinations. The items on the final examination were judged to require cognitive responses of the following types: 33 recall items, 60 understanding of concepts or principles, and 30 application items. The final examination consisted of three parts: part one composed of 58 items, part two composed of 30 items randomly selected from the unit exams (15 items taken from each form), and part three composed of 35 items designed to be somewhat easier than the items in part one. The final examination was made up of different sections to determine whether or not less difficult test items favored one or the other of the groups, whether more difficult (but still of intermediate difficulty) items favor one or the other of the groups, and whether the groups performed differently on items replicated from the two forms of the unit examinations.

Findings. The data indicate that the investigator was relatively successful in maintaining the desired levels of difficulty on the two forms of the unit examinations and on the final exam as indicated by Tables 1 and 2. In addition, item analysis of the two test forms for each exam indicated that item validity (Wood, 1961, p. 87) remained good despite variations in the item distractors. This would suggest that the more difficult items were not simply just more confusing to the students. Furthermore, responses to the questionnaire indicated that the students had not been aware of the true nature of the study nor had they knowingly changed their study habits during the course.

An analysis of variance procedure using the final examination total scores as the dependent variable and the QWT scores as a blocking variable (approximately the top, middle, and bottom one-third of the sample) to control

TABLE 1.   Means, Standard Deviations, and Difficulty Levels for the Unit Examinations.

Test	Form	No. Items	N	Mean	S.D.	Diff. Index
#1	W	40	81	23.6	4.8	.59
	G	40	74	29.2	4.4	.73
#2	W	35	81	18.8	4.5	.54
	G	35	74	25.9	3.7	.74
#3	W	35	81	17.6	3.9	.50
	G	35	74	24.8	3.3	.71
(Average All Tests)	W	——	81	20.0	——	.54
	G	——	74	26.6	——	.73

TABLE 2.   Means, Standard Deviations, Estimate of Reliability, and Difficulty Levels for the Final Examination.

		Section	#1 (58 items)			#1 & 2 (93 items)			Total Exam (123 items)			
Form	N	M	s	Diff.	M	s	Diff.	M	s	Diff.	KR_{21}
W	77	34.2	6.7	.59	59.1	9.65	.64	83.0	11.9	.67	.82
G	69	35.4	5.9	.61	60.8	8.07	.65	86.6	10.2	.70	.76

for any differences in mental ability resulted in an F ratio of 5.98 for the test difficulty factor and an F ratio of 9.46 for the QWT factor both of which are significant beyond the .05 level of confidence. An inspection of the cell means for the test difficulty factor, note Table 5, revealed the difference to be in favor of the G group (easy unit exams) in all of the cells. The largest cell mean difference between the two groups was found at the lowest one-third

TABLE 3.   Analysis of Variance Using Final Examination Total Scores as the Dependent Variable and QWT Scores as a Control Variable.

Source of Variance	SS	df	MS	F
A (Levels of Test Difficulty)	654.24	1	654.24	5.98*
B (Three levels of QWT)	2070.48	2	1035.24	9.46**
AB	494.16	2	247.08	2.26
Within Cell	15326.00	140	109.47	

$*F_{(.05\ 1,\ 140)} = 3.91$ $**F_{(.01\ 2,\ 140)} = 3.91$

QWT score level which suggests that the easy unit examinations were especially beneficial to the college students of lower ability in the sample. This analysis is reported in Table 3. An analysis of variance using only the first section final examination scores as the dependent variable with QWT scores again used as a control variable yielded an F ratio of 2.92 which is significant at the .10 level of confidence. The cell means again revealed an advantage for the G group at all levels of the QWT scores. An analysis of the remaining part scores of the final examination revealed a consistent trend in favor of the G group. Neither the varied difficulty levels of the examination parts nor the replication part (part two) appeared to influence the comparative performance of the two experimental groups.

In an effort to determine the influence of test anxiety on the score variance, an analysis of variance with the final examination total scores used as the dependent variable and with test anxiety used as a control variable (three levels of anxiety, top, middle, and bottom approximate one-third of the sample) was completed. This resulted in an F ratio of 6.87 for the test anxiety factor which is significant at the .01 level of confidence and an F ratio of 3.03 for the test difficulty factor which is significant at the .10 level. This analysis is presented in Table 4. An inspection of the cell means for this analysis revealed that the G group (easy unit exams) scored above the W group at all levels of test anxiety; the cell means for these analyses are reported in Table 5.

TABLE 4. Analysis of Variance Using Final Examination Total Scores the Dependent Variable and Test Anxiety Scores as a Control Variable.

Source of Variance				
A (Levels of Test Difficulty)	356.82	1	356.82	3.03*
B (Three Levels of Test Anxiety)	1619.29	2	809.65	6.87**
AB	1.39	2	.76	
Within Cell	15913.29	135	117.88	

$*F_{(.10\ 1,\ 135)} = 2.75$ $**F_{(.01)}\ 2 = 4.78$

TABLE 5. Cell Means for Analyses Presented.

QWT Scores as a Control Variable			Test Anxiety as a Control Variable		
Anxiety Scores			QWT Scores		
B_1 (High)	B_2 (Middle)	B_3 (Low)	B_1 (High)	B_2 (Middle)	B_3 (Low)
A_1 (Form G) 91.10	83.50	86.43	A_2 (Form W) 82.90	85.88	91.00
A_2 (Form W) 89.31	82.00	76.93	A_2 (Form W) 79.40	82.84	87.91

Discussion. The data derived from this investigation have supported the hypothesis that college students who experience less difficult unit examinations achieve better on a course final examination. Although the magnitude of the mean difference between the two groups was small, 83.0 as compared to 86.6, this would seem to be of sufficient magnitude to warrant a further investigation of this relationship especially since these findings are in contrast to those obtained by Sax and Reade. Furthermore, if test difficulty is related to student motivation, one must wonder about long-term effects of this factor in terms of the years spent in the educational process.

The data have indicated also that test anxiety is inversely associated with student achievement as measured by final examination performance. However, this factor did not account for a significant portion of the variance between the easy and difficult groups of students. Therefore, the hypothesis that students with high test anxiety profit more from experiencing relatively less difficult unit data was not supported. The interaction effects between the test difficulty factor and the test anxiety and QWT scores were not significant; however, it appeared that the students of lower ability in the sample benefited more from the less difficult course examinations than did the more capable students. In addition it should be noted that these data have not revealed what test difficulty level will result in maximal achievement, nor has it revealed why achievement was higher in the G (easy unit exam) group.

The writer suggests a set to study phenomenon as an explanation for the difference in achievement which occurred between the two groups of students. Harlow's (1949) research on learning set indicates that a relatively permanent state of motivation for certain types of responses can be developed. An analogous type of motivation or set to study could result from successful performance on test items; and perhaps less difficult tests through increased reinforcement result in a more intense set to study. This increased set to study could then in turn lead to more study efforts or more efficient studying or both.

A set to study would appear to be a more feasible explanation for the difference in achievement as compared to set as a response to a specific type of test item or a set to make careful discriminations among item alternates. A set to make careful discriminations among the item responses could feasibly develop from experiencing difficult multiple-choice items. However, the data indicated that the difficult unit examination group performed less well on all sections of the final examination. This evidence would make this explanation untenable. An explanation of difference in the presence of response interference on the test items between the two groups would also appear equally untenable for several reasons: First, feedback was provided following each unit examination which would have reduced any response interference considerably. Second, a greater difference in performance between the two groups did not appear on the replication item section (part two) of the final examination for which any interference effect would be maximum. And last, the final examination items on the first and third sections would seem to be too dissimilar, as compared to the unit test items, to result in the generalization of specific response interference between the two sets of items.

EXPERIMENT II

Procedure. This study was designed to test the hypothesis that college students who experience relatively easy unit examinations during a course will study more during that course. It was assumed that substantiation of this hypothesis would support a set to study explanation for the influence of unit test difficulty level upon student achievement.

Forty-four students enrolled in two introductory educational psychology classes at the University of Nebraska during the Summer of 1967 were selected as the sample. One class completed four unit examinations with a mean difficulty level near 50 percent, and the second class completed four unit examinations with a mean difficulty near 70 percent. The unit examinations consisted of 20–25 randomly arranged four alternative multiple-choice items. Each form of the unit examinations contained identical item stems and correct responses. As in experiment one, only the item distractors were varied on the two test forms to attain the desired difficulty levels for each test form. To control for any "motivation for grade improvement" between the two groups, each group was assigned equivalent numbers of each letter grade for their performance on each of the unit examinations. In addition as similar as possible classroom learning experiences were provided in the two classes which were taught by the same instructor.

The students were required to complete the Quick Word Test (QWT) measure of mental ability and to maintain daily records of study time during the course. Time was provided at the beginning of each class period to complete the daily records of study which were handed in to the instructor each week. The mean QWT scores for the two groups were found to be 50.5 and 50.0.

Findings. An analysis of student performance on the unit examinations revealed that the mean difficulty level of the four unit tests for the easy group was 72 percent of the total number of items correct and that the mean difficulty level of the four unit exams for the difficult group was 52 percent. The means, standard deviations, and difficulty levels for the unit examinations are reported in Table 6.

An analysis of variance procedure completed on the hours of study reported by each student from the first unit examination to the completion of the course with the QWT scores used as a control variable (top, middle, and bottom one-third of the sample) resulted in an F ratio of 11.85 for the test difficulty factor. This ratio is significant well beyond the .01 level of confidence. An inspection of the cell means revealed that the students exposed to the relatively easy unit examinations reported more hours of study within all levels of the QWT scores. Neither the interaction effect between the test difficulty and mental ability factor nor the main effect of the QWT factor yielded significant F ratios. This analysis is presented in Table 7, and the means of the treatment cells are reported in Table 8.

TABLE 6.   Means, Standard Deviations, and Difficulty Levels of the Unit Examinations.

Test Number	Form	No. Items	Mean	S.D.	Diff. Index
1	hard	25	13.5	2.8	.54
1	easy	25	17.0	2.2	.68
2	hard	25	10.6	2.4	.42
2	easy	25	18.2	3.5	.73
3	hard	25	13.0	3.0	.52
3	easy	25	18.5	3.0	.74
4	hard	20	11.7	2.8	.59
4	easy	20	14.4	2.1	.73
(Average	hard	—	12.2	—	.52
all tests)	easy	—	17.0	—	.72

TABLE 7.   Analysis of Variance with QWT Scores as a Control Variable and Reported Hours of Study as the Dependent Variable.

Source of Variance	SS	df	MS	F
A (Test Difficulty)	2715.52	1	2715.52	11.85*
B (Levels of QWT)	306.04	2	153.02	.65
AB	381.97	2	190.99	.83
Within Cell	7788.88	34	229.08	

*$F_{(.01 \ 1, \ 34)} = 7.46$

TABLE 8.   ANOVA Treatment Means for Reported Hours of Study.

	QWT Scores		
	B_1 (High)	B_2 (Middle)	B_3 (Low)
A_1 (Form G)	43.6	40.4	51.2
A_2 (Form W)	23.5	32.6	29.5

As the variances among the columns in the analysis of variance procedure differed a good deal, a t test not requiring an assumption of equality of variance was completed to determine if these differences in variance could have influenced the F test for differences between the two experimental groups (Winer, 1962, p. 36). However, this test was also significant well beyond the .01 level of confidence. The means of the two groups, 45.2 and 28.7 for this test resulted in a t value of 11.39.

Discussion. The findings supported the hypothesis that college students exposed to relatively easy unit examinations study more during a course. It would seem feasible to hypothesize that college students experiencing relatively easy unit examinations receive more reinforcement for their study efforts and consequently develop a more intense "set to study." This in turn results in an expenditure of greater amounts of time for the purpose of studying the course learning materials. However, further investigation of the unit test difficulty-college student achievement relationship needs to be done. This study was limited by small, intact group sampling procedures and by a single procedure for developing examinations of varying difficulty levels. In addition replication of the experimental conditions may reveal that the unit test difficulty-achievement relationship exists only for certain types of test items, course materials, or levels of test difficulty.

SUMMARY

Two experiments were conducted to investigate the relationship between classroom test difficulty and learning efforts and outcomes. It was reported that test construction theory and research indicate that test items should have a difficulty level near 50 percent for maximal reliability. However, opposing this statistical criterion for test construction, some educators contend that classroom tests should be less difficult for maximum motivational and achievement outcomes and that this criterion is more important for classroom unit tests than is the statistical criterion.

In the two experiments college students were exposed to unit tests of a difficulty level of either approximately 50 or 70 percent. The results of the first study indicated that students exposed to the less difficult unit exams achieved greater on the course final examination, and the results of the second study indicated that students exposed to less difficult unit exams study more during a course.

In summation the findings of this investigation have supported the classroom educators' contention that unit examination difficulty is related to student effort and achievement. Theoretically, it would seem that unit examinations need to be difficult enough to motivate students to study and to obtain a suitable level of test reliability and yet not so difficult as to result in inadequate reinforcement to maintain study efforts. Just what level of unit test difficulty is consonant with these goals was not revealed by these data, but the data do suggest that unit test difficulty level influences student achievement as well as test reliability. It was suggested that the relationship between test difficulty and study efforts and achievement be further investigated. If this relationship does exist at all grade levels and for various testing approaches, it may have a profound effect upon student motivation over a period of years.

REFERENCES

Bloom, Benjamin S. (Ed.) *Taxonomy of Educational Objectives, Handbook of Cognitive Domain.* New York: David McKay Company, Inc., 1956. 207 pp.

Borgatta, Edgar F. and Corsini, Raymond J. "The Quick Word Test (QWT) and the WAIS." *Psychological Reports* 6:201; April 1960.

Carrier, Neil A. and Jewell, Donald O. "Efficiency in Measuring the Effect of Anxiety upon Academic Performance." *Journal of Educational Psychology* 57:23–26; February 1966.

Fay, Paul J. "The Effect of the Knowledge of Marks on the Subsequent Achievement of College Work." *Journal of Educational Psychology* 54:554; October 1937.

Guilford, J. P. *Psychometric Methods.* New York: McGraw-Hill Book Company, Inc., 1954. 597 pp.

Harlow, Harry F. "The Formation of Learning Sets." *Psychological Review* 56:51–65; January 1949.

Sax, Gilbert and Reade, Marybell. "Achievement as a Function of Test Difficulty Level." *American Educational Research Journal* 1:22–25; January 1964.

Winer, Benjamin J. *Statistical Principles in Experimental Design.* New York: McGraw-Hill Book Company, 1962. 672 pp.

Wood, Dorothy A. *Test Construction.* Columbus, Ohio: Charles E. Merrill Books, Inc., 1961. 134 pp.

ANALYSIS OF COVARIANCE: AN INTRODUCTION

In chapter 8 and the previous section of this chapter, we discussed the various forms of the analysis of variance technique. We noted that analysis of variance is used in situations where differences between groups are of major concern. In a comparative study in which this technique is most often used, the object is to determine the significance of difference between means by analyzing the variance. In many instances, a basic prerequisite to adequate comparison is that the subjects used in a study have been *equated*. For example, if we are testing the effects of three instructional approaches on achievement, we would want the subjects in each group to approximate each other on the variable, or variables, that might affect their achievement other than the independent variables under study.

We can look at this in the same way as a race. If a proper judgment about who can win a race is to be made, the runners must start at the same place. The same idea applies to testing instructional approaches.

The most effective way of equalizing groups is by random assignment. In chapter 3 we discussed sampling and mentioned that the idea of sampling, applied in reverse, is random assignment. In essence, the procedure is one of randomly assigning subjects to groups in order to distribute the extraneous variables that might have an effect on the outcome of the study. If random assignment is possible, it's the best way to equalize groups.

There are many instances in behavioral science research when random assignment is not possible. Researchers working in the schools, for example, often find it impossible to manipulate students to serve their research purposes. Researchers working with political units, families, social groups, and various other subjects find it difficult to place subjects into groups at random.

When random assignment is not possible, we turn to the technique of analysis of covariance. This technique is an extension of analysis of variance and is designed to equate groups statistically. We use analysis of covariance when two or more means are to be compared and the data meet the basic assumptions for analysis of variance. This technique allows us to use intact groups and to equate our groups statistically on one or more variables that we feel will make a difference on the dependent variable. For example, if we were concerned with the effects of several instructional approaches on achievement, one variable that obviously would make a difference on the dependent variable (achievement) would be ability. In such a case, we would want to equate the groups statistically on the basis of ability using whatever measure of ability we feel most appropriate.

SAMPLE STUDY

The study that follows illustrates the use of single classification analysis of covariance utilizing one covariate. The basic model employed consists of one dependent variable (achievement), one independent variable (team approach), and one covariate (GPA).

We can see how this problem could become multiple classification by adding a second independent variable.

Effect of a Team Approach in Achieving the Objectives of an Introductory Course in Education*

"An Introduction to" is a familiar preface to a large number of courses found in most college and university catalogs. The preface denotes a beginning course designed to acquaint the student with a broad area of study, such as education, in order to provide a foundation for future specialization. In the

---

*Joe D. Cornett and Walter Butler, "The Effect of a Team Approach in Achieving the Objectives of an Introductory Course in Education," reprinted from The Journal of Educational Research 63, no. 5 (January 1970): 222–24, by permission.

field of education, introductory courses, foundation courses, and principles courses fall into this category. References to the advantages and disadvantages of the introductory course are too numerous to mention, but the literature reveals a preponderance of comments relative to the disadvantages of such courses.

A consistent criticism from both students and faculty is that, due to the broad coverage of the material included in an introductory course, it becomes too general and unequal treatment is given to the various topics. The result is often a sketchy treatment of some phases of the course and a more detailed study of other phases. This might be attributed to the idea that instructors teaching a course such as this are not normally well informed about all the subject areas in a broad field of study. Consequently, an instructor is more likely to converge on those areas in which he is best qualified and most interested.

It was assumed, then, that a team approach, utilizing instructors of competence in the areas covered, would provide a more balanced coverage of the course material and enhance the students' understanding of the breadth and depth of the course. The course selected for this study was entitled "An Introduction to Education" and was designed to achieve two objectives: (1) to provide an understanding of the teaching profession, the organization, and administration of schools, and the historical and philosophical foundations of the American school system, and (2) to assist students in deciding whether or not they wanted to become teachers. The course was offered at the sophomore level and served as a first course required of all teacher education students.

Having experienced many of the criticisms of the introductory course, the researchers decided to experiment with a team approach in an effort to provide a more balanced background for the students enrolled. Accordingly, the purpose of this study was to compare the achievement scores of students enrolled in an introductory course in education when taught by a team of instructors with achievement scores of similar students taught in traditionally arranged classes. Also, an effort was made to determine if a student's decision to become a teacher would be affected more by a team approach or the traditional approach.

PROCEDURE

It was hypothesized that those students taught by a teaching team of three instructors with special competence in the areas covered in the course would achieve significantly higher on a standardized education examination than students taught in a conventional class with one instructor. It was further hypothesized that the influence of the course on a student's decision to become a teacher was independent of the teaching technique employed. To test these hypotheses, two groups were utilized in this experiment:

The Experimental Group. This group consisted of three intact classes enrolled in the introductory course and combined into one group for the purpose of this experiment. The subjects were seventy-eight second-semester sopho-more students majoring in both elementary and secondary education. The ex-perimental approach used with this group consisted of a combination of large group presentations, small group discussions, and additional enrichment ex-periences. The instructor assigned to a particular phase of the course was considered the lead instructor for that particular unit and was responsible for all formal presentations to the large group and for planning the small group discussions.

The Control Group. This group consisted of fifty-five students enrolled in two sections of the introductory course. In an effort to minimize the factor of teacher variability, the data gathered on these two groups were combined to form one control group. One of the team instructors was involved with the control group while the other class was taught by an instructor not associated with the team. The approach used in both control groups consisted primarily of lecture, discussion, and some outside projects.

TABLE 1. Introductory Education Students' Criterion and Control Variable Means.

| Groups | N | Criterion Post-Achievement | | | Control Prior Achievement | | |
		Adjusted Means	Un-Adjusted Means	SD	(GPA)	SD
Experimental	78	72.07	72.26	73.38	2.377	2.461
Control	55	56.99	56.80	58.65	2.284	2.194

Criterion Measure

The instrument used to measure a student's understanding of the course ma-terial consisted of a standardized one-semester examination especially pre-pared for this experiment. It was based on material included in the text (1) used by all students enrolled in the course and a common syllabus used by all instructors. The examination included an equal number of questions on the three major phases of the course, the teaching profession, the organization and administration of schools, and the historical and philosophical founda-tions of American education.

The examination was constructed by an impartial group of graduate stu-dents using the text and syllabus as a guide. "Face Validity" of the test items was checked by the instructors involved. The examination was administered to a sample of like students and an item analysis was used to determine re-liability. Sample questions from each of the three areas are presented below. They are typical examples of all the questions.

The NEA is an organization open to

    a. all in education or interested in education
    b. classroom teachers only
    c. school administrators only
    d. teacher preparation personnel only
    e. classroom teachers and administrators only

Check the phrase which best describes the system of education in the United States

    a. centralized
    b. standardized
    c. federally controlled
    d. decentralized
    e. regionally operated

The Essentialists would get their aims of education from

    a. the Great Books
    b. tradition
    c. pupil interests
    d. the church
    e. pressure groups

The instrument used to determine the influence the course had on the student's decision to become a teacher was a checklist requiring the student to choose if the course had a positive influence, a negative influence, or no influence at all on his decision to become a teacher.

Three days prior to the close of the Spring semester, the examination was administered to students in the experimental and control groups. The examination was administered to all groups the same day but at different times during the day. The factor of class schedules made it necessary to follow this practice. At the same time, the students were asked to indicate the influence the course had on their decisions to become teachers. Students were instructed not to place their name on the checklist and care was taken to inform them that their grades in the course would not be affected by their responses. The time limit for the experiment covered a period of four and one-half months. This was considered long enough to get an adequate measure of the differences due to the experimental treatment.

Data Analysis

The post-achievement un-adjusted and adjusted criterion means and the control variable means are presented in Table 1. As noted in the table, the ex-

TABLE 2.   Analysis of Covariance for Achievement Differences between Two Groups of Introductory Education Students Controlling for Prior Achievement.

Source of Variation	Degree of Freedom	Sum of Squares	Mean Square	F
Between	1	4,678.67	4,678.67	
				14.40*
Within	130	42,249.00	324.99	

*Significant beyond the .01 level.

perimental group exceeded the control group by a margin of 15.46 on the examination. When the means were adjusted, the situation did not change appreciably. The two groups differed only slightly on the control variable, grade point average at the time of enrollment in the course, but enough to be considered different. Therefore, a single classification analysis of covariance, (2) was employed to determine the significance of difference between the experimental and control groups' performance on the standardized education test. The analysis of covariance treatment yielded an F value of 14.40 which was found to be significant at the .01 level. The result of this analysis is presented in Table 2.

In testing the hypothesis that the influence of the course on a student's decision to become a teacher is independent of the teaching approach, the chi-square technique was employed. This analysis resulted in a chi-square value of 3.05 which was found not to be significant when tested at the .01 level. This information is summarized in Table 3.

CONCLUSIONS

The first hypothesis tested stated that those students taught by a teaching team would achieve significantly higher on a standardized education test than

TABLE 3.   Responses of Introductory Education Students to a Question Regarding the Influence the Course Had on Their Decision to Become a Teacher.

Groups	Positive Influence	No Influence	Negative Influence	Total
Experimental	14 (18.18)	62 (58.06)	2 (1.76)	78
Control	17 (12.82)	37 (40.94)	1 (1.24)	55
Total	31	99	3	133

Chi-square of 3.05 not significant at the .01 level.

students taught in a conventional class with one instructor. The analysis of data concerned with this hypothesis yielded a significant F value of 1.40 thereby supporting this hypothesis. It can be concluded, then, that students exposed to this particular team approach achieved significantly higher on a standardized education examination than students exposed to a conventional class situation. It should be noted that the experimental group gained much of its advantage on the foundations section of the examination.

The second hypothesis tested indicated that the influence of the course on a student's decision to become a teacher is independent of the teaching approach used. A chi-square value of 3.05 was found dictating the acceptance of the second hypothesis. Therefore, it was concluded that the approach used in teaching the course was not a factor in the students' decision to become a teacher. A majority of the students enrolled in both the experimental and control groups indicated that the course had no influence of any kind on their decision.

The major limitation of this study is concerned with teacher variability. The researchers attempted to deal with this factor by combining the two control groups, but it is still questionable if adequate control was achieved. A better method would have been for the team instructors to also be instructors in the control groups.

We note from this study that the groups were compared on the basis of achievement after being equated on GPA. Table 1 in the sample study presents the adjusted and unadjusted means. Through the process of regression, the initial means are adjusted according to the relationship between the control variable and the achievement scores. We can see that the experimental group had a higher GPA; therefore, the achievement mean was adjusted downward and the control group mean adjusted upward.

Computational procedures for this technique are not presented here since our purpose for presenting analysis of covariance in this chapter is simply to acquaint you with the technique. For a description of how the technique works, more advanced texts should be consulted. We hope, however, that you will acquire a basic understanding of how this technique is used in behavioral science research.

FOR REVIEW AND FURTHER STUDY

1. The purpose of a study by Hountras and Brandt[1] was to explore the relation of student residence to academic achievement in five colleges of an

---

1. Peter T. Hountras, and Kenneth R. Brandt, "Relation of Student Residence to Academic Performance in College," *The Journal of Educational Research* 63:8 (April 1970): 351–54.

upper midwest university. Academic achievement was measured by grade-point averages. Places of residence were classified as residence halls, at home, or off-campus other than at home. The three groups of students were matched according to ACT composite standard scores and class standing. An analysis of variance was used to explore possible differences in GPA for students enrolled in the five colleges. The incomplete summary table is shown below.

Two-Way Analysis of Variance for the Differences
in GPA for Students in Five Colleges.

Source of Variation	SS	df	MS	F
Columns (C) (Colleges)			6.35	
Rows (R) (Residence)			3.80	
$R \times C$			1.43	
Within			129.24	
Total			140.82	
$N = 270$				

a. State the hypothesis appropriate for this study.
b. Complete the summary table.
c. Interpret the findings.

2. An investigation by Armand J. Galfo[2] sought to determine if (1) pupils gain more information from slide-tape audio-visual materials when sight and sound are not presented simultaneously; and (2) pupil information acquisition is influenced by whether the audio or visual message is presented first. Randomly selected groups of pupils were exposed to two experimental sequences which separated sight and sound and two control treatments which combined the audio and visual presentation. The students were either eighth- or ninth-graders, and they were grouped into three categories of mental ability level. Evaluation of learning was measured with a 120-item multiple-choice test.

Student scores on the achievement test were subjected to an analysis of variance. The following incomplete summary table shows the results.

Source of Variation	SS	df	MS	F
Treatment (T)	941	3		
Ability Level (L)	26202	2		
Grade (G)	1201	1		
$L \times G$	791	2		
$L \times T$	757	6		
$C \times T$	645	3		
$L \times G \times T$	622	6		
Within	27135	240		
Total				

2. Armand J. Galfo, "Effects of Certain Audio and Visual Presentation Sequences on Pupil Information Acquisition," *The Journal of Educational Research* 64:4 (December 1970): 172–76.

a. Complete the summary table.
b. Interpret the findings.
c. Draw appropriate conclusions.

3. A study[3] was conducted to determine the effect of putting either all girls or all boys in classes together (same-sex class organization). Seventh- and eighth-grade students were so placed in classes, and after a full school year they were evaluated in terms of academic achievement, self-discipline, self-concept, sex role identification, and attitude toward school. The portion of the study pertaining to self-concept utilized the following hypothesis.

There is no significant difference in report of self-concept of ability between a group of junior high school boys and girls after one school year in classes of the same sex.

A portion of the California Test of Personality, the "Total Personal Adjustment" section, yielded scores which are computed into the incomplete summary table below. An analysis of covariance technique was used to equate the control and experimental groups in terms of academic achievement, self-discipline, sex role identification, and attitude toward school.

Summary of Analysis of Covariance for "Total
Personal Adjustment," CTP Adjusted Posttest

Source of Variation	SS	df	MS	F
Grade (J Effect)	292.9609	1		
Sex (I Effect)	22.8008	1		
Group (K Effect)	45.0234	1		
$J \times I$	9.4883	1		
$J \times K$	139.9492	1		
$I \times K$	10.8086	1		
$J \times I \times K$	4.3516	1		
Within	7027.7031	79		
Total	7553.0859	86		

a. Complete the summary table.
b. Interpret the findings.
c. Determine if the hypothesis was supported by this data.

3. Joseph R. Ellis, and Joan F. Peterson, "Effects of Same Sex Class Organization on Junior High School Students' Academic Achievement, Self-Discipline, Self-Concept, Sex Role Identification, and Attitude Toward School," *The Journal of Educational Research* 64:10 (July-August 1971): 455–64.

10

The Chi-Square
Technique

Nonparametric statistics are a group of techniques designed to analyze data that fail to meet the assumptions for parametric techniques, i.e., distribution and variance assumptions. You will recall that correlation, t-test, and analysis of variance are employed only when certain assumptions regarding population distribution and variance can be met. Nonparametric techniques allow us to test hypotheses with data that cannot meet the assumptions necessary for parametric techniques.

In this chapter we will present only one nonparametric technique, chi-square.

CHI-SQUARE (χ^2)

Probably one of the most widely used nonparametric techniques is chi-square. This technique is used when data are frequencies rather than data that can be expressed in numerical values, such as test scores.

For example, suppose we asked a randomly selected group of one hundred people in a given community to respond to the following statement in terms of whether they agree with the statement, disagree with the statement, or have no opinion: "Additional taxes should be levied to finance needed services for persons over age 65." Due to the way the one hundred persons were selected, we would expect the responses to be different. Regardless of how they respond, the type of data we get from this is frequencies, or how many persons responded agree, disagree, or have no opinion. Final tabulation might look like this:

Agree	Disagree	No Opinion
30	50	20

We could look at the responses in more detail by considering the factor of age. Tabulating the responses according to age, the results might look like table 10–1.

TABLE 10–1.

Age/	Agree	Disagree	No Opinion
Under 30	5	22	6
30–60	5	16	6
Over 60	30	5	5

We note from both of these tables that the data we have to work with are total frequencies. The chi-square technique allows us to take data such as these and test hypotheses regarding how one distribution differs from some predetermined theoretical distribution. The use of chi-square for this purpose is called *testing goodness of fit*. The chi-square technique also allows us to test hypotheses regarding the significance of difference between and among groups on various responses. The use of chi-square for this purpose is called *testing for independence*. As we will see later in this chapter, both of these type of hypotheses are tested with the same procedure.

The Chi-Square Formula

The chi-square formula we will use in this chapter is presented below.

$$\chi^2 = \sum \frac{(O - E)^2}{E}$$

where

O = observed frequencies
E = expected frequencies

Preparing Data for Analysis

To use the chi-square formula, data must be prepared in terms of obtaining values for O and E.

Little calculation is required for obtaining observed frequencies since these simply represent the total frequency of each cell. The observed frequencies are totaled and entered in the appropriate cell similar to the results on the tax question illustrated earlier. The combination of cells create a contingency table the shape of which is determined by the number of cells. Contingency tables can be of any size depending upon the number of cells involved. For example, a 2×1 table would contain two cells, a 2×2 table would contain four cells, a 3×3 table would contain nine cells. The illustration on the responses of persons to the tax question when classified by age resulted in a 3×3 contingency table with nine cells.

To illustrate one procedure for obtaining expected frequencies, we will use a 2×2 table consisting of four cells. Hypothetical data in each cell represent observed frequencies. Values within parentheses represent expected frequencies.

18 (20.36)	24 (21.64)	42
14 (11.64)	10 (12.36)	24
32	34	66

The expected frequencies for this 2×2 table were obtained in the following manner:

$$32 \times 42 \text{ divided by } 66 = 20.36$$
$$32 \times 24 \text{ divided by } 66 = 11.64$$
$$34 \times 42 \text{ divided by } 66 = 21.64$$
$$34 \times 24 \text{ divided by } 66 = 12.36$$

We can see from this procedure that, to obtain the expected frequency for each cell, we multiply the column total by the row total and divide the result by the grand total. The sum of the expected frequencies for rows and columns is equal to the sum of the observed frequencies for rows and columns. We also note that what we are actually doing is applying the method of simple proportion to obtain the expected frequencies. With this in mind, we can say that the chi-square analysis is basically one of determining the proportionality of observed and expected frequencies.

Computation of Chi-Square

With both the observed and expected frequencies known, we can compute chi-square.

$$\chi^2 = \sum \frac{(O - E)^2}{E}$$

$$= \frac{(18 - 20.36)^2}{20.36} + \frac{(24 - 21.64)^2}{21.64} + \frac{(14 - 11.64)^2}{11.64}$$

$$+ \frac{(10 - 12.36)^2}{12.36}$$

$$= .27 + .26 + .48 + .45$$

$$= 1.46$$

To further illustrate the use and computation of chi-square, let's return to the original problem posed in this chapter. Suppose we were interested in conducting a survey in a given city regarding the increase in taxes to provide additional benefits for persons over age sixty-five. The question was posed to a representative group of persons residing in that city and the data were tabulated and classified according to age. With three options to respond and three classifications of age, the data were tabulated in a 3 × 3 table. Since we are interested in determining the significance of difference in the way the persons responded according to age, we are testing a hypothesis of independence. Put another way, we are interested in determining if the way the persons responded is independent of their ages.

We mentioned earlier that chi-square is used to test independence and to test goodness of fit. This is a situation where chi-square is used to test independence because our concern is with the way they responded according to their ages. This is probably the most frequent use for chi-square.

The results of the tabulation, the expected frequencies, and the marginal totals are presented in table 10–2.

TABLE 10–2.

Age/	Agree	Disagree	No Opinion	
Under 30	5 (13.20)	22 (14.19)	6 (5.61)	33
30–60	5 (10.80)	16 (11.61)	6 (4.59)	27
Over 60	30 (16.00)	5 (17.20)	5 (6.80)	40
	40	42	17	100

Completing the computation for chi-square:

$$\chi^2 = \frac{(O - E)^2}{E}$$

$$= \frac{(5 - 13.20)^2}{13.20} + \frac{(22 - 14.19)^2}{14.19} + \frac{(6 - 5.61)^2}{5.61} + \frac{(5 - 10.80)^2}{10.80}$$

$$+ \frac{(16 - 11.61)^2}{11.61} + \frac{(6 - 4.59)^2}{4.59} + \frac{(30 - 16)^2}{16}$$

$$+ \frac{(5 - 17.20)^2}{17.20} + \frac{(5 - 6.80)^2}{6.80}$$

$$= 5.09 + 4.30 + .03 + 3.11 + 1.66 + .43 + 12.25 + 8.65 + .48$$
$$= 36.00$$

The chi-square analysis yielded a value of 36.00. If additional questions were asked, this same procedure would be repeated and a chi-square obtained for each question.

Testing the Significance of Chi-Square

The basic procedure for testing the significance of chi-square is the same as it is for all other statistical values. We enter the chi-square table (Appendix G) with our computed value, the appropriate degrees of freedom, and the desired probability level.

Degrees of Freedom.   Degrees of freedom for chi-square are determined in the following manner.

$$df = (r - 1)(c - 1)$$

where

   r = the number of rows in the contingency table
   c = the number of columns in the contingency table

We note that sample size is not considered when determining the number of degrees of freedom as it is in the parametric techniques.

For our example problems, the degrees of freedom would be:

$$df = (3 - 1)(3 - 1)$$
$$= 4$$

With four degrees of freedom at the .05 level, our value of 36.00 is significant beyond the .05 level of significance.

Interpretation of Chi-Square

As we mentioned in the first part of this chapter, chi-square can be used to test independence or goodness of fit. The example given above illustrates the use of chi-square for independence. The chi-square of 36.00 tells us that a significant difference exists, by age, among the opinions the subjects hold regarding the issue. Stated another way, the responses are *not* independent of age. The chi-square value, however, does not tell us where the differences lie. In most instances, the researcher can simply inspect the data to determine the exact points of difference.

Chi-Square Applied to a Single Item

If the observed frequencies are classified into a single response pattern, such as a 3×1 table, we use chi-square to determine if the proportion of observed and expected frequencies are beyond what pure chance would allow.

To illustrate this point, consider the first example given in this chapter. A question was posed concerning the opinions of one-hundred subjects regarding additional taxes for old age benefits. If data were organized into a 2×1 table omitting the no opinion cell, we could use chi-square to test what is called a 50:50 hypothesis. In other words, we would begin by assuming that responses to the two categories would be equal. Chi-square could then be computed by following the procedure below.

Agree	Disagree
42 (50)	58 (50)

$$\chi^2 = \frac{(O - E)^2}{E}$$
$$= \frac{(42 - 50)^2}{50} + \frac{(58 - 50)^2}{50}$$
$$= 1.28 + 1.28$$
$$= 2.56$$

The hypothesis regarding the distribution of responses could also be tested using these data.

Degrees of freedom for this type of table would always be 1, therefore we would test the significance of this chi-square value with df = 1. Entering the table we note that with df = 1 we would need a value larger than

3.84 in order to rule the value significant. Since our value is only 2.56, we would accept the null hypothesis of no difference. We note from the table that, unlike the tables for t and F, values of χ^2 increase with the increase of df.

For most practical research purposes, a single classification problem such as the one described above can often be handled by simple percentage. It depends, of course, upon the nature of the study, but unless the chi-square value is necessary for proper interpretation, it may not need to be used.

Chi-Square When Frequencies Are Small

When relatively large samples are involved, chi-square is an extremely accurate technique. However, when any of the expected frequencies is small, say less than 10, the computed chi-square is likely to be an overestimate. Before pursuing this matter, a word about the chi-square distribution itself. When the degrees of freedom approach 30, the chi-square distribution approaches that of the normal curve. With this in mind, we need to take care that our sample distributions do not produce overestimates due to frequencies that are too small. We can guard against this by utilizing the following corrections.

When any observed frequency is less than 5, some sort of collapsing should be done in order to insure at least 5 observations in each cell. For example, a 5 × 2 table could be reduced to a 3 × 2 table to avoid the small frequencies. This situation occurs often when rating scales are used to collect data and the scales consist of 5 points or more. The problem usually occurs in the extreme points, particularly when the sample size is not large enough to insure the probability of getting 5 or more observations at the extreme points. Some loss of sensitivity might be lost but the chi-square analysis would be more accurate.

Small expected frequencies can also produce inaccurate chi-square values. As we mentioned before, when any expected frequency is less than 10, the computed chi-square is likely to be an overestimate. A correction formula, called the Yates' correction, should be applied when this situation arises. This formula is presented below.

$$\chi^2 = \sum \frac{(|O - E| - .5)^2}{E}$$

The formula allows us to take each observed frequency that is larger than the expected frequency to be reduced by .5, and each observed frequency that is less than the expected frequency to be increased by .5.

When our data so indicate we would use this formula in place of the chi-square formula presented earlier. When we apply this formula to the data in our example problem, which contains some expected frequencies less than 10, the result would be:

$$\chi^2 = \sum \frac{(|O - E| - .5)^2}{E}$$
$$= \frac{(5 - 13.20 - .5)^2}{13.20} + \frac{(22 - 14.19 - .5)^2}{14.19}$$
$$+ \frac{(6 - 5.61 - .5)^2}{5.61} + \frac{(5 - 10.80 - .5)^2}{10.80}$$
$$+ \frac{(16 - 11.61 - .5)^2}{11.61} + \frac{(6 - 4.59 - .5)^2}{4.59}$$
$$+ \frac{(30 - 16 - .5)^2}{16} + \frac{(5 - 17.20 - .5)^2}{17.20}$$
$$+ \frac{(5 - 6.80 - .5)^2}{6.80}$$
$$= 4.49 + 3.77 + .002 + 2.60 + 1.30 + .18$$
$$+ 11.39 + 7.96 + .25$$
$$= 31.94$$

We can see that this chi-square value is somewhat smaller than the one previously computed using the regular formula. Testing the hypothesis with df $= 1$, we note that the same decision is made even though the value is smaller. It is possible, however, to make an incorrect decision on a hypothesis because a correction for small frequencies was not employed.

To avoid an inaccurate decision on a hypothesis, a good rule to follow is that of combining cells when you have observed frequencies less than 5 and to employ the Yates correction when any of the expected frequencies is less than 10. This rule should be followed even though some evidence exists to support the notion that the chi-square analysis can tolerate approximately 20 percent of the expected frequencies less than 10 without jeopardizing the analysis.

Chi-Square for Goodness of Fit

The chi-square technique can also be used to determine if a set of data is normally distributed with regard to some known or theoretical distribution. The procedure is basically the same as for chi-square for independence with the exception of the manner in which the hypotheses are stated and the expected frequencies are obtained.

One of the most common uses for chi-square in this regard is to determine if a set of sample data approximates the normal distribution. The following example illustrates goodness of fit in this manner.

An Example Problem.   Let's assume that we are interested in determining if the number of hours spent preparing for a comprehensive examination by a sample of graduate students is a chance variation from a normal distribution. In a problem such as this, we would be testing a hypothesis that the sample distribution of hours spent preparing for the examination came from a normal distribution.

After selecting our sample and obtaining the desired data, we organize our data into a simple frequency distribution utilizing class intervals to conserve space and effort (table 10–3). From this distribution we esti-

TABLE 10–3.   Frequency Distribution for Time Spent Preparing for a Comprehensive Examination by 103 Graduate Students.

Time (Hours)	Number of Students
Less than 10	10
10 but less than 20	28
20 but less than 30	35
30 but less than 40	18
40 but less than 50	12

mate a mean of 25.6 and a standard deviation of 11.40. These estimates are derived by the group data method (see chapter 1).

The next step is to standardize the class boundaries by subtracting the mean from each boundary and dividing the result by the standard deviation. We accomplish this task by using the following formula:

$$z = \frac{b - \bar{X}}{s}$$

where

z = standard score (z-score)
b = upper limit of each class

We employ this formula for each class interval in the following manner.

For the first class (less than 10):

$$z_1 = \frac{10 - 25.6}{11.40}$$
$$= -1.37$$

For the second class (10 but less than 20):

$$z_2 = \frac{20 - 25.6}{11.40}$$
$$= -.49$$

For the third class (20 but less than 30):

$$z_3 = \frac{30 - 25.6}{11.40}$$
$$= .39$$

For the fourth class (30 but less than 40):

$$z_4 = \frac{40 - 25.6}{11.40}$$
$$= 1.26$$

For the fifth class (40 but less than 50):

$$z_5 = \frac{50 - 25.6}{11.40}$$
$$= 2.14$$

After the z-scores have been obtained, we take these values to the normal curve table (Appendix B) and determine the area associated by each z-score. You might want to review the material in chapter 2 before attempting this procedure.

For the first class, we find the area to the left of a z-score of -1.37 (area in the smaller portion of the curve) is .0853. This tells us that if the data are from a normal distribution with a mean of 25.6 and a standard deviation of 11.40, 8.5 percent of the sample values is the expected percentage for the first class interval.

With this information, we can obtain the expected frequency for the first class by taking the appropriate percentage of the total sample.

$$E_1 = (.0853)(103)$$
$$= 8.79$$

We now follow basically the same procedure for the other four classes. The area for the remaining classes, though, is the difference between the preceding percentage of area and the z-score for the class being computed. If problems occur in obtaining the desired area, review the procedure again in chapter 2.

For the remaining four classes, we compute the expected frequencies in the following manner.

$$E_2 = (.2268)(103)$$
$$= 25.03$$

$$E_3 = (.3396)(103)$$
$$= 34.98$$

$$E_4 = (.2445)(103)$$
$$= 25.18$$

$$E_5 = (.0876)(103)$$
$$= 9.02$$

We are now ready to enter these expected values into a chi-square table (table 10–4).

TABLE 10–4.   Chi-Square Table for Goodness of Fit.

Class	O	E
Less than 10	10	8.79
10 but less than 20	28	25.03
20 but less than 30	35	34.98
30 but less than 40	18	25.18
40 but less than 50	12	9.02

With our observed and expected frequencies obtained, we can now compute chi-square in the usual way.

$$\chi^2 = \sum \frac{(O - E)^2}{E}$$
$$= \frac{(10 - 8.79)^2}{8.79} + \frac{(28 - 25.03)^2}{25.03} + \frac{(35 - 34.98)^2}{34.98}$$
$$+ \frac{(18 - 25.18)^2}{25.18} + \frac{(12 - 9.02)^2}{9.02}$$
$$= .17 + .35 + 0 + 2.05 + .98$$
$$= 3.55$$

Degrees of Freedom.   Degrees of freedom for a goodness of fit problem will be equal to the number of classes (intervals) less one, minus the number of parameters we estimated in order to find the expected values.

For the normal distribution with an unknown mean and standard deviation, we must estimate both parameters. With this in mind, the degrees of freedom are determined by: $K - 3$, where K is the number of classes less one minus the two parameters to be estimated. For our problem, the degrees of freedom will be $4 - 2 = 2$.

Interpretation

Entering the chi-square table (Appendix G) with 2 degrees of freedom, we find the table value to be 5.99 at the .05 level. Since our calculated value of 3.55 is less than the table value of 5.99, we conclude that the normal distribution does provide a good fit to the data. In other words, we accept the null hypothesis that the data came from a normal population.

SAMPLE STUDY

The following sample study illustrates the use of chi-square for independence in a manner which is common to behavioral science research. The study concerns itself with analyzing responses to various questions with respect to two categories. In essence, the study is attempting to determine if the responses to the questions are independent of the type of recreational activity they pursue.

Since the study is rather long, some parts have been omitted to conserve space. However, all the study that deals with the chi-square analysis has been retained.

A Study of Conflict in Recreational Land Use: Snowmobiling vs. Ski-Touring*

It is well recognized that increased leisure has brought about increased conflict over the use of public recreation areas. Outdoor recreation is especially prone to conflict because it is in outdoor recreation that the values of solitude, freedom and property are deliberately sought; and it is these values which are the most vulnerable to crowding.

But it is not only crowding that is responsible for conflicts. Various forms of recreation (or activities) have proven to be incompatible. Now here is the conflict more heated than in the battle between advocates of motorized recreation vehicles and those that prefer the self-propelled forms of transport, such as hiking, canoeing, bicycling, etc. (Baldwin 1970; Dunn 1970).

---

*Timothy B. Knopp and John D. Tyger, "A Study of Conflict in Recreational Land Use: Snowmobiling vs. Ski-Touring," reprinted from *Journal of Leisure Research* 5 (Summer 1973): 6–17, by permission of the publisher.

At first glance it appears to be a simple conflict; each group is fighting to gain or retain territory. Yet the defenses each group presents for its position reveal a misunderstanding of the other's viewpoint or a basic difference in philosophy. The ORV (off road vehicle) enthusiasts often argue that they (and their machines) are entitled to the use of any public recreation area because it is "public."

Their opponents contend that certain activities alter the environment in a way that limits the opportunities available to others. The "one way" nature of the conflict probably helps to explain the lack of understanding between conflicting groups. The motorized vehicle literally destroys the quiet, undisturbed, natural environment the self-propelled recreationist is often seeking. The vehicle operator is often quite tolerant, even oblivious, of the person on foot.

Emotion generated in this confrontation is much more intense than a simple difference in choice of outdoor pursuit would seem to warrant. Recreation activities often serve as a symbolic identification for a cultural group. At a recent public hearing one of the authors heard proponents of ORVs refer to their opponents as "long-haired unemployed hippies" and "elitist millionaires." The same group often refer to themselves as "patriotic," "family people," or "hard-working middle-class citizens." The ORV user has often been stereotyped as "lower-class, uneducated and consumer oriented."

At this point the questions arise: Are the participants in these conflicting forms of recreation "different kinds of people"? Does each of these groups have a distinct set of attitudes and values? Do these attitudes help to determine which activities they select? Are these attitudes and values, in turn, associated with major cultural trends? If we can relate cultural trends to demand for recreational opportunities we will be in a better position to anticipate and reduce conflicts.

The primary objective of the study described in this paper was to investigate the relationship between participation in two forms of outdoor recreation and attitudes toward the environment and public land management. It was designed to test the following hypotheses:

• Those individuals who engage in motorized forms of recreation are less likely to have "environmentalist" values than those who prefer self-propelled forms of recreation.

• Those individuals who engage in motorized recreation are less likely to understand and/or sympathize with the concept of devoting specific recreation areas for distinct purposes than are those who prefer activities with less environmental impact.

These hypotheses were examined in Minnesota by comparing the participants in two conflicting forms of outdoor recreation—snowmobiling and ski touring. These two activities are incompatible for both physical and aesthetic reasons. Snowmobiles can ruin a ski track and may make the trail hazardous. The snowmobile itself adds an element to the environment that most ski tourers are trying to avoid (Coggeshall, 1971). A good deal of the resentment on the part of ski tourers may be due to snowmobilers being capable of using more space in a given unit of time.

This conflict has, in fact, all of the ingredients of a classic battle. The "frontier" was there for the taking. Minnesota's winters remained an untapped resource for years. The land abounded in those very elements which are becoming scarce in the urban environment: solitude, freedom, clean air, and unspoiled nature.

Both antagonists arrived on the scene at *almost* the same time. The snowmobile, in part because of the commercial sales campaign associated with its introduction, secured a four to five year advantage and has well established battlements supported by powerful economic interests.

At this point in time, it is difficult to predict the final outcome. There are some indications that the popularity of snowmobiling is leveling off: an industry spokesman stated that 75 percent of current sales are to repeat customers. Ski touring has just become a visible alternative for the general public.

Minnesota is an ideal area in which to examine this conflict. Both forms of recreation have experienced phenomenal growth during the past few years. In 1972, the number of registered snowmobiles in the state was approaching 300,000. Snowmobile manufacturing has become a $30 million industry in the state.

Ski touring has experienced a different kind of growth *sub-rosa* for many years. It wasn't until the winter of 1971–1972 that it received a large amount of exposure to the general public. During the winter of 1971–1972 almost every major magazine published an article describing the basic characteristics and appeals of ski touring. It is difficult to determine the number of participants; ski sales are probably the best measure. Sales have been roughly estimated at 20,000–30,000 pairs in the St. Paul-Minneapolis Metropolitan area. Most observers agree that participation will show a sharp increase during the 1972–1973 season.

METHODS

It is very difficult to identify the population of those who participate in a given form of recreation; thus it is almost impossible to obtain a completely unbiased sample. The only method this writer can conceive of is to randomly sample the entire population and select from that sample those who indicated that they participate. Obviously this would be very costly and inefficient.

In the case of snowmobilers, the problem was somewhat simplified in that Minnesota requires the registration of their machines. This listing, however, does not have a one-to-one relationship to the people who snowmobile. There is a degree of non-compliance, *i.e.*, unregistered snowmobiles. Snowmobile owners are not the only ones who snowmobile. An owner's children may make more use of the machine than he does. For our purposes it may be more important to sample owners than users. Those who purchase snowmobiles are making a decision which contributes the most to the growth of the sport and thus to the demand for areas and facilities.

Our sample was selected in a systematic-random fashion from a listing of approximately 250,000 registered snowmobiles, supplied by Minnesota in June of 1971. The listing was in chronological order as the requests were received; thus there is no reason to believe that a systematic selection biased the sample in any way.

Ski tourers are the only group with which we could make a relevant comparison to snowmobilers. These individuals are utilizing the same resource at the same time. However, the ski touring population is much more difficult to identify. To date, the impact of the purchase and use of their equipment has not been deemed significant enough to warrant registration.

At the time of the study there was a single large ski touring club centered in the Minneapolis-St. Paul area with members throughout Minnesota. This organization had experienced very rapid growth since its conception in 1967. The membership at the time the sample was taken consisted of approximately 50 percent new members, i.e., those who had joined in the past year. We can probably assume that most of these persons were attracted to the club because it offered a means for them to find out about an unfamiliar form of recreation. The membership was not, by and large, made up of long time participants in ski touring or club activities. The sample consisted of 100 percent of the June 1971 membership of the North Star Ski Touring Club.

As the results of this study are reported it would be well to keep in mind the character of the populations sampled; although, for the sake of efficiency, these will be referred to as "snowmobilers" and "ski tourers."

A questionnaire was prepared and mailed in June of 1971. Rate of returns (after two follow-up letters) was 70.4 percent for the snowmobile sample and 86.6 percent for the ski touring sample. In designing the questionnaire, we attempted to conceal that it had any direct concern with either snowmobilers or ski tourers. That is, we sought to obtain a measure of attitudes that would be least affected by their interest in a particular activity.

The specific items used to measure these attitudes are given in Tables 1 and 3. The respondent was asked to indicate whether he strongly agreed, agreed, disagreed, strongly disagreed or was undecided in respect to each statement. The questionnaire was introduced to the respondent to ascertain public opinions on important environmental issues. There was no indication that the results would be used to compare participants in two different forms of recreation.

Standard socioeconomic parameters were obtained and used as a basis for comparing the two samples. Both were then compared with the 1970 census data for Minnesota to determine how each group differed from the

TABLE 1. Responses to Environmental Issues: Snowmobilers and Ski Tourers, 1971.

1. We need the Alaskan oil pipline in spite of possible environmental hazards.

	(1) S.A.	(2) AGR.	(3) UND.	(4) DIS.	(5) S.D.	χ^2	p	mean	var.
Snowmobilers %	6.6	21.0	26.4	27.0	19.2	38.9	*	3.31	1.42
Ski Tourers %	0.9	7.3	21.4	28.6	41.8			4.03	1.01

2. Mass transit systems should be substituted for the automobile in our cities.

	(5) S.A.	(4) AGR.	(3) UND.	(2) DIS.	(1) S.D.	χ^2	p	mean	var.
Snowmobilers %	22.0	42.9	14.3	16.1	4.8	57.3	*	3.61	1.29
Ski Tourers %	56.8	32.3	3.6	5.0	2.3			4.36	0.88

3. Pollution is a price we have to pay for economic progress.

	(1) S.A.	(2) AGR.	(3) UND.	(4) DIS.	(5) S.D.	χ^2	p	mean	var.
Snowmobilers %	3.6	11.2	4.1	47.9	33.1	23.2	*	3.96	1.15
Ski Tourers %	1.4	4.6	2.3	35.6	56.2			4.40	0.73

4. Public monies should be spent to protect an endangered species of wildlife.

	(5) S.A.	(4) AGR.	(3) UND.	(2) DIS.	(1) S.D.	χ^2	p	mean	var.
Snowmobilers %	28.6	53.6	6.6	9.5	1.8	25.5	*	3.98	0.90
Ski Tourers %	51.4	40.0	5.0	2.3	1.4			4.38	0.64

5. Pesticides are essential and their effect on wildlife should not be a major consideration.

	(1) S.A.	(2) AGR.	(3) UND.	(4) DIS.	(5) S.D.	χ^2	p	mean	var.
Snowmobilers %	1.2	8.9	7.1	43.8	39.1	20.9	*	4.11	0.92
Ski Tourers %	0.9	1.4	7.4	32.9	57.4			4.44	0.59

6. Conservation groups should be allowed to prevent the development of flood control dams.

	(5) S.A.	(4) AGR.	(3) UND.	(2) DIS.	(1) S.D.	χ^2	p	mean	var.
Snowmobilers %	10.8	26.4	21.0	33.5	8.4	28.1	*	2.98	1.37
Ski Tourers %	22.0	33.5	26.2	15.1	3.2			3.56	1.19

7. Development of the SST should have been continued in spite of possible environmental effects because it means more jobs and a boost to the economy.

	(1) S.A.	(2) AGR.	(3) UND.	(4) DIS.	(5) S.D.	χ^2	p	mean	var.
Snowmobilers %	3.0	10.7	17.2	37.9	31.4	29.7	*	3.84	1.16
Ski Tourers %	0.5	4.1	11.0	27.1	57.3			4.37	0.87

8. Certain parkways should be closed to automobiles in order to reduce traffic and encourage walking and bicycling.

	(5) S.A.	(4) AGR.	(3) UND.	(2) DIS.	(1) S.D.	χ^2	p	mean	var.
Snowmobilers %	22.0	55.4	10.1	10.1	2.3	40.8	*	3.84	0.92
Ski Tourers %	53.6	35.4	5.4	4.6	0.9			4.36	0.72

9. Potential mineral deposits should not be left undeveloped in wilderness areas such as the Boundary Waters Canoe Area.

	(1) S.A.	(2) AGR.	(3) UND.	(4) DIS.	(5) S.D.	χ^2	p	mean	var.
Snowmobilers %	6.6	17.3	9.5	41.7	25.0	18.5	*	3.61	1.48
Ski Tourers %	4.1	4.1	9.2	20.6	61.9			4.32	1.15

*Significant at .01 level
Snowmobilers: N = 169
Ski tourers: N = 220

state population. These differences will be referred to when they offer possible explanations for differences in attitudes.

ATTITUDES TOWARD ENVIRONMENTAL ISSUES

The first set of statements was presented to solicit responses to several well publicized environmental issues. None of these concerned the use of snowmobiles. An attempt was made to avoid other issues with which the respondent may have been directly involved. Because there are so many attitudes affecting the response to each statement (which may create ambivalence within the individual), we could not expect a great deal of consistency. Nevertheless, we felt that by utilizing several issues we would have a basis for comparing the two samples.

A chi-square test was used as a measure of significance. Also, an "index" was determined by calculating a mean after assigning a value to each response. The highest numbers were attached to those responses consistent with published resolutions of groups such as the Sierra Club, Wilderness Society and other "environmentalist" organizations.

Results showed a significant and consistent difference between the samples on all nine items, i.e., the ski tourers were much more likely to conform to the environmentalist image. Both groups, however, had an index above the "undecided" level of the scale on all but one item. Without a control group it is impossible to say how these groups differed from the general population. . . .

ATTITUDES TOWARD PUBLIC RECREATION LAND MANAGEMENT

It is relatively easy for the average person to understand that a public library or a public road is intended for a specific use. Their perception of a park or other recreation land area is much more subjective. Often individuals will not comprehend that recreation is not a homogeneous entity and that to provide different experiences we must have different environments. This concept implies the administration of controls over how an area is developed and used.

In this study we utilized seven statements attempting to derive a measure of the respondent's understanding and/or sympathy with the concept that distinct areas must be provided for certain recreational uses. A higher number was assigned to responses indicating a greater degree of agreement with the concept.

Here again, as in the case of the "environmentalist" measure, the differences in the responses were both significant and consistent in direction. The ski touring sample showed much more agreement with the principle of the use of controls to maintain environments.

TABLE 4.   Responses to Public Recreation Land Management Issues: Snowmobilers and Ski Tourers, 1971.

1. In any public park or forest a person should be allowed to enjoy his
own kind of recreation.

	(1) S.A.	(2) AGR.	(3) UND.	(4) DIS.	(5) S.D.	χ^2	p	mean	var.
Snowmobilers %	10.2	31.7	3.6	46.7	7.8	82.8	*	3.10	1.50
Ski Tourers %	4.2	6.0	7.4	41.9	40.6			4.09	1.09

2. "Multiple use" in regard to our public lands means that every possible
use should be made of every acre of public land.

	(1) S.A.	(2) AGR.	(3) UND.	(4) DIS.	(5) S.D.	χ^2	p	mean	var.
Snowmobilers %	7.7	22.5	11.2	46.2	12.4	72.4	*	3.33	1.39
Ski Tourers %	1.8	5.9	8.2	33.8	50.2			4.24	0.93

3. A number of different types of recreation areas ought to be maintained
in order to provide a large number of choices for the individual, even
though this may mean some areas will get very little use.

	(5) S.A.	(4) AGR.	(3) UND.	(2) DIS.	(1) S.D.	χ^2	p	mean	var.
Snowmobilers %	8.9	50.9	13.0	24.8	2.4	84.3	*	3.39	1.06
Ski Tourers %	48.4	40.6	4.2	6.0	0.9			4.29	0.76

4. Some recreation activities should not be permitted in some areas because
they disturb other recreationists.

	(5) S.A.	(4) AGR.	(3) UND.	(2) DIS.	(1) S.D.	χ^2	p	mean	var.
Snowmobilers %	19.5	65.1	4.7	10.1	0.6	80.0	*	3.93	0.70
Ski Tourers %	64.6	29.8	1.9	2.8	0.9			4.54	0.57

5. It is possible to provide every kind of recreation opportunity within a
few miles of everyone's home.

	(1) S.A.	(2) AGR.	(3) UND.	(4) DIS.	(5) S.D.	χ^2	p	mean	var.
Snowmobilers %	3.0	13.0	4.1	61.5	18.3	11.1	**	3.79	0.97
Ski Tourers %	5.6	9.7	8.8	49.1	26.8			3.81	1.22

6. Wilderness areas, that is, areas where roads and mechanized travel are
prohibited, are only used by a few wealthy individuals; therefore the
public should not pay the cost of providing these areas.

	(1) S.A.	(2) AGR.	(3) UND.	(4) DIS.	(5) S.D.	χ^2	p	mean	var.
Snowmobilers %	11.9	24.4	13.7	31.6	18.4	124.4	*	3.20	1.74
Ski Tourers %	1.4	2.8	1.8	25.5	68.5			4.57	0.62

7. Protecting a natural environment is not worthwhile if it means keeping
out motorized transportation and therefore discouraging those who are
less physically able to enter under their own power.

	(1) S.A.	(2) AGR.	(3) UND.	(4) DIS.	(5) S.D.	χ^2	p	mean	var.
Snowmobilers %	4.8	14.3	11.9	41.7	27.4	78.1	*	3.72	1.32
Ski Tourers %	0.5	3.2	1.4	26.3	68.7			4.59	0.52

*Significant at .01 level
**Significant at .05 level
Snowmobilers: N = 169
Ski tourers: N = 220

CONCLUSIONS

Probably few participants in either snowmobiling or ski touring identify with a particular ideology; more likely they are simply trying to enjoy themselves. Still, as researchers, it may be valuable to identify a set of attitudes which can be associated with specified activities.

With the limited evidence provided by this study it is impossible to say whether attitudes determine participation or participation determines attitudes. No doubt there is some influence in both directions; although the authors would expect the latter to be dominant. Certainly there are many other factors as important as these attitudes in determining participation in recreational activities.

However, a laissez faire attitude, anything goes on public land, may help to reduce any resistance a person might have to identify with a sport as controversial as snowmobiling. An attitude of concern toward protecting the environment could have an opposite effect. All else being equal, the person who is about to choose between two forms of recreation may be swayed one way or the other by his generalized attitudes. This would be especially true if the two activities are conflicting or mutually exclusive.

REFERENCES

Baldwin, Malcolm F. 1970. The Off-Road Vehicle and Environmental Quality. Washington, D.C.: The Conservation Foundation.

Bosselman, Fred and David Callies. 1971. The Quiet Revolution in Land Use Controls, Council on Environmental Quality. Washington, D.C.: U.S. Government Printing Office.

Coggeshall, Almy D. and Harry N. Roberts. 1971. Snowmobiles and Ski Touring: A Study in Recreational Conflicts. Eastern New York Ski Touring Association.

Dunn, Diana R. 1970 Motorized Recreational Vehicles . . . On Borrowed Time. Parks and Recreation, July.

Harry, Joseph, Richard Gale and John Hendee. 1969. Conservation: An Upper-middle Class Social Movement, Journal of Leisure Research, 1 (Spring): 246–254.

FOR REVIEW AND FURTHER STUDY

1. The relationship between pupils' self-concepts (above average vs. below average) and whether they were grouped homogeneously or heteroge-

neously in the classroom was examined by Dyson.[1] The following data
were obtained from a sample of 568 seventh-grade students.

Self Concept

	Below Average	Above Average	Totals
Classroom Homogeneous	108	137	
Grouping Heterogeneous	164	159	
Totals			

   a. Complete the contingency table.
   b. Test the hypothesis of independence of self-concept and classroom
      grouping in the population sampled.
2. If a student responded to a 95-item true-false test and had 55 correct
   answers, would this differ significantly from what would be expected by
   chance?
3. An experiment[2] to test the relative effectiveness of two procedures for
   teaching an introductory education course included an investigation into
   whether either procedure was more influential on a students' decisions to
   become teacher. Responses to a question regarding the influence the
   course had on their decision to become teachers yielded results shown in
   the following incomplete table.

Groups	Positive Influence	No Influence	Negative Influence	Total
Experimental	14	62	2	
Control	17	37	1	
Total				

   a. This table would be called a ——— × ——— contingency table.
   b. Complete the contingency table.
   c. Compute chi-square (consider use of Yates' correction).
   d. What conclusion would be appropriate to the hypothesis that the in-
      fluence of the course on students' decisions to become teachers is in-
      dependent of the teaching approach?

   1. Ernest Dyson, "A Study of Ability Grouping and the Self-Concept," *The
Journal of Educational Research* 60 (1967): 403–5.
   2. Joe D. Cornett, and Walter Butler, "Effect of a Team Approach in Achieving
the Objectives of an Introductory Course in Education," *The Journal of Educational Research* 63:5 (January 1970): 222–24. (This study is described in chapter
9 of the text.)

4. Suppose a study utilized a cultural awareness test to examine concepts of American Indians, resulting in the following sample of scores. A normal distribution of scores on this test by typical Americans has a mean of 50 and standard deviation of 10. Examine the hypothesis that the population studied exhibits a normal distribution of cultural concepts.

33	76	53	71	73
18	20	74	68	69
54	57	37	58	54
47	64	39	61	40
44	75	64	43	69
81	36	67	43	73
55	33	73	32	32
19	20	61	31	33
21	78	57	65	72
52	48	19	50	34
80	51	33	47	
61	54	28	41	
60	20	43	46	
54	62	40	25	
52	55	48	23	

5. A school counselor wished to determine if the students in his school exhibited a normal distribution of academic abilities. If he tested the students with a Stanford-Binet Form M intelligence test, he might collect data as summarized in the following table.[3] The table utilizes class intervals of 10 and includes scores for 2970 students. It also shows the 2-score for each class interval and the proportionate area under the curve expected on this test. Complete the table for goodness of fit, compute chi-square, and interpret the results.

Table for Goodness of Fit,
Standard-Binet IQs, Form M

IQ	O	2	Proportionate Area	E	$O - E$	$(O - E)^2/E$
160	3 ⎫	2.645	.0041			
150	13 ⎬ 16	2.645	.0041			
140	55	2.057	.0158			
130	120	1.468	.0512			
120	330	.879	.1186			
110	610	.291	.1958			
100	719	−.298	.2316			
90	592	−.886	.1950			
80	338	−1.475	.1177			
70	130	−2.064	.0506			
60	48	−2.652	.0155			
50	7 ⎫ 12		.0040			
40	4 ⎬					
30	1 ⎭					
Totals	2970		.9999			

3. Quinn McNemar, *Psychological Statistics,* 3d ed. (New York: John Wiley and Sons, Inc., 1962), p. 232.

11

Using the Computer

The purpose of this chapter is to provide some basic instruction on how to use a computer for statistical analyses. As you have probably noticed, hand calculation for statistical problems is practically out of the question. For some types of problems, particularly those of a single classification nature, a desk calculator can accomplish the task quite well. However, when multiple classification techniques are employed and rather large sample sizes are used with single classification techniques, computation with a desk calculator can become a very time-consuming process. For more complex problems, the most efficient and accurate way of obtaining desired statistical information is through the use of a computer.

In this chapter we will look at the computer as a computational tool, a tool that can provide a service to us in computing data. We will not concern ourselves, at this point, with the computer itself other than general comments that seem necessary to explain how it is used. Again, we will approach the discussion of this subject from the standpoint of a user and look upon the computer as a rather sophisticated extension of a desk calculator that analyzes our data automatically rather than manually.

To be an effective user, we must be able to tell the computer what we want done in such a way that we obtain the desired results. Computer centers vary, of course. Each center requires the performance of some unique procedures before the computer can be used. We believe, however, that once the general procedure for using a computer is known, you will be able to make the necessary adaptations without much trouble.

STATISTICAL LIBRARIES

Much in the same way that a regular library contains reference material, the statistical library houses computer programs. A computer program is simply a predeveloped set of instructions which a computer employs to analyze data. These programs consist of detailed instructions on how the data are to be analyzed. For example, a computer program on the *t*-test is a computer language description of the *t*-test formula. With a few exceptions, computer programs are available for most of the statistical techniques commonly used by behavioral science researchers.

There are basically two ways of giving instruction to a computer. The first is to *write* a program. This approach requires that a person, using the appropriate computer language, write a specific set of instructions for the computer. For example, if a single classification analysis of variance is to be employed, the programmer must write the instructions for this procedure much in the same way as you would construct a step-by-step description in regular language. The second, and by far the most reasonable approach, is to use a set of instructions that has already been written. Our task, then, becomes one of selecting the desired program and applying the program to our data in such a way that we obtain the desired results.

Some Common Programs

Computer programs have been prepared by a variety of sources. Some are locally prepared to fit a particular kind of machine and some come from sources outside a given center and are designed to be used with a wide variety of computing machines.

One of the most popular sets of computer programs is the Biomedical Series (BIMED) developed at U.C.L.A. Although these programs were developed primarily for the medical field, they are widely used by behavioral science researchers. Most computer centers have a manual of these programs for reference which consists of detailed information regarding the types of programs available and the procedures for using them. Manuals describing other program series are also available at most centers.

An example of some of the BIMED programs available are listed below.

BMDO1D	Simple Data Description
BMDo1R	Simple Linear Regression
BMDO1V	Analysis of Variance for One-Way Design
BMDO3V	Analysis of Covariance for Factorial Design

The analysis of variance for one-way design, for example, provides the following output:

1. sums of squares for within groups, between groups, and total;
2. degrees of freedom for all sources of variation;
3. mean squares for within groups and between groups;
4. F value.

You will recall that this is the exact information needed to test a hypothesis using a single-classification analysis of variance.

A computer program does the same thing with a set of data that we could do with a desk calculator. The only difference is that a computer can do the job much more quickly and efficiently than we can using some other means.

PREPARING DATA FOR THE COMPUTER

The procedure we will follow here is that of taking a sample problem and describing the procedure for preparing the data for computer analysis.

Sample Problem

Let's assume that we are interested in making a comparison between two groups of subjects on the results of an attitude scale administered after a sharp rise in the cost of living. The comparison is to be made between a group of self-employed subjects and a group of salaried subjects. The scale is designed to measure attitudes toward the taxation of excess profits. Our hypothesis for this problem would be:

H_{o1} There will be no difference in attitudes regarding the taxation of excess profits between a group of self-employed subjects and a group of salaried subjects.

We randomly select our subjects and administer the scale. For our purposes we will assume an N of 15 for the first group and an N of 15 for the second. The size of the N is somewhat lower than we might actually use for a study of this nature but for our purposes it will suffice.

The data obtained as a result of administering the scale are presented in table 11–1.

TABLE 11–1. Attitude Scores for Two Groups of Subjects.

Group 1 (Self-employed)						Group 2 (Salaried)					
32	23	46	19	19	22	56	46	68	41	39	49
13	22	38	42	16	20	40	42	58	57	39	41
26	32	15				52	45	45			
		$\bar{X} = 25.67$						$\bar{X} = 47.87$			

Transferring Data to Cards

After our data are organized into the appropriate groups, we must transfer these data to computer cards. The computer card, or punch card, is the means used by the computer to "read" the data.

The punch card is a rectangular card consisting of eighty vertical columns and twelve horizontal rows (see figure 11–1). You will notice

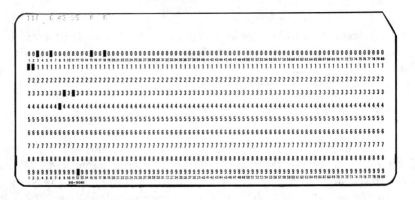

FIGURE 11–1. A Punch Card.

that only ten rows (0 through 9) are actually designated on the card. The other two rows are in the blank area above the "0" row. These rows are devoted to punching letters or certain other characters such as plus or minus.

When data are recorded on a punch card, they are punched into each column by means of a *keypunch machine* which is similar to a common typewriter. Instead of a printed character, the keypunch produces a hole in the card that corresponds to the desired value. A device called a *card reader* senses these holes and transmits the information to the computer. Thus, the punch card is simply the means for transmitting data to the computer.

Normally, data are recorded on cards by beginning at column 1 and punching sequentially the information that is to be recorded. In figure 11–1, we recorded six numbers on the card (the translation at the top serves as a check on what we have punched). These numbers, 110, 0, 43, 39, 0, 0, can be read by the punched out area on the card. The number 110, for example, occupies the first three columns and the rows corresponding to 1, 1, and 0.

When recording data on cards, decimal points are not used. These are taken care of on a card that will be described later. For example, if you wish to punch the number 42.6, you would record this number on the card as 426.

The number of columns allotted to a particular variable on the punch card is called a *field*. Depending upon the maximum size of any single observation, the appropriate field is determined. For example, the data recorded on the card in figure 11–1 contain numbers of three, two, and one digits. The field for these data, then, is three.

An important point to remember when recording data on cards is that the numbers should be "right justified." This means that the last digit of an observation should be punched as far to the right of a given field as possible. In figure 11–1, we see that the field is three and the single digit numbers, such as 0, are recorded to the far right of the field. In listing form, we would right justify these numbers in the following manner.

$$110$$
$$0$$
$$43$$
$$39$$
$$0$$
$$0$$

Using a keypunch machine is a simple task and does not require any special skill. To help you use this machine, consult an instruction booklet or seek help from computer center personnel.

For our problem we have a total of thirty scores, fifteen in the first group and fifteen in the second. We will need a card for each score, a total of thirty. Figure 11–2 illustrates how the first card in the data deck would look after punching it with the number 32 (the first score in Group 1).

Selecting a Program

Knowing that the *t*-test is the technique we wish to use, we go to the statistical library and select this program. In some cases, several *t*-test

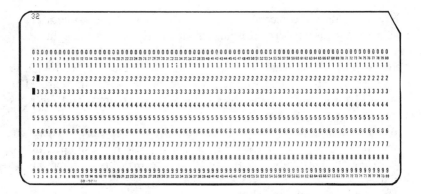

FIGURE 11–2. A Punched Card for the First Score (32) in Group 1.

programs are available. To select the one that best fits your needs, computer center personnel should be consulted. Although we want to use the computer on our own, we should not hesitate to ask for help when we need it.

Preparing Instructions for the Computer

Contrary to popular belief, a computer can do only what it is told to do. On a desk calculator, the results of a single multiplication problem can only be obtained by pressing the proper keys. In the same way, a computer must be instructed on what to do with the data you have provided.

These instructions consist of a series of punch cards containing information relative to how the computer is to read the data and what it is to do with the data.

Computer systems available to the user of statistical programs vary, making it necessary to prepare instructions according to the format specified by a particular computer center. The procedure used in one location may need to be adapted to another location. There are, however, enough common requirements that, once learned, can apply to most situations. The unique requirements can be learned by exploring your own computer center and consulting with center personnel.

For most programs, the instructional sequence, listed in the order of submission, consists of the following cards:

1. System Cards
2. Program Deck
3. Execute Card

4. Control Cards
5. Variable Format Card
6. Data Cards
7. Finish Card
8. End-of-File Card

If you were using a BIMED program, for example, specific instructions are provided for punching these cards. Instructions are also available for other types of programs.

System Cards. In order to "get on" a computer in such a way that it will run a program, a set of cards, called system cards, must be prepared. This is one stage of preparing data for the computer that almost always has to be done to local specifications because of differences in computer systems and differences in computer center requirements. However, system cards usually consist of a job card, an execute card, and a card that instructs the computer to begin operation. In many situations, the cards that pertain to the program or the system do not have to be prepared by the user as they are pre-prepared by the center and simply inserted at the appropriate place. The two system cards that normally require input from the user are the job card and the execute card.

The job card contains the program name, the user's account number, the user's name, and any other information that a given situation requires to get a job run. For our sample problem, utilizing the requirements of one system, the job card was punched in the following manner.

//SAMPROB JOB (11870020),CORNETT,CLASS=A

where

    // tells the computer that control information is to follow. // must appear in columns 1 and 2.

    CLASS=A=the priority of the job (how soon it will be run and finished)

The other information specifies the name of the job (SAMPROB; a name invented for this situation), the word "JOB" which automatically must appear, the account number, and user's name.

In essence, the job card tells who wants the program run, how it will be billed, when it will be run, and any other information needed for administrative purposes.

The execute card identifies for the computer the specific program that is to be used. The execute card for our sample problem was punched in the following manner.

// EXEC TTEST

Program Deck.   The program deck is the specific set of instructions that enables the computer to perform the desired statistical analysis. From a user's standpoint, it is not necessary to understand these instructions in that they are written in various types of computer languages. The primary concern is that the user have the data in such a form that the identified program can be used.

Control Cards.   The control cards are used to provide specific information about the data in order for the program to operate. These cards tell the computer such things as the number of variables, number of groups, number of observations, and the designation of what available options the user desires. The number of control cards needed depends upon program requirements and needs of the user. More cards would be needed for a highly complicated analysis with multiple options than would be needed with a rather simple analysis.

For our sample problem, only three control cards were punched. The first control card contained the word "PROBLM," the job name, the number of variables, the number of groups, and instructions to rewind the input unit after reading. The first control card punched is presented in figure 11–3.

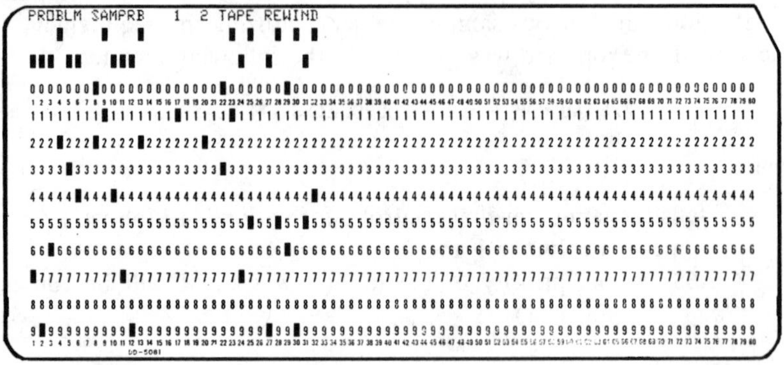

FIGURE 11–3.   A Control Card.

The card presented in figure 11–3 was punched from a set of instructions prepared specifically for this program. The instructions were:

Control Card 1:

    Col. 1– 6 "PROBLM"
           8–13 JOBNAME
         15–17 Number of Variables

      19–20 Number of Groups
      22–25 "TAPE"
      27–32 "REWIND"

You will note in figure 11–3 the information has been punched in accordance with the program instructions. The control cards for any program must be prepared according to a set of instructions indicating how and where the information should be punched on a card. As we have mentioned before, this information is found in the various program manuals.

Variable Format Cards. The variable format cards are the means by which we tell the computer how we want the data read. When we punch a five-digit number on a card, the computer must know how we want the number read. For example, the number 123.45 is punched on a data card as 12345. The variable format card allows us to specify how the number should be read since decimal points are not punched on the card.

Several formats are used to describe the way data should be read but the F-type format is one of the most frequently used. The general F-type format is as follows.

$$Fw.d$$

where

    F = indicates that the data are numeric
    w = indicates the width of a field
    d = indicates the number of digits to the right of the decimal point

The F-type format for the number 12345 if we wish it to be read 123.45, would be:

$$F5.2$$

In this case, the F indicates that the variable is numeric, 5 indicates the width of the field is 5, and the 2 indicates that it contains two digits to the right of the decimal point.

If the numbers you are working with are negative, the space occupied by the sign must be included in the width of the field. It is not necessary to sign a positive number in that if a sign is not provided the number is read as positive. The negative number -4954.2, for example, would be punched on the variable format card as follows.

$$F6.1$$

Table 11–2 illustrates the format specifications for different kinds of numbers.

TABLE 11–2.

Your Data	Punched on Card As	Format Specification
48	48	F2.0
368.45	36845	F5.2
16.386	16386	F5.3
1.36	136	F3.2
−4.32	−432	F4.2
−1381.2	−13812	F6.1

In the previous discussion, we talked about a format specification for a single number. In some cases, such as our sample problem, the data are all the same width, therefore, only one format specification needs to be made. In other instances, we may have several different types of data on the same card. When this is the case, we use the following form.

$$Fw.d, Fw.d, \ldots, Fw.d$$

For example, if we had three different kinds of data punched on each card, say IQ, GPA, and a two-digit test score, the variable format card would be punched in the following manner.

$$F3.0, F3.2, F2.0$$

Since all the data in our sample problem are two-digit numbers, the variable format card was prepared very simply as shown in figure 11–4.

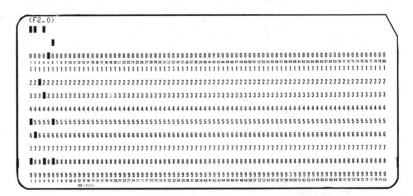

FIGURE 11–4.   A Variable Format Card.

Data Cards.   These are the cards containing your data. The procedure for transferring data to card was discussed earlier in this chapter.

Finish Card.   The purpose of a finish card is to tell the computer that the end of the data for a given group has been reached. When groups are being compared, for example, a finish card is sometimes required at the end of the data for each group. The use of this card, or its equivalent, depends upon the particular system being used.

End-of-File Card.   This is the last card and is used to tell the computer that all the necessary input has been received. At this point the computer begins to compute the program, produce a print-out, and end its attention to your program.

The finish card and the end-of-file card are normally pre-prepared by the computer center and automatically inserted into your program, therefore requiring no action on your part except to be sure that they are included.

We will mention again that the number and kinds of card needed to use a statistical program depends upon the type of program and the system requirements. With manuals available, however, this can be done without much trouble by following the instructions given for a particular program.

Beginning on this page, an example of such a set of instructions is provided. These instructions, taken from a locally prepared manual used to compute our sample problem data, tell the user what kind of information must be punched on the control cards and where it should be punched. You will find on most program descriptions a number of things that may not be applicable to your needs. In this case, simply indicate on the card the items that you want and omit punching in the columns the items that you do not want.

TTEST—TEXAS TECH T-TESTS

LIMITATIONS:

    200   VARIABLES MAXIMUM.
     20   GROUPS MAXIMUM.

OUTPUT:

    1.   VARIABLE NUMBER.
    2.   NUMBER OF OBSERVATIONS FOR EACH VARIABLE.

3. MEANS.
4. MEAN SQUARE.
5. STANDARD DEVIATION.
6. STANDARD ERROR OF THE MEAN.
7. COEFFICIENT OF VARIANCE.
8. MINIMUM VALUE.
9. MAXIMUM VALUE.
10. COEFFICIENT OF SKEWNESS.
11. COEFFICIENT OF KURTOSIS.
12. F-RATIO AND ITS PROBABILITY ADJUSTED FOR MULTIPLE GROUPS.
13. T-TEST AND ITS PROBABILITY ADJUSTED FOR MULTIPLE GROUPS.

CONTROL CARD 1:

COL. 1– 6: "PROBLM".
      8–13: JOBNAME.
     15–17: NUMBER OF VARIABLES IN THE LARGEST GROUP.
     19–20: NUMBER OF GROUPS.
     22–25: "TAPE": INPUT IS ON DATA SET 10, EITHER DISK OR TAPE.
     27–32: "REWIND": REWIND THE INPUT UNIT AFTER READING.

CONTROL CARD 2:

COL. 1– 6: "SAMPLE".
      8– 9: NUMBER OF THE GROUP.
     11–15: NUMBER OF CASES IN THE GROUP.
     17–19: "RAW": USING RAW DATA FOR THIS GROUP.
         "   ": USING "N", MEANS, AND STANDARD DEVIATIONS
                 FOR THIS GROUP.
     21–22: NUMBER OF VARIABLE ELIMINATION CARDS.
     24–25: NUMBER OF DATA ELIMINATION CARDS.
        27: NUMBER OF FORMAT CARDS FOR "N" IF NOT USING RAW
             DATA: OR NUMBER OF FORMAT CARDS IF USING RAW DATA.
        29: NUMBER OF FORMAT CARDS FOR MEANS.
        31: NUMBER OF FORMAT CARDS FOR STANDARD DEVIATIONS.

CONTROL CARD 3:

COL. 1– 6: "ELEMVA".
      3– 9: NUMBER OF VARIABLES TO BE ELIMINATED.
     11–13: NUMBER OF THE VARIABLE TO BE ELIMINATED.
     14–16:   "
     17–19:   "

CONTROL CARD 4:

    COL. 1– 6: "ELEMDA".
           8– 9: NUMBER OF VARIABLES WITH DATA TO BE ELIMINATED.
         11–13: NUMBER OF THE VARIABLE.
         14–20: DATA VALUE TO BE ELIMINATED.
         21–23: NUMBER OF THE VARIABLE.
         24–30: DATA VALUE TO BE ELIMINATED.

             ·
             ·

         71–73: NUMBER OF THE VARIABLE.
         74–80: DATA VALUE TO BE ELIMINATED.

CONTROL CARD 5:

    COL. 1–72: FORMAT OF THE DATA.
                  DATA DECK MUST FOLLOW IMMEDIATELY.

CONTROL CARD 6:

    COL. 1– 6: "FINISH".

         CONTROL CARDS 1–5 AND A DATA DECK MAY BE REPEATED AS MANY
         TIMES AS DESIRED WITH CONTROL CARD 5 FOLLOWING ONLY THE
         LAST DATA DECK.

         CONTROL CARDS 2–5 MUST BE REPEATED ONCE FOR EACH GROUP IN
         THE PROBLEM.

Sample Problem Solution

After the system and control cards were punched for our sample problem, they were submitted, along with the data deck, to the computer. The computer print-out for this problem is presented in figure 11–5. We can see from this print-out that all the information we need to make a decision on our hypothesis is present. Means and standard deviations for both groups are provided along with the F value that reveals the homogeneity of variance between these two groups. We note that this F value is not significant. Finally, we have the t value of 6.461 which is significant at the .01 level. Our hypothesis, therefore, would be rejected on the basis of a t value of 6.46 with 28 degrees of freedom.

```
*******************
*******************
**T-TEST SUMMARY TABLE**
*******************
*******************
```

```
************************************************************
************************************************************
**VAR  GROUP  N  XBAR  SD  GROUP  N  XBAR  SD  F-RATIO  P/  T-TEST  P/**
************************************************************
************************************************************
```

**VAR	GROUP	N	XBAR	SD	GROUP	N	XBAR	SD	F-RATIO	P/	T-TEST	P/**
** 1 **	2	**15	47.87	8.63	1	15	25.67	1.01	1.38	NS	6.461	01**

```
************************************************************
************************************************************
```

FIGURE 11–5.   Computer Print-Out.

For illustration purposes, we will work our sample problem with a desk calculator and compare the results.

$$
\begin{aligned}
t &= \frac{\bar{X}_1 - \bar{X}_2}{\sqrt{\dfrac{\Sigma x_1{}^2 + \Sigma x_2{}^2}{n_1 + n_2 - 2}(1/n_1 + 1/n_2)}} \\[2mm]
&= \frac{25.67 - 47.87}{\sqrt{\dfrac{1435.33 + 1043.73}{15 + 15 - 2}}(1/15 + 1/15)} \\[2mm]
&= \frac{22.20}{\sqrt{\dfrac{2479.06}{28}}(.14)} \\[2mm]
&= \frac{22.20}{3.52} \\[2mm]
&= 6.31
\end{aligned}
$$

We note a slight difference between the computer result and the desk calculator result. This is due primarily to differences in rounding. In most instances hand calculation will differ slightly from computer calculation. If these differences are great, however, the program should be run again to be sure the results are accurate. We should keep in mind that a computer will do only what it is told to do. Most errors occur from the human standpoint, either in punching data on cards or some other factor associated with giving instructions to the computer. To avoid the most common error, punching data on cards, the cards should be verified before submitting them to the computer.

FOR REVIEW AND FURTHER STUDY

Instead of providing some specific exercises at the conclusion of this chapter, we suggest that the best way to learn how to use a computer is to use it. With this in mind, get some data, real or manufactured, determine the statistical technique you wish to use, and go on an exploration trip to the computer center.

It might be well if your data are small in number and your statistical technique is uncomplicated. This will give you a better chance of completing your mission.

You will make mistakes but that is to be expected. The advantages of a working knowledge of computer use will far exceed the effort in learning how to use it.

12

Exercises in
the Selection and
Interpretation of
Statistical Analyses

This chapter is intended to provide the student with additional opportunities to apply the concepts and techniques studied in the previous chapters. The suggested activities at the end of each chapter have been provided to encourage application of the concepts and techniques explained in that particular chapter. We now come to the point of assuming the role of a researcher as he selects research and statistical techniques appropriate to the study of a problem, utilizes those techniques, and interprets the findings in relation to the identified problem or question.

The chapter will be divided into two sections. The first section will include typical studies concerned with: (1) determining relationships (simple and multiple), (2) determining differences (use of t-test, analysis of variance, and analysis of covariance), and (3) use of chi-square techniques in nonparametric statistics. The second section will be devoted to interpreting and drawing conclusions from analyses.

SELECTION

Various kinds of research studies in the behavioral sciences will be excerpted or summarized. In each case, the student should complete all or

227

selected portions of the following: (1) state the problem, (2) write a hypothesis suitable to the problem, (3) identify the kinds of data that will be needed to examine the hypothesis and show how the data might be acquired, and (4) select the appropriate technique for analysis of the data to be acquired. To compare proposed treatment of a study to the way it was actually carried out, reference to the original description of the study is recommended.

A. A study was designed to evaluate certain hypotheses in respect to the structure of attitudes, and the relation of these attitudes to the political beliefs and voting patterns of Communists and Fascists in Great Britain. One part of the study was concerned with determining if Communists and Fascists were different in terms of being classified as radical or conservative. An instrument identified as "Melvin's Amplified Form of Eysenck's R and T Scale" was used to determine individual differences in radical or conservative persuasion.[1]

B. Another part of the Eysenck and Coulter study compared Communists, Fascists, and an "average" group of citizens as being classified as radical or conservative.

C. A study of automobile accidents and injuries included an attempt to determine the relationship between the age of the driver and seat belt use.[2]

D. A group of counselor educators wished to determine if there would be a significant difference in learning among students who were given a choice of learning counseling theories by means of three different forms of instructional materials: prose-text, linear programmed instruction, or branching programmed instruction.[3]

E. It has been stated that the expectancies of teachers affects the achievement of students. A study designed to test this theory seeks to determine if teachers' expectations of significant progress by some students would cause those students to make more progress in learning than other students of similar ability. A recent study of this theory utilized a procedure in which teachers were given fictitious information indicating

---

1. H. J. Eysenck, and Thelma T. Coulter, "The Personality and Attitudes of Working Class British Communists and Fascists," *The Journal of Social Psychology*, June 1972, pp. 59–73.

2. Frank J. Vilardo, "Vehicle Damage Scale for Traffic Accident Investigators: An Investigation of Its Use and Potential for Predicting Driver Injury," *Journal of Safety Research*, December 1973, pp. 229–237.

3. Avraham Scherman, and Marion Scherman, "Free-Choice, Final Performance and Attitudes Toward Different Types of Programmed Instruction," *Journal of Education*, February 1973, pp. 56–63.

that certain students in classes of educationally disadvantaged boys and girls had exceptional latent ability, according to a test which they had been given.[4]

F. Assume that a particular school district wishes to determine which one of three academic abilities tests best predicts teacher grades in four subject areas (English, mathematics, science, and social studies).

G. Research was conducted to determine if concepts of school law could be effectively taught, using simulated materials presented audio-tutorially, to preservice teachers. The researcher wished to evaluate differences in learning with this teaching technique as compared to learning with traditional lecture methods. He also wished to determine if two other variables, either individually or in combination, significantly affected learning in this situation. The other variables were: (a) having completed student teaching, and (b) college grade-point average.[5]

H. To compare effectiveness of seven teaching methods according to attention to the speaker, topic, course, and college was the purpose of a study utilizing "consciousness sampling" to supply necessary data. Consciousness sampling is a technique whereby subjects are caught by surprise and asked in effect, "What was it you were thinking about in the split second before I surprised you." This sampling was carried out while the seven teaching methods being studied were in use: lecture, discussions, buzz sessions, panel, student-led exercise, problem solving, and movies. The study included two major purposes: (1) comparison of the seven teaching methods according to whether students' attention during the class was on the speaker, the course, the topic, college life, or time (past, present, future); (2) comparison of these results according to whether the students were undergraduate or graduate.[6]

I. The relationship between teacher understanding of basic mathematical concepts and pupils' use of abilities to master arithmetic was investigated to determine the importance of teacher understanding to student learning in mathematics classes. Data for the study were gathered by giving three tests and one inventory to students (California Achievement Test, Arithmetic, 1951, Form AA and Form BB; California Achievement Test,

4. Glen E. Mendels, and James P. Flanders, "Teachers' Expectations and Pupil Performance," *American Educational Research Journal* 10:3 (Summer 1973): 203–11.

5. Richard P. Manatt, "A Comparison of Audio-Tutorial and Lecture Methods in Teaching," *The Journal of Educational Research* 69:9 (May-June 1970): 414–18.

6. James R. Schoen, "Use of Consciousness Sampling to Study Teaching Methods," *The Journal of Educational Research* 63:9 (May-June 1970): 387–90.

Reading, 1951, Form AA; Henmon-Nelson Test of Mental Ability; and an Arithmetic Interest Inventory). These tests yielded correlations between arithmetic interest, arithmetic achievement, reading achievement, and mental ability. The Glennon Test of Basic Mathematical Understandings was administered to teachers.[7]

J. A major purpose of a study of aging blacks in North Carolina was to compare the responses of males and females to questions about which spouse made certain kinds of decisions. Subjects were asked whether husband or wife usually made a certain kind of decision or if the decision was shared equally. Items included were:

> Making major household decisions
> Making and paying bills
> Buying life or burial insurance
> Job husband should take
> Job wife should take
> To work or not to work
> Amount to be spent on food
> Doctor to obtain in illnesses.[8]

K. Researchers studying graduate school admission requirements desired to compare university undergraduate grades with scores on the Graduate Record Examination. If a high correlation existed, there would seem to be little justification for using both criteria to make decisions about graduate school admission. Intercorrelations of the eight semesters of undergraduate grades were obtained. Controls for sex and college enrollment within the university were desired. The Graduate Record Examination includes three major divisions: verbal aptitude, quantitative aptitude, and an advanced test to measure achievement in the student's major field of study.[9]

L. A study is proposed to determine the relationship between type of undergraduate school attended and later success in graduate school. As a part of the study, it is desired to determine how the size of students' home towns affects the relationship between type of undergraduate school attended and success in graduate school.

---

7. Harrell Bassham, "Teacher Understanding and Pupil Efficiency in Mathematics—A Study of Relationship," *The Arithmetic Teacher*, November 1962, pp. 383–87.

8. Jacquelyne Johnson Jackson, "Marital Life Among Aging Blacks," *The Family Coordinator* 21:1 (January 1972): 21–27.

9. Lloyd G. Humphreys and Thomas Taber, "Postdiction Study of the Graduate Record Examination and Eight Semesters of College Grades," *Journal of Educational Measurement* 10:3 (Fall 1973): 179–84.

M. A study of divorce is designed to determine if couples receiving premarital counseling, postmarital counseling, and no counseling differ in divorce rate. Controls for age, ethnic group, and socioeconomic status are desired.

N. A study seeks to determine if the height distribution is normal among Japanese adults who, as children under age 5, sustained radiation injury from the atomic bombing of World War II.

INTERPRETATION

The examples included in this section will provide the student with opportunities to interpret data and other information collected and processed in the course of carrying out several kinds of studies. Attention should be given to appropriateness of research methods and statistical treatment, conclusions to be drawn from the study, significance level of conclusions, limitations and reservations relative to conclusions, and the like.

A. In study D by Scherman and Scherman (page 228), evaluation instruments to measure retention of factual information when the different forms of instructional materials were used resulted in scores showing gains in factual knowledge. Analysis of variance yielded the following table of information.

Analysis of Variance Test for Gainscore Effects

Source of Variation	SS	df	MS	F
Between Groups	2502.03	3	834.01	9.72
Within Groups	11325.60	132	85.80	
Total	13827.63	135		

What conclusions may be drawn from interpretation of the table?

B. Twenty-six Mississippi children were tested with the Wechsler Preschool and Primary Scale of Intelligence (WPPSI) and the Stanford-Binet Intelligence Scale, Form L-M, to assess the usefulness of the WPPSI with culturally disadvantaged, lower socioeconomic children. One of the hypotheses for this study stated that no significant difference would exist between the WPPSI scores (verbal, performance, and full scale) and Stanford-Binet, Form L-M scores. The following table shows the t ratios between these scores. Determine the validity of the hypothesis according to these t-scores.[10]

SCALE	t
Verbal	11.629
Performance	0.015
Full Scale	13.043

C. The predictive validity of reading readiness scores for school achievement in the primary grades was investigated in two different school systems. The Metropolitan Readiness Test and the Metropolitan Achievement Test were used in one district (District A). In the other district (District B) the Ginn Pre-Reading Test and Stanford Achievement Test were used. The following table shows the relationship of composite readiness scores (Metropolitan) and achievement scores (Metropolitan) in

Grade	Word Meaning	Word Discrimination	Reading	Spelling	Language
1	.55	.47	.70	N.A.	N.A.
2	.59	.49	.59	.45	N.A.
3	.56	.50	.52	.44	.57

$N = 100$

the first three grades of District A. The next table shows the relationship of composite readiness scores (Ginn) and achievement scores (Stanford) in grades two and four of District B. Determine the significance of the

Grade	Word Meaning	Paragraph Meaning	Spelling	Word Study Skills	Language	Battery Composite
2	−.07	−.06	−.04	.05	.12	.11
4	.22	.08	−.02	.12	.06	N.A.

$N = 103$

---

[10] Erwin L. Shatus, "Validation of the Wechsler Preschool and Primary Scale of Intelligence with the Stanford-Binet Form L-M, on Culturally Deprived Children," *The Southern Journal of Educational Research* 4:1 (January 1970): 18–36.

relationship shown between reading readiness test scores and reading achievement scores.[11]

D. In the study by Ashburn, correlation coefficients (point-biserial) were computed between composite readiness scores and sex in school districts A and B. They were as follows:

A   .04

B   .01

Interpret these findings.

E. An attempt was made to delineate ability, achievement, and personality variables which differentiate students having positive attitudes toward school from those with negative attitudes. The California Study Methods Survey (CSMS) was used to measure student attitudes toward school. Forty-six students who scored at least 1.3 SD above the national mean on the attitudes toward school scale of the CSMS were designated as the positive group, and sixty-five who scored at least 1.3 SD below the normative mean were designated the negative group. Various instruments were used to measure ability, achievement, and personality variables of the students in the two groups. The first table on page 234 shows the means and t ratios for the two groups.[12]

F. The study by Hountras and Brandt mentioned in Case 1 of chapter 9 also analyzed differences in ACT composite standard scores among students of five colleges in a university according to their type of residence (residence hall, at home, or off-campus other than at home). Write appropriate hypotheses for this aspect of the study, complete the summary table on page 234, and make appropriate interpretations.

G. In order to compare the knowledge of human sexuality acquired by students in various fields of study, their SKI (Sex Knowledge Inventory) scores were analyzed.[13] These scores had been obtained by various researchers from medical students, law students, students at the Wurzweiler School of Social Work, and the general population of college students. The table on page 234 summarizes the score data.

---

11. Patricia Sue Ashburn, "Predictive Validity of Beginning Readiness in Relation to Reading Achievement in Primary Grades in Selected Southern Mississippi Schools," *The Southern Journal of Educational Research* 3:1 (January 1969): 59–70.

12. Robert L. Williams, "Personality, Ability, and Achievement Correlates of Scholastic Attitudes," *The Journal of Educational Research* 63:9 (May-June 1970): 401–3.

13. Naomi R. Abramowitz, "Human Sexuality in the Social Work Curriculum," *The Family Coordinator* 20:4 (October 1971): 349–54.

Means and t Ratios for Attitudinal Groups (Ex. E)

Dependent Variables	t	df	Satisfied Mean	Dis-satisfied Mean	Normative Mean	SD
Language IQ	6.61†	119	114.19	98.46	100.00	16.00
Non-language IQ	3.24*	119	106.66	98.73	100.00	16.00
Total IQ	5.82†	119	110.66	98.78	100.00	16.00
Reading Achievement[1]	4.82†	119	112.69	100.15		
Mathematics Achievement[1]	4.05†	116	115.40	103.36		
Physical Self	3.93†	117	72.32	66.58	71.78	7.67
Moral—ethical Self	4.30†	117	70.80	64.61	70.33	8.70
Personal Self	5.17†	117	67.25	59.81	64.55	7.41
Family Self	4.08†	117	71.08	65.12	70.83	8.43
Social Self	3.79†	117	69.49	64.03	68.14	7.86
Total Self-concept	5.08†	117	349.94	320.55	345.57	30.70
Bell Adjustment[2]	−8.26†	115	38.71	66.96		
Grade Point Average	6.37†	115	87.00	78.21		

*p .01. †p .001.
1. Achievement indices were computed by dividing S's achievement age by his chronological age to obtain an Achievement Quotient (AQ).
2. Masculinity–femininity indices were deleted from the total Bell scores.

Two-Way Analysis of Variance for the Differences in ACT
Composite Standard Scores for Students
in Five Colleges (Ex. F)

Source of Variation	SS	df	MS	F
Columns (C) (Colleges)	545.59	4	136.40	
Rows (R) (Residence)	1.78	2	.89	
$R \times C$	2.52	8	.32	
Within	2462.28	255	9.66	
Total				

A Comparison of W.S.S.W. Student SKI Scores
with Other Professional Students (Ex. G)

Professional School	Mean Score	N	S.D.
W.S.S.W.—Beginning	53.6	18	6.0
W.S.S.W.—Advanced	56.9	17	4.0
Shatin's Study of Freshman Medical Students	59.5		5.59
Sheppe and Hain's Study			
Freshman Medical Students	61.9	50	5.79
Fourth Year Medical Students	69.0	31	3.04
Freshman Law Students	59.7	41	7.31
Third Year Law Students	61.3	19	5.16
Standard Mean of College Population	55		

What conclusions may be drawn from this study?

H. Thirty couples having marital problems were randomly assigned to three groups: (a) a control group receiving no treatment; (b) a group receiving eight hours of programmed instruction on communication in marriage; and (c) a group receiving eight hours of counseling emphasizing marital communication.[14] Reconciliation decisions following treatments were as indicated below.

Comparisons Between Groups on Posttreatment Reconciliation Agreements

Group	Reconciliation	No Reconciliation
Control	3	7
Programmed Text	5	5
Control	3	7
Counseled	9	1
Programmed Text	5	5
Counseled	9	1

Using the proper analytical calculations (note small frequencies) compare the results of the treatments and propose conclusions.

I. Elkind, Deblinger, and Adler[15] sought to determine if the conditions under which a test of creativity was given might affect the results of the testing. Two conditions were varied. One procedure took thirty-two students from either an interesting or uninteresting activity and gave them the creativity test (motivating-condition). The other procedure tested half of the children under the "uninteresting" condition first and the "interesting" condition second, whereas the reverse was followed for the other half of the group (order-of-motivating condition). These two conditions thus became the within subjects variables. The between subjects variable was termed the "groups-under-order-of-motivating-condition." F-values obtained were:

Motivating condition	51.56
Order of motivating condition	2.14
Groups under order of motivating condition	1.20

What conclusions seem warranted on the basis of this study?

---

14. Margaret E. Hickman, and Bruce A. Baldwin, "Use of Programmed Instruction to Improve Communication in Marriage," *The Family Coordinator* 20:2 (April 1971): 121–25.

15. David Elkind, Joann Deblinger, and David Adler, "Motivation and Creativity: The Context Effect," *American Educational Research Journal* 7:3 (May 1970): 351–56.

J. It was hypothesized that kindergarten children who participated in Project Head Start would be superior in the following verbal communication abilities: (a) ability in telling a story, (b) ability to structure sentences, (c) enunciation.[16] The following tables show the ratings obtained on these skills from children in a Head Start group and a matched sample of children who did not go through a Head Start program. Interpret these findings.

Verbal Ability: Telling a Story

Story-telling Rating	Number of Children Receiving Each Rating	
	Head Start (35)	Non-Head Start (35)
4	10	4
3	11	7
2	6	10
1	7	11
0	1	3

Ability to Structure Sentences

Scale Rating for Sentence Structure Used	Number of Children Receiving Each Rating	
	Head Start (35)	Non-Head Start (35)
3	22	11
2	9	14
1	3	5
0	1	5

Enunciation Ratings

Clarity of Speech Rating	Number of Children Receiving Rating	
	Head Start (35)	Non-Head Start (35)
2	22	15
1	13	20

16. Eleanor S. Kaplan, " 'Head Start' Experience and the Development of Skills and Abilities in Kindergarten Children," (mimeographed.)

K. Hunkins "sought to determine whether a dominant use in social studies text-type materials of analysis and evaluation questions, as defined by Bloom's *Taxonomy,* would effectively stimulate the development of sixth grade pupils' social studies achievement." The overall hypothesis tested, stated in null form, was:

> Use of text-type materials employing questions requiring "analysis" and "evaluation" will not result in differences in sixth grade pupils' social studies achievement when compared with the use of text-type materials incorporating questions requiring the recall of knowledge in relationship to pupils' (a) reading level, (b) sex, and (c) the interaction between these variables.[17]

Analysis of covariance treatment of the data yielded the following summary. Draw conclusions.

Source of Variation	Original		Adjusted			
	d.f.	S.S.	d.f.	S.S.	M.S.	F
Treatment	1	12.06	1	10.05	10.05	9.85
Reading level	3	133.55	3	65.02	21.67	21.24
Sex	1	.92	1	.92	.92	.90
Treatment × reading level	3	.49	3	.23	.07	.06
Treatment × sex	1	.75	1	.26	.26	.25
Reading level × sex	3	2.29	3	.63	.21	.20
Treatment × reading level × sex	3	8.06	3	7.21	2.40	2.35
Within groups	244	269.88	243	247.98	1.02	

L. A study at the University of Illinois[18] examined "the degree to which measures of aptitude and undergraduate preparation obtained before the beginning of doctoral study are predictive of the 'success' of psychology graduate students." Criterion measures included course grades and progress and potential ratings at the end of the first year of graduate study, Graduate Record Examination scores (verbal aptitude, quantitative aptitude, and advanced test in psychology), indicators of foreign language facility, undergraduate grades, and rated quality of student's undergraduate school. Success ratings six years after the students began their graduate work provided the long-term criterion.

The tables on pages 238–40 summarize the results of the study and analysis of relationships. How might they be interpreted?

17. Francis P. Hunkins, "The Influence of Analysis and Evaluation Questions on Achievement in Sixth Grade Social Studies," *Educational Leadership Research Supplement,* January 1968, pp. 326–32.

18. J. Richard Hackman, Nancy Wiggins, and Alan R. Bass, "Prediction of Long-Term Success in Doctoral Work in Psychology," *Educational and Psychological Measurement* 30 (1970): 365–74.

Predictor-Criterion Relationships

	Core Content Course I	Core Content Course II	Core Quantitative Course I	Core Quantitative Course II	End of Year GPA	Self-reports: Speed to Degree	Self-reports: Plans to Continue	Faculty ratings: Making Normal Progress	Faculty ratings: Encourage toward Ph.D.	Long-term Criterion Global Assessment of "success" six years after enrollment
Aptitude and Ability										
GRE-Verbal	.30*	.14	.26	.03	.22	.45*	.23	.21	.20	.19
GRE-Quant.	−.12	−.05	.56*	.50*	.15	.40*	.03	.29	.23	.32*
GRE-Advanced (Psych.)	.35*	.24	.13	−.14	.23	.23	.16	.08	.12	−.11
Foreign Languages facility										
No. languages spoken	−.42*	.05	.19	.28	.04	−.04	−.39*	−.04	.10	−.21
No. languages read	−.29	.29	.28	.33*	.19	.07	−.47*	.01	.28	−.25
No. hours language taken as undergrad.	−.10	.07	−.03	−.13	−.06	−.20	−.25	−.03	−.02	−.34*
Undergraduate grades										
GPA last two yrs.	.24	.29	−.04	.07	.28	.02	−.04	−.08	.05	−.22
GPA psychology	.24	.31*	.04	.22	.34*	.14	.20	.21	.07	−.05
GPA mathematics	.13	.13	.06	.21	.22	.20	−.14	−.02	.22	−.28
GPA phys. science	−.12	.01	−.07	−.08	−.19	−.17	.00	−.32*	−.24	−.50*
GPA biology	.06	.14	−.22	.03	.04	−.09	−.14	−.32*	−.05	−.31*
GPA sociology	.11	.13	−.19	.29	.20	.12	.02	−.09	.17	−.02
Rated Quality Undergrad. School	.00	−.13	.21	.16	.15	.30*	.16	.31*	.08	.43*

$N = 42$.
*$p = <.05$.

Relationships among the Predictors

	1	2	3	4	5	6	7	8	9	10	11	12	13
1. GRE-V	—												
2. GRE-Q	.24	—											
3. GRE-A	.60*	-.02	—										
4. Number of languages spoken	-.25	.10	-.33*	—									
5. Number of languages read	-.03	.20	-.06*	.65*	—								
6. Number of undergraduate hours of language	-.05	.05	.21	-.02	.20	—							
7. GPA-overall	.04	-.22	.18	.04	-.11	.14	—						
8. GPA-Psych	.16	-.18	.15	.02	-.04	.04	.75*	—					
9. GPA-Math	-.27	.00	-.07	.17	.12	.11	.52*	.35*	—				
10. GPA-Science	-.17	-.17	.08	.17	.07	.20	.27	.15	.39*	—			
11. GPA-Biology	-.16	-.19	-.14	.30*	.12	-.15	.48*	.28	.51*	.52*	—		
12. GPA-Sociology	-.26	.07	-.08	.18	.13	.22	.49*	.39*	.65*	.40*	.34*	—	
13. Quality of undergraduate school	.22	.30*	.24	.20	-.09	-.20	-.33*	-.26	-.39*	-.25*	-.28	-.35*	—

$N = 42$.
*$p < .05$.

Relationships between First-year and Long-term Criteria

End-of-first-year Criteria	Global assessment of "success" six years after enrollment
Course Grades	
Core Content Course I	.28
Core Content Course II	−.08
Core Quantitative Course I	.19
Core Quantitative Course II	.28*
End-of-year GPA	.24
Self-reports	
Speed to degree	.50*
Plans to continue	.45*
Faculty ratings	
Making normal progress	.56*
Encourage toward Ph.D.	.35*

$N = 42$.
*$p < .05$ (one-tailed).

Practice Problems

The problems presented in this section of the text are designed to provide practice in computing the various statistical measures and techniques. The problems are keyed to each chapter and the answers are provided at the end of the section.

CHAPTER 1

1. Find the mean and median for the following group of salaries. Which would be the most useful measure for use in salary negotiations?

$15,000	6,900
7,500	13,500
7,250	6,700
6,500	8,950
10,650	

2. Find the mean and median of the data in the following frequency distribution.

X	f	X	f
30	1	23	6
29	1	22	4
28	0	21	2
27	0	20	0
26	3	19	2
25	5	18	0
24	6	17	1

3. Find the mean and median of the following scores.
   A. 24, 18, 19, 12, 23, 20, 21, 22
   B. 20, 16, 12, 19, 16, 18, 16
   C. 24, 18, 19, 20, 22, 25, 23, 12

4. Construct a histogram for the following data.

Scores	f	Scores	f
20–24	1	55–59	8
25–29	1	60–64	6
30–34	0	65–69	7
35–39	3	70–74	4
40–44	5	75–79	4
45–49	6	80–84	2
50–54	6	85–89	1

5. Construct a frequency distribution using the data below. Group the data using intervals of four.

65	41	48	80	64	66
67	67	64	59	68	76
72	68	76	60	72	67
75	94	39	48	63	61
71	61	54	57	61	27
59	69	78	62	57	65
68	86	46	64	57	68

6. Construct a bar graph using the following data representing the average number of workers absent from work per day.

Monday	46.3
Tuesday	30.8
Wednesday	36.2
Thursday	26.0
Friday	31.4

CHAPTER 2

1. Determine the standard deviation for the following set of data.

80	88
92	83
75	71
57	87
97	65
77	92
86	82
90	84
67	

2. Determine the variance of the data in problem 1.

3. Compute the standard deviation for the following data.

16	9
14	9
13	8
12	7
12	7
12	7
11	6
10	4

4. Compute the variance for the data in problem 3.

5. Compute the standard deviation for the following data.

750	620
710	580
690	570
680	550
660	510

6. Subtract 500 from each score in problem 5 and compute the standard deviation again.

7. Given the following data with a standard deviation of 78.00 and a mean of 632, convert each to a z-score.

   a. 750   f. 620
   b. 710   g. 580
   c. 690   h. 570
   d. 680   i. 550
   e. 660   j. 510

8. Given the following z-scores, determine the area under the curve for all scores greater than and less than each score.

   a. 1.52
   b. .61
   c. −2.15
   d. −.97
   e. 2.71

9. Find the corresponding area from the mean to each score.

   a. .35
   b. −1.74
   c. −.85
   d. 1.40
   e. 3.09

10. Find the area under the curve:

from	to
a. .42	1.04
b. −1.06	−1.75
c. −.94	2.11
d. −.52	1.30
e. −1.61	.47

CHAPTER 6

1. Ten persons made the following scores on two simple tests. Compute a Pearson r for these data.

Subject	Test 1	Test 2
1	25	12
2	24	16
3	22	10
4	21	14
5	20	12
6	18	10
7	17	9
8	16	8
9	15	7
10	13	2

2. Compute the degrees of freedom for problem 1.

3. Using the data in problem 1, test the hypothesis $r = 0$ at the 0.5 level.

4. Determine the degree of relationship between the following two sets of data using the Pearson r.

X	Y
32	11
31	17
30	16
29	15
29	15
27	16
27	13
27	12
25	9
23	9
22	13
21	9
20	11
18	11
17	10

5. Compute the degrees of freedom for problem 4.

6. Using the data in problem 4, test the hypothesis $r = 0$ at the .05 level.

7. Estimate the point biserial coefficient, using the graph, for the following data.

Test Score	Number Answering a Single Question Correctly	Number Answering a Single Question Incorrectly
10	3	1
9	5	2
8	6	0
7	8	2
6	7	5
5	9	4
4	3	3
3	4	7
2	1	6
1	3	8
0	2	9

8. Compute an equation to predict test scores with the following information. Determine an equation for predicting both X from Y and Y from X.

$$\Sigma X = 191 \qquad \Sigma Y = 100 \qquad \Sigma XY = 2030 \qquad N = 10$$
$$\Sigma X^2 = 3789 \qquad \Sigma Y^2 = 1138 \qquad r = .8630$$

9. Using the information below, compute an equation for predicting Y scores from X scores and X scores from Y scores.

$$\Sigma X = 130 \qquad \Sigma Y = 100 \qquad \Sigma XY = 1440 \qquad N = 10$$
$$\Sigma X^2 = 1878 \qquad \Sigma Y^2 = 1138 \qquad r = .87$$

10. Compute a Spearman *rho* for the following data.

Subject	X	Y	Subject	X	Y
1	100	23	9	84	14
2	98	20	10	81	16
3	95	25	11	79	21
4	90	19	12	76	18
5	88	12	13	76	16
6	87	22	14	72	13
7	87	20	15	70	12
8	85	17			

11. Compute a Pearson *r* for the data in problem 10 and compare your answers.

12. Twelve different speeches on the same topic have been scored by two judges. What is the correlation between the ranking of the two judges?

Speaker	Judge 1	Judge 2
1	49	28
2	44	18
3	37	14
4	48	21
5	51	23
6	30	13
7	40	16
8	44	16
9	34	13
10	48	21
11	40	15
12	31	12

CHAPTER 8

1. Two groups of subjects were given the same test with the following results.

   $\bar{X}_1 = 10.33$ $\bar{X}_2 = 9.23$
   $\Sigma X_1{}^2 = 226.61$ $\Sigma X_2{}^2 = 212.31$
   $N_1 = 12$ $N_2 = 13$

   a. Compute a t value for these data.
   b. Test a null hypothesis at the .05 level.

2. Two groups of subjects were exposed to a different version of an experiment on perception. Is there a significant difference between the means of the two groups?

Group 1	Group 2
16	14
14	8
12	7
12	6
10	4
8	4
6	12
4	

3. Compute a t on the data in problem 2 using the separate variance formula and compare the results.

4. Given the following data:

   $\bar{X}_1 = 26.66$ $\bar{X}_2 = 26.14$
   $\Sigma X_1{}^2 = 14.50$ $\Sigma X_1{}^2 = 76.80$
   $N_1 = 10$ $N_2 = 20$

a. Test the hypothesis $\sigma_1^2 = \sigma_2^2$
b. Compute a t value.

5. Given the following three random samples:

A	B	C
15	24	20
20	22	22
26	20	30
24	21	27
	34	
	18	

a. Compute an F value.
b. Test the null hypothesis with regard to mean differences.

6. Given the following three random samples:

A	B	C
20	22	12
10	20	12
20	31	6
15	18	11
18	22	6

a. Compute an F value.
b. Test the null hypothesis at the .05 level.
c. Using the Scheffé Test, what means differ significantly from each other?

7. Test a null hypothesis on the following data.

1	2	3	4	5
18	18	4	7	9
13	9	13	3	16
21	15	11	11	26
14	25	11	11	21
25	14	15	7	18
14	6	15	13	11
7	12	11	10	14
20	9	12	10	13

CHAPTER 10

1. A single die is thrown 72 times. Does a significant difference exist between the expected and observed outcomes?

Die	O	E
2	3	2
3	7	4
4	2	6
5	7	8
6	3	10
7	10	12
8	14	10
9	10	8
10	5	6
11	6	4
12	5	2

2. The following data are the results of a survey on men's and women's preference for football and basketball.

	Basketball	Football
Men	35	100
Women	60	80

a. Compute a χ^2.
b. Compute the degrees of freedom.
c. Test the appropriate hypothesis at the .05 level.

3. Below are the responses made by two groups on an item from an attitude test.

Group	Agree	No Opinion	Disagree
1	18	11	19
2	14	10	14

a. Compute a χ^2.
b. Test the appropriate hypothesis at the .05 level.

Answers to Practice Problems

CHAPTER 1

1. mean $= 9,217$
   median $= 7,500$

2. mean $= 23.52$
   median $= 24.00$

3. mean   median
   a. 19.88   20.50
   b. 16.71   16.00
   c. 20.38   21.00

CHAPTER 2

1. $s = 10.85$

2. $s^2 = 117.72$

3. $s = 3.25$

4. $s^2 = 10.56$

5. $s = 78.00$

6. $s = 78.00$

7. a. 1.51
    b. 1.00
    c. .74
    d. .62
    e. .36
    f. −.15
    g. −.67
    h. −1.90
    i. −1.05
    j. −1.56

8. Area <   Area >
    a. .9357   .0643
    b. .7257   .2743
    c. .0158   .9842
    d. .1660   .8340
    e. .9966   .0034

9. a. .1368
    b. .4591
    c. .3023
    d. .4192
    e. .4987

10. a. .1880
    b. .1045
    c. .8090
    d. .6017
    e. .6271

CHAPTER 6

1. $r = .86$

2. d.s. $= 8$

3. Reject at the .05

4. $r = .62$

5. d.s. $= 13$

6. Reject at the .05

7. $r_{pb} = $ Approx. .46

8. $Y^1 = -6.24 + .85(X)$
   $X^1 = 10.4 + .87(Y)$

9. $Y^1 = .31 + .74(X)$
   $X^1 = 2.8 + 1.02(Y)$

10. $rho = .66$

12. $rho = .95$

CHAPTER 8

1. a. $t = .3595$
   b. Accept the null hypothesis

2. $t = .5676$

4. a. $F = 2.51$
   b. $t = 5.03$

5. a. $F = .6248$
   b. Accept the null hypothesis

6. a. $F = 12.501$
   b. Significant difference between X_1 and X_3

7. $F = 3.25$

CHAPTER 10

1. $\chi^2 = 18.55$

2. a. $\chi^2 = 8.72$
   b. d.s. $= 1$
   c. Chi-square is significant

3. a. $\chi^2 = .142$
   b. Chi-square is not significant

Appendix A

Table of Squares and Square Roots

Number	Square	Square Root	Number	Square	Square Root
1	1	1.000	51	26 01	7.141
2	4	1.414	52	27 04	7.211
3	9	1.732	53	28 09	7.280
4	16	2.000	54	29 16	7.348
5	25	2.236	55	30 25	7.416
6	36	2.449	56	31 36	7.483
7	49	2.646	57	32 49	7.550
8	64	2.828	58	33 64	7.616
9	81	3.000	59	34 81	7.681
10	1 00	3.162	60	36 00	7.746
11	1 21	3.317	61	37 21	7.810
12	1 44	3.464	62	38 44	7.874
13	1 69	3.606	63	39 69	7.937
14	1 96	3.742	64	40 96	8.000
15	2 25	3.873	65	42 25	8.062
16	2 56	4.000	66	43 56	8.124
17	2 89	4.123	67	44 89	8.185
18	3 24	4.243	68	46 24	8.246
19	3 61	4.359	69	47 61	8.307
20	4 00	4.472	70	49 00	8.367
21	4 41	4.583	71	50 41	8.426
22	4 84	4.690	72	51 84	8.485
23	5 29	4.796	73	53 29	8.544
24	5 76	4.899	74	54 76	8.602
25	6 25	5.000	75	56 25	8.660
26	6 76	5.099	76	57 76	8.718
27	7 29	5.196	77	59 29	8.775
28	7 84	5.292	78	60 84	8.832
29	8 41	5.385	79	62 41	8.888
30	9 00	5.477	80	64 00	8.944
31	9 61	5.568	81	65 61	9.000
32	10 24	5.657	82	67 24	9.055
33	10 89	5.745	83	68 89	9.110
34	11 56	5.831	84	70 56	9.165
35	12 25	5.916	85	72 25	9.220
36	12 96	6.000	86	73 96	9.274
37	13 69	6.083	87	75 69	9.327
38	14 44	6.164	88	77 44	9.381
39	15 21	6.245	89	79 21	9.434
40	16 00	6.325	90	81 00	9.487
41	16 81	6.403	91	82 81	9.539
42	17 64	6.481	92	84 64	9.592
43	18 49	6.557	93	86 49	9.644
44	19 36	6.633	94	88 36	9.695
45	20 25	6.708	95	90 25	9.747
46	21 16	6.782	96	92 16	9.798
47	22 09	6.856	97	94 09	9.849
48	23 04	6.928	98	96 04	9.899
49	24 01	7.000	99	98 01	9.950
50	25 00	7.071	100	1 00 00	10.000

Number	Square	Square Root	Number	Square	Square Root
101	1 02 01	10.050	151	2 28 01	12.288
102	1 04 04	10.100	152	2 31 04	12.329
103	1 06 09	10.149	153	2 34 09	12.369
104	1 08 16	10.198	154	2 37 16	12.410
105	1 10 25	10.247	155	2 40 25	12.450
106	1 12 36	10.296	156	2 43 36	12.490
107	1 14 49	10.344	157	2 46 49	12.530
108	1 16 64	10.392	158	2 49 64	12.570
109	1 18 81	10.440	159	2 52 81	12.610
110	1 21 00	10.488	160	2 56 00	12.649
111	1 23 21	10.536	161	2 59 21	12.689
112	1 25 44	10.583	162	2 62 44	12.728
113	1 27 69	10.630	163	2 65 69	12.767
114	1 29 96	10.677	164	2 68 96	12.806
115	1 32 25	10.724	165	2 72 25	12.845
116	1 34 56	10.770	166	2 75 56	12.884
117	1 36 89	10.817	167	2 78 89	12.923
118	1 39 24	10.863	168	2 82 24	12.961
119	1 41 61	10.909	169	2 85 61	13.000
120	1 44 00	10.954	170	2 89 00	13.038
121	1 46 41	11.000	171	2 92 41	13.077
122	1 48 84	11.045	172	2 95 84	13.115
123	1 51 29	11.091	173	2 99 29	13.153
124	1 53 76	11.136	174	3 02 76	13.191
125	1 56 25	11.180	175	3 06 25	13.229
126	1 58 76	11.225	176	3 09 76	13.266
127	1 61 29	11.269	177	3 13 29	13.304
128	1 63 84	11.314	178	3 16 84	13.342
129	1 66 41	11.358	179	3 20 41	13.379
130	1 69 00	11.402	180	3 24 00	13.416
131	1 71 61	11.446	181	3 27 61	13.454
132	1 74 24	11.489	182	3 31 24	13.491
133	1 76 89	11.533	183	3 34 89	13.528
134	1 79 56	11.576	184	3 38 56	13.565
135	1 82 25	11.619	185	3 42 25	13.601
136	1 84 96	11.662	186	3 45 96	13.638
137	1 87 69	11.705	187	3 49 69	13.675
138	1 90 44	11.747	188	3 53 44	13.711
139	1 93 21	11.790	189	3 57 21	13.748
140	1 96 00	11.832	190	3 61 00	13.784
141	1 98 81	11.874	191	3 64 81	13.820
142	2 01 64	11.916	192	3 68 64	13.856
143	2 04 49	11.958	193	3 72 49	13.892
144	2 07 36	12.000	194	3 76 36	13.928
145	2 10 25	12.042	195	3 80 25	13.964
146	2 13 16	12.083	196	3 84 16	14.000
147	2 16 09	12.124	197	3 88 09	14.036
148	2 19 04	12.166	198	3 92 04	14.071
149	2 22 01	12.207	199	3 96 01	14.107
150	2 25 00	12.247	200	4 00 00	14.142

Number	Square	Square Root	Number	Square	Square Root
201	4 04 01	14.177	251	6 30 01	15.843
202	4 08 04	14.213	252	6 35 04	15.875
203	4 12 09	14.248	253	6 40 09	15.906
204	4 16 16	14.283	554	6 45 16	15.937
205	4 20 25	14.318	255	6 50 25	15.969
206	4 24 36	14.353	256	6 55 36	16.000
207	4 28 49	14.387	257	6 60 49	16.031
208	4 32 64	14.422	258	6 65 64	16.062
209	4 36 81	14.457	259	6 70 81	16.093
210	4 41 00	14.491	260	6 76 00	16.125
211	4 45 21	14.526	261	6 81 21	16.155
212	4 49 44	14.560	262	6 86 44	16.186
213	4 53 69	14.595	263	6 91 69	16.217
214	4 57 96	14.629	264	6 96 96	16.248
215	4 62 25	14.663	265	7 02 25	16.279
216	4 66 56	14.697	266	7 07 56	16.310
217	4 70 89	14.731	267	7 12 89	16.340
218	4 75 24	14.765	268	7 18 24	16.371
219	4 79 61	14.799	269	7 23 61	16.401
220	4 84 00	14.832	270	7 29 00	16.432
221	4 88 41	14.866	271	7 34 41	16.462
222	4 92 84	14.900	272	7 39 84	16.492
223	4 97 29	14.933	273	7 45 29	16.523
224	5 01 76	14.967	274	7 50 76	16.553
225	5 06 25	15.000	275	7 56 25	16.583
226	5 10 76	15.033	276	7 61 76	16.613
227	5 15 29	15.067	277	7 67 29	16.643
228	5 19 84	15.100	278	7 72 84	16.673
229	5 24 41	15.133	279	7 78 41	16.703
230	5 29 00	15.166	280	7 84 00	16.733
231	5 33 61	15.199	281	7 89 61	16.763
232	5 38 24	15.232	282	7 95 24	16.793
233	5 42 89	15.264	283	8 00 89	16.823
234	5 47 56	15.297	284	8 06 56	16.852
235	5 52 25	15.330	285	8 12 25	16.882
236	5 56 96	15.362	286	8 17 96	16.912
237	5 61 69	15.395	287	8 23 69	16.941
238	5 66 44	15.427	288	8 29 44	16.971
239	5 71 21	15.460	289	8 35 21	17.000
240	5 76 00	15.492	290	8 41 00	17.029
241	5 80 81	15.524	291	8 46 81	17.059
242	5 85 64	15.556	292	8 52 64	17.088
243	5 90 49	15.588	293	8 58 49	17.117
244	5 95 36	15.620	294	8 64 36	17.146
245	6 00 25	15.652	295	8 70 25	17.176
246	6 05 16	15.684	296	8 76 16	17.205
247	6 10 09	15.716	297	8 82 09	17.234
248	6 15 04	15.748	298	8 88 04	17.263
249	6 20 01	15.780	299	8 94 01	17.292
250	6 25 00	15.811	300	9 00 00	17.321

NUMBER	SQUARE	SQUARE ROOT	NUMBER	SQUARE	SQUARE ROOT
301	9 06 01	17.349	351	12 32 01	18.735
302	9 12 04	17.378	352	12 39 04	18.762
303	9 18 09	17.407	353	12 46 09	18.788
304	9 24 16	17.436	354	12 53 16	18.815
305	9 30 25	17.464	355	12 60 25	18.841
306	9 36 36	17.493	356	12 67 36	18.868
307	9 42 49	17.521	357	12 74 49	18.894
308	9 48 64	17.550	358	12 81 64	18.921
309	9 54 81	17.578	359	12 88 81	18.947
310	9 61 00	17.607	360	12 96 00	18.974
311	9 67 21	17.635	361	13 03 21	19.000
312	9 73 44	17.664	362	13 10 44	19.026
313	9 79 69	17.692	363	13 17 69	19.053
314	9 85 96	17.720	364	13 24 96	19.079
315	9 92 25	17.748	365	13 32 25	19.105
316	9 98 56	17.776	366	13 39 56	19.131
317	10 04 89	17.804	367	13 46 89	19.157
318	10 11 24	17.833	368	13 54 24	19.183
319	10 17 61	17.861	369	13 61 61	19.209
320	10 24 00	17.889	370	13 69 00	19.235
321	10 30 41	17.916	371	13 76 41	19.261
322	10 36 84	17.944	372	13 83 84	19.287
323	10 43 29	17.972	373	13 91 29	19.313
324	10 49 76	18.000	374	13 98 76	19.339
325	10 56 25	18.028	375	14 06 25	19.365
326	10 62 76	18.055	376	14 13 76	19.391
327	10 69 29	18.083	377	14 21 29	19.416
328	10 75 84	18.111	378	14 28 84	19.442
329	10 82 41	18.138	379	14 36 41	19.468
330	10 89 00	18.166	380	14 44 00	19.494
331	10 95 61	18.193	381	14 51 61	19.519
332	11 02 24	18.221	382	14 59 24	19.545
333	11 08 89	18.248	383	14 66 89	19.570
334	11 15 56	18.276	384	14 74 56	19.596
335	11 22 25	18.303	385	14 82 25	19.621
336	11 28 96	18.330	386	14 89 96	19.647
337	11 35 69	18.358	387	14 97 69	19.672
338	11 42 44	18.385	388	15 05 44	19.698
339	11 49 21	18.412	389	15 13 21	19.723
340	11 56 00	18.439	390	15 21 00	19.748
341	11 62 81	18.466	391	15 28 81	19.774
342	11 69 64	18.493	392	15 36 64	19.799
343	11 76 49	18.520	393	15 44 49	19.824
344	11 83 36	18.547	394	15 52 36	19.849
345	11 90 25	18.574	395	15 60 25	19.875
346	11 97 16	18.601	396	15 68 16	19.900
347	12 04 09	18.628	397	15 76 09	19.925
348	12 11 04	18.655	398	15 84 04	19.950
349	12 18 01	18.682	399	15 92 01	19.975
350	12 25 00	18.708	400	16 00 00	20.000

Number	Square	Square Root	Number	Square	Square Root
401	16 08 01	20.025	451	20 34 01	21.237
402	16 16 04	20.050	452	20 43 04	21.260
403	16 24 09	20.075	453	20 52 09	21.284
404	16 32 16	20.100	454	20 61 16	21.307
405	16 40 25	20.125	455	20 70 25	21.331
406	16 48 36	20.149	456	20 79 36	21.354
407	16 56 49	20.174	457	20 88 49	21.378
408	16 64 64	20.199	458	20 97 64	21.401
409	16 72 81	20.224	459	21 06 81	21.424
410	16 81 00	20.248	460	21 16 00	21.448
411	16 89 21	20.273	461	21 25 21	21.471
412	16 97 44	20.298	462	21 34 44	21.494
413	17 05 69	20.322	463	21 43 69	21.517
414	17 13 96	20.347	464	21 52 96	21.541
415	17 22 25	20.372	465	21 62 25	21.564
416	17 30 56	20.396	466	21 71 56	21.587
417	17 38 89	20.421	467	21 80 89	21.610
418	17 47 24	20.445	468	21 90 24	21.633
419	17 55 61	20.469	469	21 99 61	21.656
420	17 64 00	20.494	470	22 09 00	21.679
421	17 72 41	20.518	471	22 18 41	21.703
422	17 80 84	20.543	472	22 27 84	21.726
423	17 89 29	20.567	473	22 37 29	21.749
424	17 97 76	20.591	474	22 46 76	21.772
425	18 06 25	20.616	475	22 56 25	21.794
426	18 14 76	20.640	476	22 65 76	21.817
427	18 23 29	20.664	477	22 75 29	21.840
428	18 31 84	20.688	478	22 84 84	21.863
429	18 40 41	20.712	479	22 94 41	21.886
430	18 49 00	20.736	480	23 04 00	21.909
431	18 57 61	20.761	481	23 13 61	21.932
432	18 66 24	20.785	482	23 23 24	21.954
433	18 74 89	20.809	483	23 32 89	21.977
434	18 83 56	20.833	484	23 42 56	22.000
435	18 92 25	20.857	485	23 52 25	22.023
436	19 00 96	20.881	486	23 61 96	22.045
437	19 09 69	20.905	487	23 71 69	22.068
438	19 18 44	20.928	488	23 81 44	22.091
439	19 27 21	20.952	489	23 91 21	22.113
440	19 36 00	20.976	490	24 01 00	22.136
441	19 44 81	21.000	491	24 10 81	22.159
442	19 53 64	21.024	492	24 20 64	22.181
443	19 62 49	21.048	493	24 30 49	22.204
444	19 71 36	21.071	494	24 40 36	22.226
445	19 80 25	21.095	495	24 50 25	22.249
446	19 89 16	21.119	496	24 60 16	22.271
447	19 98 09	21.142	497	24 70 09	22.293
448	20 07 04	21.166	498	24 80 04	22.316
449	20 16 01	21.190	499	24 90 01	22.338
450	20 25 00	21.213	500	25 00 00	22.361

Number	Square	Square Root	Number	Square	Square Root
501	25 10 01	22.383	551	30 36 01	23.473
502	25 20 04	22.405	552	30 47 04	23.495
503	25 30 09	22.428	553	30 58 09	23.516
504	25 40 16	22.450	554	30 69 16	23.537
505	25 50 25	22.472	555	30 80 25	23.558
506	25 60 36	22.494	556	30 91 36	23.580
507	25 70 49	22.517	557	31 02 49	23.601
508	25 80 64	22.539	558	31 13 64	23.622
509	25 90 81	22.561	559	31 24 81	23.643
510	26 01 00	22.583	560	31 36 00	23.664
511	26 11 21	22.605	561	31 47 21	23.685
512	26 21 44	22.627	562	31 58 44	23.707
513	26 31 69	22.650	563	31 69 69	23.728
514	26 41 96	22.672	564	31 80 96	23.749
515	26 52 25	22.694	565	31 92 25	23.770
516	26 62 56	22.716	566	32 03 56	23.791
517	26 72 89	22.738	567	32 14 89	23.812
518	26 83 24	22.760	568	32 26 24	23.833
519	26 93 61	22.782	569	32 37 61	23.854
520	27 04 00	22.804	570	32 49 00	23.875
521	27 14 41	22.825	571	32 60 41	23.896
522	27 24 84	22.847	572	32 71 84	23.917
523	27 35 29	22.869	573	32 83 29	23.937
524	27 45 76	22.891	574	32 94 76	23.958
525	27 56 25	22.913	575	33 06 25	23.979
526	27 66 76	22.935	576	33 17 76	24.000
527	27 77 29	22.956	577	33 29 29	24.021
528	27 87 84	22.978	578	33 40 84	24.042
529	27 98 41	23.000	579	33 52 41	24.062
530	28 09 00	23.022	580	33 64 00	24.083
531	28 19 61	23.043	581	33 75 61	24.104
532	28 30 24	23.065	582	33 87 24	24.125
533	28 40 89	23.087	583	33 98 89	24.145
534	28 51 56	23.108	584	34 10 56	24.166
535	28 62 25	23.130	585	34 22 25	24.187
536	28 72 96	23.152	586	34 33 96	24.207
537	28 83 69	23.173	587	34 45 69	24.228
538	28 94 44	23.195	588	34 57 44	24.249
539	29 05 21	23.216	589	34 69 21	24.269
540	29 16 00	23.238	590	34 81 00	24.290
541	29 26 81	23.259	591	34 92 81	24.310
542	29 37 64	23.281	592	35 04 64	24.331
543	29 48 49	23.302	593	35 16 49	24.352
544	29 59 36	23.324	594	35 28 36	24.372
545	29 70 25	23.345	595	35 40 25	24.393
546	29 81 16	23.367	596	35 52 16	24.413
547	29 92 09	23.388	597	35 64 09	24.434
548	30 03 04	23.409	598	35 76 04	24.454
549	30 14 01	23.431	599	35 88 01	24.474
550	30 25 00	23.452	600	36 00 00	24.495

NUMBER	SQUARE	SQUARE ROOT	NUMBER	SQUARE	SQUARE ROOT
601	36 12 01	24.515	651	42 38 01	25.515
602	36 24 04	24.536	652	42 51 04	25.534
603	36 36 09	24.556	653	42 64 09	25.554
604	36 48 16	24.576	654	42 77 16	25.573
605	36 60 25	24.597	655	42 90 25	25.593
606	36 72 36	24.617	656	43 03 36	25.612
607	36 84 49	24.637	657	43 16 49	25.632
608	36 96 64	24.658	658	43 29 64	25.652
609	37 08 81	24.678	659	43 42 81	25.671
610	37 21 00	24.698	660	43 56 00	25.690
611	37 33 21	24.718	661	43 69 21	25.710
612	37 45 44	24.739	662	43 82 44	25.729
613	37 57 69	24.759	663	43 95 69	25.749
614	37 69 96	24.779	664	44 08 96	25.768
615	37 82 25	24.799	665	44 22 25	25.788
616	37 94 56	24.819	666	44 35 56	25.807
617	38 06 89	24.839	667	44 48 89	25.826
618	38 19 24	24.860	668	44 62 24	25.846
619	38 31 61	24.880	669	44 75 61	25.865
620	38 44 00	24.900	670	44 89 00	25.884
621	38 56 41	24.920	671	45 02 41	25.904
622	38 68 84	24.940	672	45 15 84	25.923
623	38 81 29	24.960	673	45 29 29	25.942
624	38 93 76	24.980	674	45 42 76	25.962
625	39 06 25	25.000	675	45 56 25	25.981
626	39 18 76	25.020	676	45 69 76	26.000
627	39 31 29	25.040	677	45 83 29	26.019
628	39 43 84	25.060	678	45 96 84	26.038
629	39 56 41	25.080	679	46 10 41	26.058
630	39 69 00	25.100	680	46 24 00	26.077
631	39 81 61	25.120	681	46 37 61	26.096
632	39 94 24	25.140	682	46 51 24	26.115
633	40 06 89	25.159	683	46 64 89	26.134
634	40 19 56	25.179	684	46 78 56	26.153
635	40 32 25	25.199	685	46 92 25	26.173
636	40 44 96	25.219	686	47 05 96	26.192
637	40 57 69	25.239	687	47 19 69	26.211
638	40 70 44	25.259	688	47 33 44	26.230
639	40 83 21	25.278	689	47 47 21	26.249
640	40 96 00	25.298	690	47 61 00	26.268
641	41 08 81	25.318	691	47 74 81	26.287
642	41 21 64	25.338	692	47 88 64	26.306
643	41 34 49	25.357	693	48 02 49	26.325
644	41 47 36	25.377	694	48 16 36	26.344
645	41 60 25	25.397	695	48 30 25	26.363
646	41 73 16	25.417	696	48 44 16	26.382
647	41 86 09	25.436	697	48 58 09	26.401
648	41 99 04	25.456	698	48 72 04	26.420
649	42 12 01	25.475	699	48 86 01	26.439
650	42 25 00	25.495	700	49 00 00	26.458

Number	Square	Square Root	Number	Square	Square Root
701	49 14 01	26.476	751	56 40 01	27.404
702	49 28 04	26.495	752	56 55 04	27.423
703	49 42 09	26.514	753	56 70 09	27.441
704	49 56 16	26.533	754	56 85 16	27.459
705	49 70 25	26.552	755	57 00 25	27.477
706	49 84 36	26.571	756	57 15 36	27.495
707	49 98 49	26.589	757	57 30 49	27.514
708	50 12 64	26.608	758	57 45 64	27.532
709	50 26 81	26.627	759	57 60 81	27.550
710	50 41 00	26.646	760	57 76 00	27.568
711	50 55 21	26.665	761	57 91 21	27.586
712	50 69 44	26.683	762	58 06 44	27.604
713	50 83 69	26.702	763	58 21 69	27.622
714	50 97 96	26.721	764	58 36 96	27.641
715	51 12 25	26.739	765	58 52 25	27.659
716	51 26 56	26.758	766	58 67 56	27.677
717	51 40 89	26.777	767	58 82 89	27.695
718	51 55 24	26.796	768	58 98 24	27.713
719	51 69 61	26.814	769	59 13 61	27.731
720	51 84 00	26.833	770	59 29 00	27.749
721	51 98 41	26.851	771	59 44 41	27.767
722	52 12 84	26.870	772	59 59 84	27.785
723	52 27 29	26.889	773	59 75 29	27.803
724	52 41 76	26.907	774	59 90 76	27.821
725	52 56 25	26.926	775	60 06 25	27.839
726	52 70 76	26.944	776	60 21 76	27.857
727	52 85 29	26.963	777	60 37 29	27.875
728	52 99 84	26.981	778	60 52 84	27.893
729	53 14 41	27.000	779	60 68 41	27.911
730	53 29 00	27.019	780	60 84 00	27.928
731	53 43 61	27.037	781	60 99 61	27.946
732	53 58 24	27.055	782	61 15 24	27.964
733	53 72 89	27.074	783	61 30 89	27.982
734	53 87 56	27.092	784	61 46 56	28.000
735	54 02 25	27.111	785	61 62 25	28.018
736	54 16 96	27.129	786	61 77 96	28.036
737	54 31 69	27.148	787	61 93 69	28.054
738	54 46 44	27.166	788	62 09 44	28.071
739	54 61 21	27.185	789	62 25 21	28.089
740	54 76 00	27.203	790	62 41 00	28.107
741	54 90 81	27.221	791	62 56 81	28.125
742	55 05 64	27.240	792	62 72 64	28.142
743	55 20 49	27.258	793	62 88 49	28.160
744	55 35 36	27.276	794	63 04 36	28.178
745	55 50 25	27.295	795	63 20 25	28.196
746	55 65 16	27.313	796	63 36 16	28.213
747	55 80 09	27.331	797	63 52 09	28.231
748	55 95 04	27.350	798	63 68 04	28.249
749	56 10 01	27.368	799	73 84 01	28.267
750	56 25 00	27.386	800	64 00 00	28.284

Number	Square	Square Root	Number	Square	Square Root
801	64 16 01	28.302	851	72 42 01	29.172
802	64 32 04	28.320	852	72 59 04	29.189
803	64 48 09	28.337	853	72 76 09	29.206
804	64 64 16	28.355	854	72 93 16	29.223
805	64 80 25	28.373	855	73 10 25	29.240
806	64 96 36	28.390	856	73 27 36	29.257
807	65 12 49	28.408	857	73 44 49	29.275
808	65 28 64	28.425	858	73 61 64	29.292
809	65 44 81	28.443	859	73 78 81	29.309
810	65 61 00	28.460	860	73 96 00	29.326
811	65 77 21	28.478	861	74 13 21	29.343
812	65 93 44	28.496	862	74 30 44	29.360
813	66 09 69	28.513	863	74 47 69	29.377
814	66 25 96	28.531	864	74 64 96	29.394
815	66 42 25	28.548	865	74 82 25	29.411
816	66 58 56	28.566	866	74 99 56	29.428
817	66 74 89	28.583	867	75 16 89	29.445
818	66 91 24	28.601	868	75 34 24	29.462
819	67 07 61	28.618	869	75 51 61	29.479
820	67 24 00	28.636	870	75 69 00	29.496
821	67 40 41	28.653	871	75 86 41	29.513
822	67 56 84	28.671	872	76 03 84	29.530
823	67 73 29	28.688	873	76 21 29	29.547
824	67 89 76	28.705	874	76 38 76	29.563
825	68 06 25	28.723	875	76 56 25	29.580
826	68 22 76	28.740	876	76 73 76	29.597
827	68 39 29	28.758	877	76 91 29	29.614
828	68 55 84	28.775	878	77 08 84	29.631
829	68 72 41	28.792	879	77 26 41	29.648
830	68 89 00	28.810	880	77 44 00	29.665
831	69 05 61	28.827	881	77 61 61	29.682
832	69 22 24	28.844	882	77 79 24	29.698
833	69 38 89	28.862	883	77 96 89	29.715
834	69 55 56	28.879	884	78 14 56	29.732
835	69 72 25	28.896	885	78 32 25	29.749
836	69 88 96	28.914	886	78 49 96	29.766
837	70 05 69	28.931	887	78 67 69	29.783
838	70 22 44	28.948	888	78 85 44	29.799
839	70 39 21	28.965	889	79 03 21	29.816
840	70 56 00	28.983	890	79 21 00	29.833
841	70 72 81	29.000	891	79 38 81	29.850
842	70 89 64	29.017	892	79 56 64	29.866
843	71 06 49	29.034	893	79 74 49	29.883
844	71 23 36	29.052	894	79 92 36	29.900
845	71 40 25	29.069	895	80 10 25	29.917
846	71 57 16	29.086	896	80 28 16	29.933
847	71 74 09	29.103	897	80 46 09	29.950
848	71 91 04	29.120	898	80 64 04	29.967
849	72 08 01	29.138	899	80 82 01	29.983
850	72 25 00	29.155	900	81 00 00	30.000

NUMBER	SQUARE	SQUARE ROOT	NUMBER	SQUARE	SQUARE ROOT
901	81 18 01	30.017	951	90 44 01	30.838
902	81 36 04	30.033	952	90 63 04	30.854
903	81 54 09	30.050	953	90 82 09	30.871
904	81 72 16	30.067	954	91 01 16	30.887
905	81 90 25	30.083	955	91 20 25	30.903
906	82 08 36	30.100	956	91 39 36	30.919
907	82 26 49	30.116	957	91 58 49	30.935
908	82 44 64	30.133	958	91 77 64	30.952
909	82 62 81	30.150	959	91 96 81	30.968
910	82 81 00	30.166	960	92 16 00	30.984
911	82 99 21	30.183	961	92 35 21	31.000
912	83 17 44	30.199	962	92 54 44	31.016
913	83 35 69	30.216	963	92 73 69	31.032
914	83 53 96	30.232	964	92 92 96	31.048
915	83 72 25	30.249	965	93 12 25	31.064
916	83 90 56	30.265	966	93 31 56	31.081
917	84 08 89	30.282	967	93 50 89	31.097
918	84 27 24	30.299	968	93 70 24	31.113
919	84 45 61	30.315	969	93 89 61	31.129
920	84 64 00	30.332	970	94 09 00	31.145
921	84 82 41	30.348	971	94 28 41	31.161
922	85 00 84	30.364	972	94 47 84	31.177
923	85 19 29	30.381	973	94 67 29	31.193
924	85 37 76	30.397	974	94 86 76	31.209
925	85 56 25	30.414	975	95 06 25	31.225
926	85 74 76	30.430	976	95 25 76	31.241
927	85 93 29	30.447	977	95 45 29	31.257
928	86 11 84	30.463	978	95 64 84	31.273
929	86 30 41	30.480	979	95 84 41	31.289
930	86 49 00	30.496	980	96 04 00	31.305
931	86 67 61	30.512	981	96 23 61	31.321
932	86 86 24	30.529	982	96 43 24	31.337
933	87 04 89	30.545	983	96 62 89	31.353
934	87 23 56	30.561	984	96 82 56	31.369
935	87 42 25	30.578	985	97 02 25	31.385
936	87 60 96	30.594	986	97 21 96	31.401
937	87 79 69	30.610	987	97 41 69	31.417
938	87 98 44	30.627	988	97 61 44	31.432
939	88 17 21	30.643	989	97 81 21	31.448
940	88 36 00	30.659	990	98 01 00	31.464
941	88 54 81	30.676	991	98 20 81	31.480
942	88 73 64	30.692	992	98 40 64	31.496
943	88 92 49	30.708	993	98 60 49	31.512
944	89 11 36	30.725	994	98 80 36	31.528
945	89 30 25	30.741	995	99 00 25	31.544
946	89 49 16	30.757	996	99 20 16	31.559
947	89 68 09	30.773	997	99 40 09	31.575
948	89 87 04	30.790	998	99 60 04	31.591
949	90 06 01	30.806	999	99 80 01	31.607
950	90 25 00	30.822	1000	100 00 00	31.623

Appendix B

Areas and Ordinates of the Normal Curve in Terms of x/σ

(A) z	(B) area between mean and z	(C) area beyond z	(A) z	(B) area between mean and z	(C) area beyond z	(A) z	(B) area between mean and z	(C) area beyond z
0.00	.0000	.5000	0.55	.2088	.2912	1.10	.3643	.1357
0.01	.0040	.4960	0.56	.2123	.2877	1.11	.3665	.1335
0.02	.0080	.4920	0.57	.2157	.2843	1.12	.3686	.1314
0.03	.0120	.4880	0.58	.2190	.2810	1.13	.3708	.1292
0.04	.0160	.4840	0.59	.2224	.2776	1.14	.3729	.1271
0.05	.0199	.4801	0.60	.2257	.2743	1.15	.3749	.1251
0.06	.0239	.4761	0.61	.2291	.2709	1.16	.3770	.1230
0.07	.0279	.4721	0.62	.2324	.2676	1.17	.3790	.1210
0.08	.0319	.4681	0.63	.2357	.2643	1.18	.3810	.1190
0.09	.0359	.4641	0.64	.2389	.2611	1.19	.3830	.1170
0.10	.0398	.4602	0.65	.2422	.2578	1.20	.3849	.1151
0.11	.0438	.4562	0.66	.2454	.2546	1.21	.3869	.1131
0.12	.0478	.4522	0.67	.2486	.2514	1.22	.3888	.1112
0.13	.0517	.4483	0.68	.2517	.2483	1.23	.3907	.1093
0.14	.0557	.4443	0.69	.2549	.2451	1.24	.3925	.1075
0.15	.0596	.4404	0.70	.2580	.2420	1.25	.3944	.1056
0.16	.0636	.4364	0.71	.2611	.2389	1.26	.3962	.1038
0.17	.0675	.4325	0.72	.2642	.2358	1.27	.3980	.1020
0.18	.0714	.4286	0.73	.2673	.2327	1.28	.3997	.1003
0.19	.0753	.4247	0.74	.2704	.2296	1.29	.4015	.0985
0.20	.0793	.4207	0.75	.2734	.2266	1.30	.4032	.0968
0.21	.0832	.4168	0.76	.2764	.2236	1.31	.4049	.0951
0.22	.0871	.4129	0.77	.2794	.2206	1.32	.4066	.0934
0.23	.0910	.4090	0.78	.2823	.2177	1.33	.4082	.0918
0.24	.0948	.4052	0.79	.2852	.2148	1.34	.4099	.0901
0.25	.0987	.4013	0.80	.2881	.2119	1.35	.4115	.0885
0.26	.1026	.3974	0.81	.2910	.2090	1.36	.4131	.0869
0.27	.1064	.3936	0.82	.2939	.2061	1.37	.4147	.0853
0.28	.1103	.3897	0.83	.2967	.2033	1.38	.4162	.0838
0.29	.1141	.3859	0.84	.2995	.2005	1.39	.4177	.0823
0.30	.1179	.3821	0.85	.3023	.1977	1.40	.4192	.0808
0.31	.1217	.3783	0.86	.3051	.1949	1.41	.4207	.0793
0.32	.1255	.3745	0.87	.3078	.1922	1.42	.4222	.0778
0.33	.1293	.3707	0.88	.3106	.1894	1.43	.4236	.0764
0.34	.1331	.3669	0.89	.3133	.1867	1.44	.4251	.0749
0.35	.1368	.3632	0.90	.3159	.1841	1.45	.4265	.0735
0.36	.1406	.3594	0.91	.3186	.1814	1.46	.4279	.0721
0.37	.1443	.3557	0.92	.3212	.1788	1.47	.4292	.0708
0.38	.1480	.3520	0.93	.3238	.1762	1.48	.4306	.0694
0.39	.1517	.3483	0.94	.3264	.1736	1.49	.4319	.0681
0.40	.1554	.3446	0.95	.3289	.1711	1.50	.4332	.0668
0.41	.1591	.3409	0.96	.3315	.1685	1.51	.4345	.0655
0.42	.1628	.3372	0.97	.3340	.1660	1.52	.4357	.0643
0.43	.1664	.3336	0.98	.3365	.1635	1.53	.4370	.0630
0.44	.1700	.3300	0.99	.3389	.1611	1.54	.4382	.0618
0.45	.1736	.3264	1.00	.3413	.1587	1.55	.4394	.0606
0.46	.1772	.3228	1.01	.3438	.1562	1.56	.4406	.0594
0.47	.1808	.3192	1.02	.3461	.1539	1.57	.4418	.0582
0.48	.1844	.3156	1.03	.3485	.1515	1.58	.4429	.0571
0.49	.1879	.3121	1.04	.3508	.1492	1.59	.4441	.0559
0.50	.1915	.3085	1.05	.3531	.1469	1.60	.4452	.0548
0.51	.1950	.3050	1.06	.3554	.1446	1.61	.4463	.0537
0.52	.1985	.3015	1.07	.3577	.1423	1.62	.4474	.0526
0.53	.2019	.2981	1.08	.3599	.1401	1.63	.4484	.0516
0.54	.2054	.2946	1.09	.3621	.1379	1.64	.4495	.0505

(A)	(B)	(C)	(A)	(B)	(C)	(A)	(B)	(C)
z	area between mean and z	area beyond z	z	area between mean and z	area beyond z	z	area between mean and z	area beyond z
1.65	.4505	.0495	2.22	.4868	.0132	2.79	.4974	.0026
1.66	.4515	.0485	2.23	.4871	.0129	2.80	.4974	.0026
1.67	.4525	.0475	2.24	.4875	.0125	2.81	.4975	.0025
1.68	.4535	.0465	2.25	.4878	.0122	2.82	.4976	.0024
1.69	.4545	.0455	2.26	.4881	.0119	2.83	.4977	.0023
1.70	.4554	.0446	2.27	.4884	.0116	2.84	.4977	.0023
1.71	.4564	.0436	2.28	.4887	.0113	2.85	.4978	.0022
1.72	.4573	.0427	2.29	.4890	.0110	2.86	.4979	.0021
1.73	.4582	.0418	2.30	.4893	.0107	2.87	.4979	.0021
1.74	.4591	.0409	2.31	.4896	.0104	2.88	.4980	.0020
1.75	.4599	.0401	2.32	.4898	.0102	2.89	.4981	.0019
1.76	.4608	.0392	2.33	.4901	.0099	2.90	.4981	.0019
1.77	.4616	.0384	2.34	.4904	.0096	2.91	.4982	.0018
1.78	.4625	.0375	2.35	.4906	.0094	2.92	.4982	.0018
1.79	.4633	.0367	2.36	.4909	.0091	2.93	.4983	.0017
1.80	.4641	.0359	2.37	.4911	.0089	2.94	.4984	.0016
1.81	.4649	.0351	2.38	.4913	.0087	2.95	.4984	.0016
1.82	.4656	.0344	2.39	.4916	.0084	2.96	.4985	.0015
1.83	.4664	.0336	2.40	.4918	.0082	2.97	.4985	.0015
1.84	.4671	.0329	2.41	.4920	.0080	2.98	.4986	.0014
1.85	.4678	.0322	2.42	.4922	.0078	2.99	.4986	.0014
1.86	.4686	.0314	2.43	.4925	.0075	3.00	.4987	.0013
1.87	.4693	.0307	2.44	.4927	.0073	3.01	.4987	.0013
1.88	.4699	.0301	2.45	.4929	.0071	3.02	.4987	.0013
1.89	.4706	.0294	2.46	.4931	.0069	3.03	.4988	.0012
1.90	.4713	.0287	2.47	.4932	.0068	3.04	.4988	.0012
1.91	.4719	.0281	2.48	.4934	.0066	3.05	.4989	.0011
1.92	.4726	.0274	2.49	.4936	.0064	3.06	.4989	.0011
1.93	.4732	.0268	2.50	.4938	.0062	3.07	.4989	.0011
1.94	.4738	.0262	2.51	.4940	.0060	3.08	.4990	.0010
1.95	.4744	.0256	2.52	.4941	.0059	3.09	.4990	.0010
1.96	.4750	.0250	2.53	.4943	.0057	3.10	.4990	.0010
1.97	.4756	.0244	2.54	.4945	.0055	3.11	.4991	.0009
1.98	.4761	.0239	2.55	.4946	.0054	3.12	.4991	.0009
1.99	.4767	.0233	2.56	.4948	.0052	3.13	.4991	.0009
2.00	.4772	.0228	2.57	.4949	.0051	3.14	.4992	.0008
2.01	.4778	.0222	2.58	.4951	.0049	3.15	.4992	.0008
2.02	.4783	.0217	2.59	.4952	.0048	3.16	.4992	.0008
2.03	.4788	.0212	2.60	.4953	.0047	3.17	.4992	.0008
2.04	.4793	.0207	2.61	.4955	.0045	3.18	.4993	.0007
2.05	.4798	.0202	2.62	.4956	.0044	3.19	.4993	.0007
2.06	.4803	.0197	2.63	.4957	.0043	3.20	.4993	.0007
2.07	.4808	.0192	2.64	.4959	.0041	3.21	.4993	.0007
2.08	.4812	.0188	2.65	.4960	.0040	3.22	.4994	.0006
2.09	.4817	.0183	2.66	.4961	.0039	3.23	.4994	.0006
2.10	.4821	.0179	2.67	.4962	.0038	3.24	.4994	.0006
2.11	.4826	.0174	2.68	.4963	.0037	3.25	.4994	.0006
2.12	.4830	.0170	2.69	.4964	.0036	3.30	.4995	.0005
2.13	.4834	.0166	2.70	.4965	.0035	3.35	.4996	.0004
2.14	.4838	.0162	2.71	.4966	.0034	3.40	.4997	.0003
2.15	.4842	.0158	2.72	.4967	.0033	3.45	.4997	.0003
2.16	.4846	.0154	2.73	.4968	.0032	3.50	.4998	.0002
2.17	.4850	.0150	2.74	.4969	.0031	3.60	.4998	.0002
2.18	.4854	.0146	2.75	.4970	.0030	3.70	.4999	.0001
2.19	.4857	.0143	2.76	.4971	.0029	3.80	.4999	.0001
2.20	.4861	.0139	2.77	.4972	.0028	3.90	.49995	.00005
2.21	.4864	.0136	2.78	.4973	.0027	4.00	.49997	.00003

Appendix C

Table of Random Numbers

Row	1	2	3	4	5	6	7	8	9	10	11	12	13	14	15	16	17	18	19
1	9	8	9	6	9	9	0	9	6	3	2	3	3	8	6	8	4	4	2
2	3	5	6	1	7	4	1	3	2	6	8	6	0	4	7	5	2	0	3
3	4	0	6	1	6	9	6	1	5	9	5	4	5	4	8	6	7	4	0
4	6	5	6	3	1	6	8	6	7	2	0	7	2	3	2	1	5	0	9
5	2	4	9	7	9	1	0	3	9	6	7	4	1	5	4	9	6	9	8
6	7	6	1	2	7	5	6	9	4	8	4	2	8	5	2	4	1	8	0
7	8	2	1	3	4	7	4	6	3	0	7	5	0	9	2	9	0	6	1
8	6	9	5	6	5	6	0	9	0	7	7	1	4	1	8	3	1	9	3
9	7	2	1	9	9	8	0	1	6	1	6	2	3	6	9	5	5	8	4
10	2	9	0	7	3	0	8	9	6	3	3	8	5	5	6	5	2	0	9
11	9	3	5	4	5	7	4	0	3	0	1	0	4	3	3	9	5	3	2
12	9	7	5	7	9	4	8	6	8	7	6	1	6	8	2	5	5	5	3
13	4	1	7	8	6	8	1	0	5	8	8	6	1	6	8	2	9	0	4
14	5	0	8	3	3	4	5	4	4	2	5	3	0	4	9	6	1	2	3
15	3	5	0	2	9	4	1	0	0	3	9	0	5	8	6	0	9	9	6
16	0	3	8	2	3	5	1	0	1	0	6	8	5	2	4	8	0	3	8
17	1	7	2	9	1	2	7	8	4	7	0	3	3	1	5	8	2	7	3
18	5	0	5	7	9	5	8	7	8	9	3	5	3	4	4	6	1	1	3
19	7	7	3	3	5	3	6	1	3	2	8	5	4	1	4	8	3	9	0
20	1	0	9	1	3	8	2	5	3	0	3	8	0	9	3	3	0	4	5
21	1	3	8	5	1	8	5	9	4	1	9	3	9	3	6	5	9	8	4
22	8	6	4	7	8	7	5	9	4	1	9	3	9	3	6	5	9	8	4
23	0	6	9	6	5	1	0	3	2	6	7	7	4	9	6	0	3	4	0
24	7	6	7	4	7	0	8	3	8	7	3	2	5	1	2	4	2	9	7
25	3	2	3	8	1	3	1	8	7	4	5	9	0	0	2	4	1	2	1
26	9	2	1	6	4	2	3	8	7	6	2	6	2	6	4	8	1	0	1
27	3	7	4	2	2	8	1	7	8	0	6	0	0	0	3	2	2	9	7
28	0	7	8	0	8	5	1	5	2	6	5	8	7	5	3	0	5	9	6
29	7	4	2	3	3	2	6	0	0	6	5	2	2	3	6	3	9	0	4
30	1	8	2	7	5	9	5	3	6	5	2	9	9	1	1	7	3	4	3
31	4	3	1	8	7	0	6	0	8	6	5	0	1	0	4	0	6	1	5
32	8	5	8	0	6	1	4	1	2	0	4	4	1	4	7	6	3	5	1
33	4	5	8	5	0	4	5	8	3	9	2	8	7	8	9	0	8	4	3
34	5	0	2	5	4	9	2	2	1	1	0	0	5	4	8	7	6	4	0
35	0	8	1	7	0	6	3	3	4	7	6	2	6	8	9	3	4	1	4
36	2	5	9	3	4	6	0	7	5	2	0	0	9	6	0	8	2	2	5
37	2	1	3	1	3	7	8	9	8	4	9	3	8	0	2	2	1	8	1
38	3	8	8	6	8	5	1	3	3	4	6	7	2	6	3	4	8	6	7
39	0	9	9	8	5	9	8	4	4	2	2	1	1	0	1	7	6	1	3
40	2	2	3	5	3	9	7	4	4	2	1	4	0	5	8	2	3	0	8

									Column Number												
20	21	22	23	24	25	26	27	28	29	30	31	32	33	34	35	36	37	38	39	40	Row
0	9	7	1	1	9	1	2	7	3	5	1	8	4	0	4	1	0	6	0	3	1
8	3	7	7	9	1	4	9	9	5	9	2	0	1	6	1	2	6	6	7	0	2
2	5	6	3	7	8	3	3	8	4	3	9	3	9	0	0	9	8	3	5	2	3
4	7	0	8	6	6	5	9	6	2	7	3	5	9	0	1	8	0	9	6	9	4
0	9	8	7	3	5	6	8	8	1	2	0	2	3	2	6	4	3	1	9	7	5
5	1	8	8	4	7	0	1	7	6	8	2	1	6	3	2	1	8	1	8	3	6
1	3	7	8	6	9	5	4	1	7	3	8	7	1	5	6	5	6	4	3	6	7
5	9	0	1	5	2	8	6	5	5	7	8	1	8	7	1	2	4	0	4	1	8
2	2	5	5	2	1	8	6	9	8	9	8	0	5	8	9	9	4	1	3	4	9
1	3	4	2	8	5	0	7	9	8	4	3	5	8	0	9	4	6	6	0	5	10
2	6	8	6	6	4	7	1	5	1	6	4	6	7	6	0	8	7	3	5	2	11
8	6	0	1	4	2	9	8	6	8	0	7	6	5	1	9	1	3	7	0	3	12
9	5	7	0	9	8	7	6	9	0	6	5	4	0	3	6	5	6	3	5	0	13
2	2	3	4	7	8	0	2	0	8	0	3	4	9	2	5	7	7	8	6	4	14
2	4	6	1	0	5	0	6	1	4	9	4	7	3	9	1	7	6	4	5	8	15
6	3	4	8	1	6	9	5	6	2	0	4	6	1	6	8	1	9	9	1	1	16
9	0	5	1	3	6	1	9	5	4	1	2	5	4	2	9	5	6	2	4	0	17
3	6	7	0	3	5	3	7	4	1	7	5	4	8	3	7	4	8	5	7	2	18
4	3	6	6	3	6	3	0	0	9	4	2	2	5	1	8	9	5	1	9	7	19
1	0	6	9	0	2	7	3	9	8	4	0	6	9	8	2	3	2	8	0	4	20
9	1	3	5	7	9	6	2	4	3	4	6	4	9	1	3	1	7	5	2	2	21
6	4	2	2	2	1	4	5	2	2	8	3	2	1	2	6	6	0	1	8	9	22
7	2	6	9	0	7	5	3	2	5	6	2	7	6	3	8	1	4	1	5	1	23
8	2	8	2	4	4	4	2	9	1	9	8	3	4	4	1	0	4	6	9	6	24
7	3	1	4	3	0	4	7	1	3	7	4	8	6	7	3	2	6	6	2	0	25
0	6	4	5	8	3	1	4	8	1	8	3	1	6	4	3	0	2	8	7	3	26
4	2	2	8	3	2	1	9	3	0	1	7	5	9	0	9	1	2	5	8	2	27
2	9	8	7	2	0	6	4	0	2	7	1	3	1	6	8	7	0	9	2	5	28
0	8	0	5	6	8	2	4	3	6	1	3	5	2	3	5	9	8	6	2	1	29
0	1	7	6	1	5	7	9	0	3	5	3	4	2	4	8	5	6	4	0	6	30
5	1	9	8	5	2	4	5	1	7	5	3	2	4	6	7	9	9	6	7	2	31
0	3	6	6	3	7	8	6	9	7	2	8	9	0	7	2	9	4	0	8	6	32
5	0	0	0	2	0	8	9	0	1	0	6	2	0	4	6	9	6	5	4	9	33
1	9	4	4	2	6	4	2	4	1	0	2	7	9	6	8	7	5	6	9	3	34
0	0	5	3	8	3	2	7	5	0	4	7	6	4	6	3	0	4	7	5	3	35
6	2	6	2	0	6	0	1	4	8	9	6	5	9	7	3	6	7	6	5	4	36
6	3	9	0	3	5	0	6	1	2	0	5	9	7	3	2	5	9	3	0	2	37
9	7	3	3	5	4	0	6	4	9	4	7	9	1	4	3	9	7	7	1	8	38
1	9	6	2	9	4	2	9	7	0	3	8	9	5	7	0	6	9	7	2	5	39
5	9	4	5	8	6	2	3	0	6	2	9	8	6	3	0	4	1	0	7	6	40

Appendix D

Values of r
for Different Levels of Significance

df	LEVEL OF SIGNIFICANCE FOR ONE-TAILED TEST			
	.05	.025	.01	.005
	LEVEL OF SIGNIFICANCE FOR TWO-TAILED TEST			
	.10	.05	.02	.01
1	.988	.997	.9995	.9999
2	.900	.950	.980	.990
3	.805	.878	.934	.959
4	.729	.811	.882	.917
5	.669	.754	.833	.874
6	.622	.707	.789	.834
7	.582	.666	.750	.798
8	.549	.632	.716	.765
9	.521	.602	.685	.735
10	.497	.576	.658	.708
11	.476	.553	.634	.684
12	.458	.532	.612	.661
13	.441	.514	.592	.641
14	.426	.497	.574	.623
15	.412	.482	.558	.606
16	.400	.468	.542	.590
17	.389	.456	.528	.575
18	.378	.444	.516	.561
19	.369	.433	.503	.549
20	.360	.423	.492	.537
21	.352	.413	.482	.526
22	.344	.404	.472	.515
23	.337	.396	.462	.505
24	.330	.388	.453	.496
25	.323	.381	.445	.487
26	.317	.374	.437	.479
27	.311	.367	.430	.471
28	.306	.361	.423	.463
29	.301	.355	.416	.456
30	.296	.349	.409	.449
35	.275	.325	.381	.418
40	.257	.304	.358	.393
45	.243	.288	.338	.372
50	.231	.273	.322	.354
60	.211	.250	.295	.325
70	.195	.232	.274	.302
80	.183	.217	.256	.283
90	.173	.205	.242	.267
100	.164	.195	.230	.254

Abridged from Table VII of Fisher and Yates, *Statistical Tables for Biological, Agricultural, and Medical Research* published by Oliver & Boyd Ltd., Edinburgh. Used with permission of the publisher.

Appendix E

Table of t Values

df	Level of significance for one-tailed test					
	.10	.05	.025	.01	.005	.0005
	Level of significance for two-tailed test					
df	.20	.10	.05	.02	.01	.001
1	3.078	6.314	12.706	31.821	63.657	636.619
2	1.886	2.920	4.303	6.965	9.925	31.598
3	1.638	2.353	3.182	4.541	5.841	12.941
4	1.533	2.132	2.776	3.747	4.604	8.610
5	1.476	2.015	2.571	3.365	4.032	6.859
6	1.440	1.943	2.447	3.143	3.707	5.959
7	1.415	1.895	2.365	2.998	3.499	5.405
8	1.397	1.860	2.306	2.896	3.355	5.041
9	1.383	1.833	2.262	2.821	3.250	4.781
10	1.372	1.812	2.228	2.764	3.169	4.587
11	1.363	1.796	2.201	2.718	3.106	4.437
12	1.356	1.782	2.179	2.681	3.055	4.318
13	1.350	1.771	2.160	2.650	3.012	4.221
14	1.345	1.761	2.145	2.624	2.977	4.140
15	1.341	1.753	2.131	2.602	2.947	4.073
16	1.337	1.746	2.120	2.583	2.921	4.015
17	1.333	1.740	2.110	2.567	2.898	3.965
18	1.330	1.734	2.101	2.552	2.878	3.922
19	1.328	1.729	2.093	2.539	2.861	3.883
20	1.325	1.725	2.086	2.528	2.845	3.850
21	1.323	1.721	2.080	2.518	2.831	3.819
22	1.321	1.717	2.074	2.508	2.819	3.792
23	1.319	1.714	2.069	2.500	2.807	3.767
24	1.318	1.711	2.064	2.492	2.797	3.745
25	1.316	1.708	2.060	2.485	2.787	3.725
26	1.315	1.706	2.056	2.479	2.779	3.707
27	1.314	1.703	2.052	2.473	2.771	3.690
28	1.313	1.701	2.048	2.467	2.763	3.674
29	1.311	1.699	2.045	2.462	2.756	3.659
30	1.310	1.697	2.042	2.457	2.750	3.646
40	1.303	1.684	2.021	2.423	2.704	3.551
60	1.296	1.671	2.000	2.390	2.660	3.460
120	1.289	1.658	1.980	2.358	2.617	3.373
∞	1.282	1.645	1.960	2.326	2.576	3.291

Abridged from Table III of Fisher and Yates, *Statistical Tables for Biological, Agricultural and Medical Research* published by Oliver & Boyd Ltd., Edinburgh. Used with permission of the publisher.

Appendix F

The 5% (Roman Type) and 1% (Boldface Type) Points for the Distribution of F

NUMERATOR df

Each cell lists the 5% (Roman) point over the 1% (Boldface) point, shown here as "5% / 1%".

DENOMINATOR df	1	2	3	4	5	6	7	8	9	10	11	12	14	16	20	24	30	40	50	75	100	200	500	∞
1	161 / 4,052	200 / 4,999	216 / 5,403	225 / 5,625	230 / 5,764	234 / 5,859	237 / 5,928	239 / 5,981	241 / 6,022	242 / 6,056	243 / 6,082	244 / 6,106	245 / 6,142	246 / 6,169	248 / 6,208	249 / 6,234	250 / 6,258	251 / 6,286	252 / 6,302	253 / 6,323	253 / 6,334	254 / 6,352	254 / 6,361	254 / 6,366
2	18.51 / 98.49	19.00 / 99.00	19.16 / 99.17	19.25 / 99.25	19.30 / 99.30	19.33 / 99.33	19.36 / 99.34	19.37 / 99.36	19.38 / 99.38	19.39 / 99.40	19.40 / 99.41	19.41 / 99.42	19.42 / 99.43	19.43 / 99.44	19.44 / 99.45	19.45 / 99.46	19.46 / 99.47	19.47 / 99.48	19.47 / 99.48	19.48 / 99.49	19.49 / 99.49	19.49 / 99.49	19.50 / 99.50	19.50 / 99.50
3	10.13 / 34.12	9.55 / 30.82	9.28 / 29.46	9.12 / 28.71	9.01 / 28.24	8.94 / 27.91	8.88 / 27.67	8.84 / 27.49	8.81 / 27.34	8.78 / 27.23	8.76 / 27.13	8.74 / 27.05	8.71 / 26.92	8.69 / 26.83	8.66 / 26.69	8.64 / 26.60	8.62 / 26.50	8.60 / 26.41	8.58 / 26.35	8.57 / 26.27	8.56 / 26.23	8.54 / 26.18	8.54 / 26.14	8.53 / 26.12
4	7.71 / 21.20	6.94 / 18.00	6.59 / 16.69	6.39 / 15.98	6.26 / 15.52	6.16 / 15.21	6.09 / 14.98	6.04 / 14.80	6.00 / 14.66	5.96 / 14.54	5.93 / 14.45	5.91 / 14.37	5.87 / 14.24	5.84 / 14.15	5.80 / 14.02	5.77 / 13.93	5.74 / 13.83	5.71 / 13.74	5.70 / 13.69	5.68 / 13.61	5.66 / 13.57	5.65 / 13.52	5.64 / 13.48	5.63 / 13.46
5	6.61 / 16.26	5.79 / 13.27	5.41 / 12.06	5.19 / 11.39	5.05 / 10.97	4.95 / 10.67	4.88 / 10.45	4.82 / 10.27	4.78 / 10.15	4.74 / 10.05	4.70 / 9.96	4.68 / 9.89	4.64 / 9.77	4.60 / 9.68	4.56 / 9.55	4.53 / 9.47	4.50 / 9.38	4.46 / 9.29	4.44 / 9.24	4.42 / 9.17	4.40 / 9.13	4.38 / 9.07	4.37 / 9.04	4.36 / 9.02
6	5.99 / 13.74	5.14 / 10.92	4.76 / 9.78	4.53 / 9.15	4.39 / 8.75	4.28 / 8.47	4.21 / 8.26	4.15 / 8.10	4.10 / 7.98	4.06 / 7.87	4.03 / 7.79	4.00 / 7.72	3.96 / 7.60	3.92 / 7.52	3.87 / 7.39	3.84 / 7.31	3.81 / 7.23	3.77 / 7.14	3.75 / 7.09	3.72 / 7.02	3.71 / 6.99	3.69 / 6.94	3.68 / 6.90	3.67 / 6.88
7	5.59 / 12.25	4.74 / 9.55	4.35 / 8.45	4.12 / 7.85	3.97 / 7.46	3.87 / 7.19	3.79 / 7.00	3.73 / 6.84	3.68 / 6.71	3.63 / 6.62	3.60 / 6.54	3.57 / 6.47	3.52 / 6.35	3.49 / 6.27	3.44 / 6.15	3.41 / 6.07	3.38 / 5.98	3.34 / 5.90	3.32 / 5.85	3.29 / 5.78	3.28 / 5.75	3.25 / 5.70	3.24 / 5.67	3.23 / 5.65
8	5.32 / 11.26	4.46 / 8.65	4.07 / 7.59	3.84 / 7.01	3.69 / 6.63	3.58 / 6.37	3.50 / 6.19	3.44 / 6.03	3.39 / 5.91	3.34 / 5.82	3.31 / 5.74	3.28 / 5.67	3.23 / 5.56	3.20 / 5.48	3.15 / 5.36	3.12 / 5.28	3.08 / 5.20	3.05 / 5.11	3.03 / 5.06	3.00 / 5.00	2.98 / 4.96	2.96 / 4.91	2.94 / 4.88	2.93 / 4.86
9	5.12 / 10.56	4.26 / 8.02	3.86 / 6.99	3.63 / 6.42	3.48 / 6.06	3.37 / 5.80	3.29 / 5.62	3.23 / 5.47	3.18 / 5.35	3.13 / 5.26	3.10 / 5.18	3.07 / 5.11	3.02 / 5.00	2.98 / 4.92	2.93 / 4.80	2.90 / 4.73	2.86 / 4.64	2.82 / 4.56	2.80 / 4.51	2.77 / 4.45	2.76 / 4.41	2.73 / 4.36	2.72 / 4.33	2.71 / 4.31
10	4.96 / 10.04	4.10 / 7.56	3.71 / 6.55	3.48 / 5.99	3.33 / 5.64	3.22 / 5.39	3.14 / 5.21	3.07 / 5.06	3.02 / 4.95	2.97 / 4.85	2.94 / 4.78	2.91 / 4.71	2.86 / 4.60	2.82 / 4.52	2.77 / 4.41	2.74 / 4.33	2.70 / 4.25	2.67 / 4.17	2.64 / 4.12	2.61 / 4.05	2.59 / 4.01	2.56 / 3.96	2.55 / 3.93	2.54 / 3.91
11	4.84 / 9.65	3.98 / 7.20	3.59 / 6.22	3.36 / 5.67	3.20 / 5.32	3.09 / 5.07	3.01 / 4.88	2.95 / 4.74	2.90 / 4.63	2.86 / 4.54	2.82 / 4.46	2.79 / 4.40	2.74 / 4.29	2.70 / 4.21	2.65 / 4.10	2.61 / 4.02	2.57 / 3.94	2.53 / 3.86	2.50 / 3.80	2.47 / 3.74	2.45 / 3.70	2.42 / 3.66	2.41 / 3.62	2.40 / 3.60
12	4.75 / 9.33	3.88 / 6.93	3.49 / 5.95	3.26 / 5.41	3.11 / 5.06	3.00 / 4.82	2.92 / 4.65	2.85 / 4.50	2.80 / 4.39	2.76 / 4.30	2.72 / 4.22	2.69 / 4.16	2.64 / 4.05	2.60 / 3.98	2.54 / 3.86	2.50 / 3.78	2.46 / 3.70	2.42 / 3.61	2.40 / 3.56	2.36 / 3.49	2.35 / 3.46	2.32 / 3.41	2.31 / 3.38	2.30 / 3.36
13	4.67 / 9.07	3.80 / 6.70	3.41 / 5.74	3.18 / 5.20	3.02 / 4.86	2.92 / 4.62	2.84 / 4.44	2.77 / 4.30	2.72 / 4.19	2.67 / 4.10	2.63 / 4.02	2.60 / 3.96	2.55 / 3.85	2.51 / 3.78	2.46 / 3.67	2.42 / 3.59	2.38 / 3.51	2.34 / 3.42	2.32 / 3.37	2.28 / 3.30	2.26 / 3.27	2.24 / 3.21	2.22 / 3.18	2.21 / 3.16

Reprinted from Snedecor, *Statistical Methods*, 5th ed. (Ames, Iowa: Iowa State University Press, 1956), with permission of the publisher. Copyright © 1956 Iowa State University Press, Ames, Iowa.

NUMERATOR df

DENOMINATOR df	1	2	3	4	5	6	7	8	9	10	11	12	14	16	20	24	30	40	50	75	100	200	500	∞
14	4.60 / 8.86	3.74 / 6.51	3.34 / 5.56	3.11 / 5.03	2.96 / 4.69	2.85 / 4.46	2.77 / 4.28	2.70 / 4.14	2.65 / 4.03	2.60 / 3.94	2.56 / 3.86	2.53 / 3.80	2.48 / 3.70	2.44 / 3.62	2.39 / 3.51	2.35 / 3.43	2.31 / 3.34	2.27 / 3.26	2.24 / 3.21	2.21 / 3.14	2.19 / 3.11	2.16 / 3.06	2.14 / 3.02	2.13 / 3.00
15	4.54 / 8.68	3.68 / 6.36	3.29 / 5.42	3.06 / 4.89	2.90 / 4.56	2.79 / 4.32	2.70 / 4.14	2.64 / 4.00	2.59 / 3.89	2.55 / 3.80	2.51 / 3.73	2.48 / 3.67	2.43 / 3.56	2.39 / 3.48	2.33 / 3.36	2.29 / 3.29	2.25 / 3.20	2.21 / 3.12	2.18 / 3.07	2.15 / 3.00	2.12 / 2.97	2.10 / 2.92	2.08 / 2.89	2.07 / 2.87
16	4.49 / 8.53	3.63 / 6.23	3.24 / 5.29	3.01 / 4.77	2.85 / 4.44	2.74 / 4.20	2.66 / 4.03	2.59 / 3.89	2.54 / 3.78	2.49 / 3.69	2.45 / 3.61	2.42 / 3.55	2.37 / 3.45	2.33 / 3.37	2.28 / 3.25	2.24 / 3.18	2.20 / 3.10	2.16 / 3.01	2.13 / 2.96	2.09 / 2.89	2.07 / 2.86	2.04 / 2.80	2.02 / 2.77	2.01 / 2.75
17	4.45 / 8.40	3.59 / 6.11	3.20 / 5.18	2.96 / 4.67	2.81 / 4.34	2.70 / 4.10	2.62 / 3.93	2.55 / 3.79	2.50 / 3.68	2.45 / 3.59	2.41 / 3.52	2.38 / 3.45	2.33 / 3.35	2.29 / 3.27	2.23 / 3.16	2.19 / 3.08	2.15 / 3.00	2.11 / 2.92	2.08 / 2.86	2.04 / 2.79	2.02 / 2.76	1.99 / 2.70	1.97 / 2.67	1.96 / 2.65
18	4.41 / 8.28	3.55 / 6.01	3.16 / 5.09	2.93 / 4.58	2.77 / 4.25	2.66 / 4.01	2.58 / 3.85	2.51 / 3.71	2.46 / 3.60	2.41 / 3.51	2.37 / 3.44	2.34 / 3.37	2.29 / 3.27	2.25 / 3.19	2.19 / 3.07	2.15 / 3.00	2.11 / 2.91	2.07 / 2.83	2.04 / 2.78	2.00 / 2.71	1.98 / 2.68	1.95 / 2.62	1.93 / 2.59	1.92 / 2.57
19	4.38 / 8.18	3.52 / 5.93	3.13 / 5.01	2.90 / 4.50	2.74 / 4.17	2.63 / 3.94	2.55 / 3.77	2.48 / 3.63	2.43 / 3.52	2.38 / 3.43	2.34 / 3.36	2.31 / 3.30	2.26 / 3.19	2.21 / 3.12	2.15 / 3.00	2.11 / 2.92	2.07 / 2.84	2.02 / 2.76	2.00 / 2.70	1.96 / 2.63	1.94 / 2.60	1.91 / 2.54	1.90 / 2.51	1.88 / 2.49
20	4.35 / 8.10	3.49 / 5.85	3.10 / 4.94	2.87 / 4.43	2.71 / 4.10	2.60 / 3.87	2.52 / 3.71	2.45 / 3.56	2.40 / 3.45	2.35 / 3.37	2.31 / 3.30	2.28 / 3.23	2.23 / 3.13	2.18 / 3.05	2.12 / 2.94	2.08 / 2.86	2.04 / 2.77	1.99 / 2.69	1.96 / 2.63	1.92 / 2.56	1.90 / 2.53	1.87 / 2.47	1.85 / 2.44	1.84 / 2.42
21	4.32 / 8.02	3.47 / 5.78	3.07 / 4.87	2.84 / 4.37	2.68 / 4.04	2.57 / 3.81	2.49 / 3.65	2.42 / 3.51	2.37 / 3.40	2.32 / 3.31	2.28 / 3.24	2.25 / 3.17	2.20 / 3.07	2.15 / 2.99	2.09 / 2.88	2.05 / 2.80	2.00 / 2.72	1.96 / 2.63	1.93 / 2.58	1.89 / 2.51	1.87 / 2.47	1.84 / 2.42	1.82 / 2.38	1.81 / 2.36
22	4.30 / 7.94	3.44 / 5.72	3.05 / 4.82	2.82 / 4.31	2.66 / 3.99	2.55 / 3.76	2.47 / 3.59	2.40 / 3.45	2.35 / 3.35	2.30 / 3.26	2.26 / 3.18	2.23 / 3.12	2.18 / 3.02	2.13 / 2.94	2.07 / 2.83	2.03 / 2.75	1.98 / 2.67	1.93 / 2.58	1.91 / 2.53	1.87 / 2.46	1.84 / 2.42	1.81 / 2.37	1.80 / 2.33	1.78 / 2.31
23	4.28 / 7.88	3.42 / 5.66	3.03 / 4.76	2.80 / 4.26	2.64 / 3.94	2.53 / 3.71	2.45 / 3.54	2.38 / 3.41	2.32 / 3.30	2.28 / 3.21	2.24 / 3.14	2.20 / 3.07	2.14 / 2.97	2.10 / 2.89	2.04 / 2.78	2.00 / 2.70	1.96 / 2.62	1.91 / 2.53	1.88 / 2.48	1.84 / 2.41	1.82 / 2.37	1.79 / 2.32	1.77 / 2.28	1.76 / 2.26
24	4.26 / 7.82	3.40 / 5.61	3.01 / 4.72	2.78 / 4.22	2.62 / 3.90	2.51 / 3.67	2.43 / 3.50	2.36 / 3.36	2.30 / 3.25	2.26 / 3.17	2.22 / 3.09	2.18 / 3.03	2.13 / 2.93	2.09 / 2.85	2.02 / 2.74	1.98 / 2.66	1.94 / 2.58	1.89 / 2.49	1.86 / 2.44	1.82 / 2.36	1.80 / 2.33	1.76 / 2.27	1.74 / 2.23	1.73 / 2.21
25	4.24 / 7.77	3.38 / 5.57	2.99 / 4.68	2.76 / 4.18	2.60 / 3.86	2.49 / 3.63	2.41 / 3.46	2.34 / 3.32	2.28 / 3.21	2.24 / 3.13	2.20 / 3.05	2.16 / 2.99	2.11 / 2.89	2.06 / 2.81	2.00 / 2.70	1.96 / 2.62	1.92 / 2.54	1.87 / 2.45	1.84 / 2.40	1.80 / 2.32	1.77 / 2.29	1.74 / 2.23	1.72 / 2.19	1.71 / 2.17
26	4.22 / 7.72	3.37 / 5.53	2.98 / 4.64	2.74 / 4.14	2.59 / 3.82	2.47 / 3.59	2.39 / 3.42	2.32 / 3.29	2.27 / 3.17	2.22 / 3.09	2.18 / 3.02	2.15 / 2.96	2.10 / 2.86	2.05 / 2.77	1.99 / 2.66	1.95 / 2.58	1.90 / 2.50	1.85 / 2.41	1.82 / 2.36	1.78 / 2.28	1.76 / 2.25	1.72 / 2.19	1.70 / 2.15	1.69 / 2.13

NUMERATOR df

Den. df	1	2	3	4	5	6	7	8	9	10	11	12	14	16	20	24	30	40	50	75	100	200	500	∞
27	4.21 7.68	3.35 5.49	2.96 4.60	2.73 4.11	2.57 3.79	2.46 3.56	2.37 3.39	2.30 3.26	2.25 3.14	2.20 3.06	2.16 2.98	2.13 2.93	2.08 2.83	2.03 2.74	1.97 2.63	1.93 2.55	1.88 2.47	1.84 2.38	1.80 2.33	1.76 2.25	1.74 2.21	1.71 2.16	1.68 2.12	1.67 2.10
28	4.20 7.64	3.34 5.45	2.95 4.57	2.71 4.07	2.56 3.76	2.44 3.53	2.36 3.36	2.29 3.23	2.24 3.11	2.19 3.03	2.15 2.95	2.12 2.90	2.06 2.80	2.02 2.71	1.96 2.60	1.91 2.52	1.87 2.44	1.81 2.35	1.78 2.30	1.75 2.22	1.72 2.18	1.69 2.13	1.67 2.09	1.65 2.06
29	4.18 7.60	3.33 5.42	2.93 4.54	2.70 4.04	2.54 3.73	2.43 3.50	2.35 3.33	2.28 3.20	2.22 3.08	2.18 3.00	2.14 2.92	2.10 2.87	2.05 2.77	2.00 2.68	1.94 2.57	1.90 2.49	1.85 2.41	1.80 2.32	1.77 2.27	1.73 2.19	1.71 2.15	1.68 2.10	1.65 2.06	1.64 2.03
30	4.17 7.56	3.32 5.39	2.92 4.51	2.69 4.02	2.53 3.70	2.42 3.47	2.34 3.30	2.27 3.17	2.21 3.06	2.16 2.98	2.12 2.90	2.09 2.84	2.04 2.74	1.99 2.66	1.93 2.55	1.89 2.47	1.84 2.38	1.79 2.29	1.76 2.24	1.72 2.16	1.69 2.13	1.66 2.07	1.64 2.03	1.62 2.01
32	4.15 7.50	3.30 5.34	2.90 4.46	2.67 3.97	2.51 3.66	2.40 3.42	2.32 3.25	2.25 3.12	2.19 3.01	2.14 2.94	2.10 2.86	2.07 2.80	2.02 2.70	1.97 2.62	1.91 2.51	1.86 2.42	1.82 2.34	1.76 2.25	1.74 2.20	1.69 2.12	1.67 2.08	1.64 2.02	1.61 1.98	1.59 1.96
34	4.13 7.44	3.28 5.29	2.88 4.42	2.65 3.93	2.49 3.61	2.38 3.38	2.30 3.21	2.23 3.08	2.17 2.97	2.12 2.89	2.08 2.82	2.05 2.76	2.00 2.66	1.95 2.58	1.89 2.47	1.84 2.38	1.80 2.30	1.74 2.21	1.71 2.15	1.67 2.08	1.64 2.04	1.61 1.98	1.59 1.94	1.57 1.91
36	4.11 7.39	3.26 5.25	2.86 4.38	2.63 3.89	2.48 3.58	2.36 3.35	2.28 3.18	2.21 3.04	2.15 2.94	2.10 2.86	2.06 2.78	2.03 2.72	1.98 2.62	1.93 2.54	1.87 2.43	1.82 2.35	1.78 2.26	1.72 2.17	1.69 2.12	1.65 2.04	1.62 2.00	1.59 1.94	1.56 1.90	1.55 1.87
38	4.10 7.35	3.25 5.21	2.85 4.34	2.62 3.86	2.46 3.54	2.35 3.32	2.26 3.15	2.19 3.02	2.14 2.91	2.09 2.82	2.05 2.75	2.02 2.69	1.96 2.59	1.92 2.51	1.85 2.40	1.80 2.32	1.76 2.22	1.71 2.14	1.67 2.08	1.63 2.00	1.60 1.97	1.57 1.90	1.54 1.86	1.53 1.84
40	4.08 7.31	3.23 5.18	2.84 4.31	2.61 3.83	2.45 3.51	2.34 3.29	2.25 3.12	2.18 2.99	2.12 2.88	2.07 2.80	2.04 2.73	2.00 2.66	1.95 2.56	1.90 2.49	1.84 2.37	1.79 2.29	1.74 2.20	1.69 2.11	1.66 2.05	1.61 1.97	1.59 1.94	1.55 1.88	1.53 1.84	1.51 1.81
42	4.07 7.27	3.22 5.15	2.83 4.29	2.59 3.80	2.44 3.49	2.32 3.26	2.24 3.10	2.17 2.96	2.11 2.86	2.06 2.77	2.02 2.70	1.99 2.64	1.94 2.54	1.89 2.46	1.82 2.35	1.78 2.26	1.73 2.17	1.68 2.08	1.64 2.02	1.60 1.94	1.57 1.91	1.54 1.85	1.51 1.80	1.49 1.78
44	4.06 7.24	3.21 5.12	2.82 4.26	2.58 3.78	2.43 3.46	2.31 3.24	2.23 3.07	2.16 2.94	2.10 2.84	2.05 2.75	2.01 2.68	1.98 2.62	1.92 2.52	1.88 2.44	1.81 2.32	1.76 2.24	1.72 2.15	1.66 2.06	1.63 2.00	1.58 1.92	1.56 1.88	1.52 1.82	1.50 1.78	1.48 1.75
46	4.05 7.21	3.20 5.10	2.81 4.24	2.57 3.76	2.42 3.44	2.30 3.22	2.22 3.05	2.14 2.92	2.09 2.82	2.04 2.73	2.00 2.66	1.97 2.60	1.91 2.50	1.87 2.42	1.80 2.30	1.75 2.22	1.71 2.13	1.65 2.04	1.62 1.98	1.57 1.90	1.54 1.86	1.51 1.80	1.48 1.76	1.46 1.72
48	4.04 7.19	3.19 5.08	2.80 4.22	2.56 3.74	2.41 3.42	2.30 3.20	2.21 3.04	2.14 2.90	2.08 2.80	2.03 2.71	1.99 2.64	1.96 2.58	1.90 2.48	1.86 2.40	1.79 2.28	1.74 2.20	1.70 2.11	1.64 2.02	1.61 1.96	1.56 1.88	1.53 1.84	1.50 1.78	1.47 1.73	1.45 1.70

DENOMINATOR df

NUMERATOR df

Denominator df	1	2	3	4	5	6	7	8	9	10	11	12	14	16	20	24	30	40	50	75	100	200	500	∞
50	4.03 / 7.17	3.18 / 5.06	2.79 / 4.20	2.56 / 3.72	2.40 / 3.41	2.29 / 3.18	2.20 / 3.02	2.13 / 2.88	2.07 / 2.78	2.02 / 2.70	1.98 / 2.62	1.95 / 2.56	1.90 / 2.46	1.85 / 2.39	1.78 / 2.26	1.74 / 2.18	1.69 / 2.10	1.63 / 2.00	1.60 / 1.94	1.55 / 1.86	1.52 / 1.82	1.48 / 1.76	1.46 / 1.71	1.44 / 1.68
55	4.02 / 7.12	3.17 / 5.01	2.78 / 4.16	2.54 / 3.68	2.38 / 3.37	2.27 / 3.15	2.18 / 2.98	2.11 / 2.85	2.05 / 2.75	2.00 / 2.66	1.97 / 2.59	1.93 / 2.53	1.88 / 2.43	1.83 / 2.35	1.76 / 2.23	1.72 / 2.15	1.67 / 2.06	1.61 / 1.96	1.58 / 1.90	1.52 / 1.82	1.50 / 1.78	1.46 / 1.71	1.43 / 1.66	1.41 / 1.64
60	4.00 / 7.08	3.15 / 4.98	2.76 / 4.13	2.52 / 3.65	2.37 / 3.34	2.25 / 3.12	2.17 / 2.95	2.10 / 2.82	2.04 / 2.72	1.99 / 2.63	1.95 / 2.56	1.92 / 2.50	1.86 / 2.40	1.81 / 2.32	1.75 / 2.20	1.70 / 2.12	1.65 / 2.03	1.59 / 1.93	1.56 / 1.87	1.50 / 1.79	1.48 / 1.74	1.44 / 1.68	1.41 / 1.63	1.39 / 1.60
65	3.99 / 7.04	3.14 / 4.95	2.75 / 4.10	2.51 / 3.62	2.36 / 3.31	2.24 / 3.09	2.15 / 2.93	2.08 / 2.79	2.02 / 2.70	1.98 / 2.61	1.94 / 2.54	1.90 / 2.47	1.85 / 2.37	1.80 / 2.30	1.73 / 2.18	1.68 / 2.09	1.63 / 2.00	1.57 / 1.90	1.54 / 1.84	1.49 / 1.76	1.46 / 1.71	1.42 / 1.64	1.39 / 1.60	1.37 / 1.56
70	3.98 / 7.01	3.13 / 4.92	2.74 / 4.08	2.50 / 3.60	2.35 / 3.29	2.23 / 3.07	2.14 / 2.91	2.07 / 2.77	2.01 / 2.67	1.97 / 2.59	1.93 / 2.51	1.89 / 2.45	1.84 / 2.35	1.79 / 2.28	1.72 / 2.15	1.67 / 2.07	1.62 / 1.98	1.56 / 1.88	1.53 / 1.82	1.47 / 1.74	1.45 / 1.69	1.40 / 1.62	1.37 / 1.56	1.35 / 1.53
80	3.96 / 6.96	3.11 / 4.88	2.72 / 4.04	2.48 / 3.56	2.33 / 3.25	2.21 / 3.04	2.12 / 2.87	2.05 / 2.74	1.99 / 2.64	1.95 / 2.55	1.91 / 2.48	1.88 / 2.41	1.82 / 2.32	1.77 / 2.24	1.70 / 2.11	1.65 / 2.03	1.60 / 1.94	1.54 / 1.84	1.51 / 1.78	1.45 / 1.70	1.42 / 1.65	1.38 / 1.57	1.35 / 1.52	1.32 / 1.49
100	3.94 / 6.90	3.09 / 4.82	2.70 / 3.98	2.46 / 3.51	2.30 / 3.20	2.19 / 2.99	2.10 / 2.82	2.03 / 2.69	1.97 / 2.59	1.92 / 2.51	1.88 / 2.43	1.85 / 2.36	1.79 / 2.26	1.75 / 2.19	1.68 / 2.06	1.63 / 1.98	1.57 / 1.89	1.51 / 1.79	1.48 / 1.73	1.42 / 1.64	1.39 / 1.59	1.34 / 1.51	1.30 / 1.46	1.28 / 1.43
125	3.92 / 6.84	3.07 / 4.78	2.68 / 3.94	2.44 / 3.47	2.29 / 3.17	2.17 / 2.95	2.08 / 2.79	2.01 / 2.65	1.95 / 2.56	1.90 / 2.47	1.86 / 2.40	1.83 / 2.33	1.77 / 2.23	1.72 / 2.15	1.65 / 2.03	1.60 / 1.94	1.55 / 1.85	1.49 / 1.75	1.45 / 1.68	1.39 / 1.59	1.36 / 1.54	1.31 / 1.46	1.27 / 1.40	1.25 / 1.37
150	3.91 / 6.81	3.06 / 4.75	2.67 / 3.91	2.43 / 3.44	2.27 / 3.14	2.16 / 2.92	2.07 / 2.76	2.00 / 2.62	1.94 / 2.53	1.89 / 2.44	1.85 / 2.37	1.82 / 2.30	1.76 / 2.20	1.71 / 2.12	1.64 / 2.00	1.59 / 1.91	1.54 / 1.83	1.47 / 1.72	1.44 / 1.66	1.37 / 1.56	1.34 / 1.51	1.29 / 1.43	1.25 / 1.37	1.22 / 1.33
200	3.89 / 6.76	3.04 / 4.71	2.65 / 3.88	2.41 / 3.41	2.26 / 3.11	2.14 / 2.90	2.05 / 2.73	1.98 / 2.60	1.92 / 2.50	1.87 / 2.41	1.83 / 2.34	1.80 / 2.28	1.74 / 2.17	1.69 / 2.09	1.62 / 1.97	1.57 / 1.88	1.52 / 1.79	1.45 / 1.69	1.42 / 1.62	1.35 / 1.53	1.32 / 1.48	1.26 / 1.39	1.22 / 1.33	1.19 / 1.28
400	3.86 / 6.70	3.02 / 4.66	2.62 / 3.83	2.39 / 3.36	2.23 / 3.06	2.12 / 2.85	2.03 / 2.69	1.96 / 2.55	1.90 / 2.46	1.85 / 2.37	1.81 / 2.29	1.78 / 2.23	1.72 / 2.12	1.67 / 2.04	1.60 / 1.92	1.54 / 1.84	1.49 / 1.74	1.42 / 1.64	1.38 / 1.57	1.32 / 1.47	1.28 / 1.42	1.22 / 1.32	1.16 / 1.24	1.13 / 1.19
1000	3.85 / 6.66	3.00 / 4.62	2.61 / 3.80	2.38 / 3.34	2.22 / 3.04	2.10 / 2.82	2.02 / 2.66	1.95 / 2.53	1.89 / 2.43	1.84 / 2.34	1.80 / 2.26	1.76 / 2.20	1.70 / 2.09	1.65 / 2.01	1.58 / 1.89	1.53 / 1.81	1.47 / 1.71	1.41 / 1.61	1.36 / 1.54	1.30 / 1.44	1.26 / 1.38	1.19 / 1.28	1.13 / 1.19	1.08 / 1.11
∞	3.84 / 6.64	2.99 / 4.60	2.60 / 3.78	2.37 / 3.32	2.21 / 3.02	2.09 / 2.80	2.01 / 2.64	1.94 / 2.51	1.88 / 2.41	1.83 / 2.32	1.79 / 2.24	1.75 / 2.18	1.69 / 2.07	1.64 / 1.99	1.57 / 1.87	1.52 / 1.79	1.46 / 1.69	1.40 / 1.59	1.35 / 1.52	1.28 / 1.41	1.24 / 1.36	1.17 / 1.25	1.11 / 1.15	1.00 / 1.00

Appendix G

Table of χ^2 Values

df	.90	.80	.70	.50	.30	.20	.10	.05	.02	.01	.001
1	.016	.064	.15	.46	1.07	1.64	2.71	3.84	5.41	6.64	10.83
2	.21	.45	.71	1.39	2.41	3.22	4.60	5.99	7.82	9.21	13.82
3	.58	1.00	1.42	2.37	3.66	4.64	6.25	7.82	9.84	11.34	16.27
4	1.06	1.65	2.20	3.36	4.88	5.99	7.78	9.49	11.67	13.28	18.46
5	1.61	2.34	3.00	4.35	6.06	7.29	9.24	11.07	13.39	15.09	20.52
6	2.20	3.07	3.83	5.35	7.23	8.56	10.64	12.59	15.03	16.81	22.46
7	2.83	3.82	4.67	6.35	8.38	9.80	12.02	14.07	16.62	18.48	24.32
8	3.49	4.59	5.53	7.34	9.52	11.03	13.36	15.51	18.17	20.09	26.12
9	4.17	5.38	6.39	8.34	10.66	12.24	14.68	16.92	19.68	21.67	27.88
10	4.86	6.18	7.27	9.34	11.78	13.44	15.99	18.31	21.16	23.21	29.59
11	5.58	6.99	8.15	10.34	12.90	14.63	17.28	19.68	22.62	24.72	31.26
12	6.30	7.81	9.03	11.34	14.01	15.81	18.55	21.03	24.05	26.22	32.91
13	7.04	8.63	9.93	12.34	15.12	16.98	19.81	22.36	25.47	27.69	34.53
14	7.79	9.47	10.82	13.34	16.22	18.15	21.06	23.68	26.87	29.14	36.12
15	8.55	10.31	11.72	14.34	17.32	19.31	22.31	25.00	28.26	30.58	37.70
16	9.31	11.15	12.62	15.34	18.42	20.46	23.54	26.30	29.63	32.00	39.29
17	10.08	12.00	13.53	16.34	19.51	21.62	24.77	27.59	31.00	33.41	40.75
18	10.86	12.86	14.44	17.34	20.60	22.76	25.99	28.87	32.35	34.80	42.31
19	11.65	13.72	15.35	18.34	21.69	23.90	27.20	30.14	33.69	36.19	43.82
20	12.44	14.58	16.27	19.34	22.78	25.04	28.41	31.41	35.02	37.57	45.32
21	13.24	15.44	17.18	20.34	23.86	26.17	29.62	32.67	36.34	38.93	46.80
22	14.04	16.31	18.10	21.24	24.94	27.30	30.81	33.92	37.66	40.29	48.27
23	14.85	17.19	19.02	22.34	26.02	28.43	32.01	35.17	38.97	41.64	49.73
24	15.66	18.06	19.94	23.34	27.10	29.55	33.20	36.42	40.27	42.98	51.18
25	16.47	18.94	20.87	24.34	28.17	30.68	34.38	37.65	41.57	44.31	52.62
26	17.29	19.82	21.79	25.34	29.25	31.80	35.56	38.88	42.86	45.64	54.05
27	18.11	20.70	22.72	26.34	30.32	32.91	36.74	40.11	44.14	46.96	55.48
28	18.94	21.59	23.65	27.34	31.39	34.03	37.92	41.34	45.42	48.28	56.89
29	19.77	22.48	24.58	28.34	32.46	35.14	39.09	42.56	46.69	49.59	58.30
30	20.60	23.36	25.51	29.34	33.53	36.25	40.26	43.77	47.96	50.89	59.70

Abridged from Table IV of Fisher and Yates, *Statistical Tables for Biological, Agricultural, and Medical Research* published by Oliver & Boyd Ltd., Edinburgh. With permission of the publishers.

Index